DAY BY DAY
WE MAGNIFY YOU

DAY BY DAY
WE MAGNIFY YOU

Daily Readings for the Entire Year

*Selected from the Writings of
Martin Luther*

Revised Edition

MARSHALL D. JOHNSON, EDITOR

AUGSBURG BOOKS
MINNEAPOLIS

DAY BY DAY WE MAGNIFY YOU
Daily Readings for the Entire Year

Cover art: Let the Children Come Unto Me, Cranach, Lucas the Elder (1472-
1553). Photo © Bildarchiv Preussischer Kulturbesitz / Art Resource, N.Y.
Cover design: Designworks / Tim Green.
Interior design: Michelle L. N. Cook

Library of Congress Cataloging-in-Publication Data
Luther, Martin, 1483-1546.
  Day by day we magnify you : daily readings for the entire year : selected from the
writings of Martin Luther / Marshall D. Johnson, editor.—Rev. ed.
      p. cm.
  Includes bibliographical references and index.
  ISBN 978-0-8066-8014-9 (alk. paper)
  1. Devotional calendars. I. Johnson, Marshall D. II. Title.
  BR331.E6 2008
  242'.3—dc22   2008017884

Manufactured in the U.S.A.

Contents

A NOTE FROM THE PUBLISHER

Christians of all traditions regard constancy in prayer and worship as a hallmark and safeguard of faith. Thus Martin Luther (1483–1546) wrote about Mary, who first sang the hymn "My soul magnifies the Lord" (Luke 1:46): "Mary's heart remains the same at all times; she lets God have his will with her and draws from it all only a good comfort, joy, and trust in God. Thus we too should do; that would be to sing a right *Magnificat*."

Readers should not be surprised to learn that Luther was a man of his day. Glimpses of the social, ecclesial, military, and political situation of the sixteenth century can be seen in a number of the selections in this book, along with an especially graphic sense of the personality of evil. But more impressive are the central emphases of Luther's piety that shine forth in these extracts—his focus on Jesus Christ and the cross and also his concern that believers develop a mature sense of Christian behavior.

The original edition of this collection of daily readings, arranged according to the church year and selected from the enormous quantity of writings of Luther, was widely used when it appeared in the United Kingdom in 1946 and in North America in 1950 (it was reissued in 1982). It has become a classic of Christian spirituality.

This new edition is revised in several ways so as to be more useful to the prayer life of contemporary readers:

- The English-language style is updated to reflect the usage of the twenty-first century.
- Cross-references to Luther's Works, American Edition, with volume numbers and page numbers, are made whenever the extract occurs there.
- Designations of the parts of the church year are those widely used in North America today.
- A response—a prayer thought, a scripture verse, or a discussion topic—is added for each day.

We offer this revised edition in the conviction that Luther's words of spiritual counsel can help Christians of all traditions to grow in grace and remain constant in prayer and worship.

Biblical passages are from the New Revised Standard Version of the Bible (NRSV), unless otherwise indicated (RSV refers to the Revised Standard Version). A few translations are adjusted to reflect Luther's reading; all of these are so identified. The Weimar edition of Luther's writings is abbreviated WA and the Erlangen edition EA. *Tischreden* refers to the "Table Talk" of the reformer, and LW refers to Luther's Works, American Edition.

Several of the Christian festivals are "movable"; that is, they fall on different days of the secular calendar from year to year. The movable date of Easter determines the length of seasons of Epiphany and Pentecost. This means that in some years you will not use all of the readings in this book for some of the weeks of Epiphany and Pentecost.

The title, *Day by Day We Magnify You*, is a phrase from the ancient Christian hymn "*Te Deum.*"

Advent

The Coming of the Lord

Matthew 21:1-9

Rejoice greatly, O daughter Zion!
Shout aloud, O daughter Jerusalem!
Lo, your king comes to you;
triumphant and victorious is he,
humble and riding on a donkey,
on a colt, the foal of a donkey.
(Zechariah 9:9)

Yes indeed, he will be a king, but a poor and wretched king who does not at all look like a king—if he is judged by the outward might and splendor in which kings and princes like to array themselves.

He leaves to other kings the castles, palaces, gold, and wealth, and he lets them eat and drink, dress and build more daintily than other folks. But what Christ the poor beggar-king knows, they do not know. He helps not against *one* sin only but against *all* my sin; and not against *my* sin only, but against *the whole world's* sin. He comes to take away not sickness only, but death; and not *my* death only, but *the whole world's* death. The prophet said: Tell the daughter of Zion that she should be not offended at his humble advent but should shut her eyes and open her ears and perceive not how he rides there so beggarly but listen to what is said and preached about this poor king. His wretchedness and poverty are manifest, for he comes riding on a donkey like a beggar, having neither saddle nor spurs. But that he will take from us sin, overcome death, endow us with eternal bliss and eternal life—this cannot be seen. Therefore you must hear and believe.

Sermon for the First Sunday in Advent, 1533.   WA 37:201f.

Lift my eyes, Lord God, above the shallow values of our time.
Help me see your presence even in the humble things of life. Amen.

Your King Comes

He will reign over the house of Jacob forever,
and of his kingdom there will be no end.
(Luke 1:33)

He is your king, the king promised to you, whose own you are. He and no other shall rule over you, but in spirit and not after worldly rule. This is he for whom you longed from the beginning. This is he for whom your dear ancestors were yearning and crying with heartfelt desire. From all the things that until now have burdened, oppressed, and imprisoned you, he will redeem you and will set you free.

Oh, what comfortable words for a believing heart, for apart from Christ we are thrown under the heel of many furious tyrants, who are not kings but murderers, under whom we suffer great pain and fear. Such are the devil, the flesh, the world, sin and the law, and death and hell, by which the wretched conscience is oppressed and held in harsh confinement, leading a bitter and fearful life.

But when we with strong faith receive this king into our inmost hearts, we are saved. Sin, death, hell, and all distress we dread no longer, for we know well, and do not doubt, that this king is a master over life and death, over sin and grace, over hell and heaven, and that all things are in his hands. What great things are contained in these few words, "Lo, your king." Such superabundant great blessings does the poor donkey rider and disdained king bestow. These things neither reason nor nature can comprehend, but faith alone.

Sermon for the First Sunday in Advent, 1522. WA 10/1(ii):27f.

We wait, O Lord, with eager longing for the redemption
of the people of God. Amen.

He Comes to You

I will come in to you and eat with you, and you with me.
(Revelation 3:20)

He comes to you. Yes, you do not go to him, neither do you send for him. He is too high for you and too far away. All your wealth and wit, your toil and labor, will not bring you near him, lest you pride yourself that your merit and worthiness have brought him to thee. Dear friend, all your merit and worthiness are struck down, and there is nothing on your side but sheer undeserving and unworthiness, and on his side pure grace and mercy. Here we in our poverty come together with the Lord in his unsearchable riches.

Therefore learn here from the gospel what happens when God begins to build us into his likeness and what is the beginning of saintliness. There is no other beginning than that your king comes to you and begins his work in you. You do not seek him; he seeks you. You do not find him; he finds you. Your faith comes of him, not of yourself. Where he does not come, you must stay outside. And where there is no gospel, there is no God, but sheer sin and destruction. Therefore ask not where to begin a godly life; there is no beginning but there this king comes and is preached.

Sermon for the First Sunday in Advent, 1522.   *WA 10/1(ii):78ff.*

Where, O Lord God, can I flee from your presence? Wherever I go,
you are already there. Amen.

The Advent of Christ Is Rich in Mercy

Blessed be the Lord God of Israel,
for he has looked favorably on his people and redeemed them.
(Luke 1:68)

In his first advent God came in a cruel, thick black cloud with fire, smoke, and thunder; with a great sound of trumpets, so fierce that the children of Israel were filled with fear and dead, and said to Moses, "You speak to us . . . , but do not let God speak to us, or we will die" (Exodus 20:19). At that time God gave them the law. The law is cruel; we do not like to hear it. The law is such a terror to our reason that at times we fall into instant despair. It is so heavy a burden that the conscience knows not where to turn or what to do.

By contrast, Christ in his advent is not terrifying but meek; not fierce like God in the Old Testament, but meek and merciful like a human being. He does not come on the mountain but in the city. On Sinai he came with terror and with thunder and lightning; now he comes with meekness and with hymns of praise. There he came with the great sound of trumpets; here he comes weeping over the city of Jerusalem. There he came with fear; here he comes with consolation, joy, and love. Here you find the difference between the law and the gospel: The law commands while the gospel gives all things freely. The law causes anger and hate; the gospel gives grace. At the first advent the children of Israel fled before the voice of God, but now our desire to hear it cannot be stilled, because it is so sweet. Therefore, when you are anxious and troubled, do not run to Mount Sinai, looking to the law for help. Neither think that you yourselves have power to atone, but rather look for help in Jerusalem, that is, in the gospel that says, "Your sins are forgiven; go and sin no more" (see John 5:14).

Sermon for Palm Sunday, 1522.   WA 10/3:67

I know and am grateful, O Lord,
that your steadfast love endures forever. Amen.

The Fullness of Time

But when the fullness of the time had come, God sent his Son,
born of a woman, born under the law.
(Galatians 4:4)

Because the law can give us neither justification nor faith, and nature with all its toil can gain us nothing, St. Paul now preaches him who in our place has won for us such faith, and who is a master in justification. For justification did not come to us easily, but at great cost; it was paid by God's own Son. Hence the apostle writes, "When the fullness of the time had come," that is, when the time of our bondage had come to an end.

For the Jews that time was fulfilled with Christ's advent in the flesh, and in like manner it is still being fulfilled in our daily life, whenever we are illumined through faith, so that our serfdom and toil under the law come to an end. For Christ's advent in the flesh would be useless unless it produced in us such a spiritual advent of faith. He came in the flesh in order to bring about such an advent in the spirit. For to all who before or after believed in his coming in the flesh in this way, even to them he has come. Therefore, in virtue of such faith, to the faithful ones of the past his coming was ever present.

From the beginning of time to the end of the world, everything must depend on this coming in the flesh, whereby we are set free from bondage, whenever, wherever, and in whomever such faith is found. And the fullness of time comes for everyone who begins to believe in Christ as the one whose advent was promised before all times and who has now come.

Sermon for the Sunday after Christmas, 1522.   WA 10/1(i):352ff.

And now, O Lord, what do I hope for? My hope is in you. Amen.

He Is Despised—A Hidden King

Lift up your heads, O gates!
and be lifted up, O ancient doors!
that the King of glory may come in.
(Psalm 24:7)

Indeed, that very glory is hidden. Therefore to him the gates are locked, and no one wants to let him in. Those in high places resist him with all their strength, but it does not help them. He is a mighty king of the cross, yet under this very cross his glory is hidden.

"Who is the king of glory?" Thus it will happen to him. "Who," they will say, "is this heretic, this agitator of the people?" They apply such names to the king. Who is the king of glory? They speak these words with bitterest scorn, and show the greatest contempt for that king. How absurd a thing it is that he is called a king of glory!

Christ still comes—in those who are the least of his servants to those who are the greatest of this world; in those who are despised to those who are praised; in his fools to the wise. But not only do they keep him out and shut the door, but they even hunt him down and scoff at him; they still oppose Christ and his Word, but they will never overpower him. For he is the Lord of hosts. He is now the king of glory, for he remains the king of glory eternally, and the heavenly hosts and the saints on earth worship and serve him.

Exposition of the first Twenty-five Psalms, 1530. WA 31/1:373

Fill me again, O Lord, with the joy of your coming,
and let me respond with praise. Amen.

But to All Who Received Him . . .

But to all who received him, who believed in his name,
he gave power to become children of God.
(John 1:12)

Here you learn what a great glory is accomplished by the Son of God in his coming among those who receive him, have faith in him, and believe him to be the one sent by God to help the world. This is to be the new work and a new way, that he will give the power and the right to become children of God to them who believe in his name.

There you have it in sum and substance. By no other way, manner, or means may we come to such high honor, such wondrous freedom and power, as to be made children of God, save alone through the knowledge of Christ, and through faith in him. This glory is preached and offered unto us year by year and day by day, and it is so great that no one, whoever it may be, can meditate enough on it, much less tell it in their own words—that we, through our first birth from the time of Adam, poor, condemned, and miserable sinners, should come to this high honor and glory, that the eternal and almighty God should be our Father and we his children, Christ our brother and we his joint heirs, and that the dear angels should be—not our masters—but our servants and our brothers. It is so great and overwhelming that all who ponder it deeply are so astounded that they say, "Beloved, can it be so, and is it true?"

Therefore the Holy Spirit must be master in this matter. The Spirit must write this knowledge in our hearts and witness to our minds that it is Yes and Amen, that we through faith in Christ are children of God, now and forevermore.

Exposition of John 1, 1537.   WA 46:610f.

I know, O Lord, that all who are led by the Spirit are your children.
Keep me faithful all the days of my life. Amen.

He Comes at the Day of Judgment
Luke 21:25-36

And this is the judgment, that the light has come into the world, and people loved darkness rather than light because their deeds were evil. (John 3:19)

Christ asserts here, "This is the judgment, that the light has come into the world." As if he were to say, "It is a grand and blessed light that shines into your hearts and says, 'Do not fear the wrath of God, for God is gracious to you.' Even if your sin and your conscience plague and oppress you and you stand in awe of God's judgment, you must realize that all has been changed and that judgment has been abolished. Instead of harboring fear of the last judgment, you must yearn and long for it, since it does not denote your judgment at all but your redemption." At that time we shall be delivered from the last enemy, death (1 Corinthians 15:26); our bodies will rise again from the grave. Devil, death, and worms will cease; and God's disfavor will end. This judgment will draw you from the grave and deliver you from all evil. Therefore the day of judgment will be a time of rejoicing for you, far more so than the wedding day is for the bride; for this terrible day has been converted into a happy and desirable day for you. Thus all is well if you believe. But those who love darkness more than light will experience the reverse. They must live in dread of the last day. For the believer, the thought of this day is comforting, since condemnation and the terrible judgment are gone.

Sermons on the Gospel of St. John   *LW* 22:384

On that great day, O Lord, sustain me with your powerful word. Amen.

God's Merciful Warning

Be on guard so that your hearts are not weighed down
with dissipation and drunkenness and the worries of this life,
and that day catch you unexpectedly.
(Luke 21:34)

God in his great mercy does not will that the day of judgment should suddenly overtake us, and so, out of grace, he honors us with a merciful warning. God causes his Word to be preached to us, calls us to repentance, and offers us in Christ forgiveness of all our sins. God gives a sure promise that pain and guilt shall be abolished if we believe in his Son. He commands us to continue in our calling and to do our work well. If we obey him in doing so, he in no way grudges us food and drink or that we are happy and of good cheer. For eat and drink we must if we are to live on this earth. But we must not be forgetful of God and the life to come. Is not this a good and holy God, in that he looks on us with so fatherly a love? He ever speaks to us like a father to his children, and he says, "Dear children, repent; believe in my Son whom I have sent to you. Be holy and obedient, and faithful servants in your work; then eat and drink and use the earthly goods with which I have blessed you. But take care that you use the world and its passing goods like a man who is awaiting the last trumpet; so that when it peals and when the last thunders resound you are prepared and ready, walking in holy ways and with a godly spirit. If you live like that, you are in no danger."

Sermons from the year 1545.   WA 49:743

Your word, O LORD, is a lamp to my feet and a light to my path. Amen.
(Psalm 119:105)

Your Kingdom Come

Your kingdom come.
(Matthew 6:10)

This prayer does two things: it humbles us and it uplifts us. It *humbles* us in that it makes us confess openly that God's kingdom is not yet come to us. When earnestly contemplated and thoughtfully prayed, this is frightening, and it will surely grieve and pain every devout heart. For we must infer from this petition that we are still rejected, bereft of our most beloved homeland.

This involves two woeful and deplorable losses. The first is that God the Father is bereft of his kingdom in us, and that he who is and should be Lord of everything should through us alone be kept from such lofty power and honor. This must without doubt pain all who love God well and truly. The other loss is ours. It consists in this, that we are still kept in misery, in foreign lands among such mighty foes.

Second, when such thoughts have humbled us and shown us our misery, *consolation* follows, and our kind Master, our Lord Jesus, teaches us to pray and petition for rescue from our misery and not despair. Those who confess that they themselves are hindering God's kingdom from coming and plaintively pray that it may come to them will, because of their penitence and prayer, be pardoned by God.

That is why we do not pray, "Let us come into your kingdom," as if we should run after it, but "May your kingdom come to us." For the grace of God and his kingdom, with all the virtues thereof, must come to us, if ever we are to inherit it. Of ourselves we can never come to the kingdom. Similarly, Christ came to us from heaven to earth; we did not ascend from earth into heaven to him.

Exposition of the Lord's Prayer.   WA 2:95f.

Let your kingdom come to me that
I might follow your way, Lord God. Amen.

Your Redemption Is Drawing Near

Now when these things begin to take place, stand up
and raise your heads, because your redemption is drawing near.
(Luke 21:28)

This is indeed the true Master, who can interpret the signs rightly, not like astrologers and fortune tellers who read nothing but evil in them and so frighten people. For he tells nothing but good. And in those signs, which for the wise and the worldly signify nothing but destruction, which we must flee and fear, he can discern all that is good, and can find there those blessed words "your redemption," and so have a comforting picture for which the heart should long above all things. For what else do the words "your redemption" mean than that you who are now in bondage to the power of Satan, who attacks you with all his arrows so that you are beset and oppressed by the world and threatened by all kinds of peril and want, out of which neither you yourself nor anyone can help you, will be saved and set free by your Lord Jesus in heaven, and will be brought where you will be a master over devil, hell, and death, so that they all must lie at your feet? Why then should you be afraid of those signs and fear them? Why should you not rather greet them with joy?

We should willingly receive the comfort of knowing that he will surely come and will show by these signs that he is near.

Sermon for the Second Sunday in Advent, 1531.   WA 34/2:470ff.

Keep me ever mindful, Lord God, of your steadfast love,
especially in times of great distress. Amen.

Children of Light

Let us live honorably, as in the day.
(Romans 13:13)

No one does dark deeds while it is day; otherwise everyone would stand abashed before his neighbor. Hence all persons appear to be honest. There is a saying that "night knows no shame." This is true, and it is the reason why we do by night deeds for which we should blush by day. The day is chaste and makes us to walk in the way of honor. Likewise also Christians should live their lives and behave in such a way that they need feel no shame at any of their works, even though all the world should see them. For if our lives and works are such that we are loath to let our deeds be seen or heard openly and before everyone, we certainly are not living the Christian life.

You can see from this how much we need such an exhortation and warning to be wakeful and to put on the armor of light. How many true Christians can be found at this moment who could allow all their doings to come to light? But what manner of Christian life is it that we hypocrites live, if we cannot have our ways laid open before our neighbors, when they are actually long since laid bare before God and his angels and all creatures, and at the day of judgment will be known to everyone? Therefore Christians should live as they wish to be known by all persons and at the last day. Live as children of light (Ephesians 5:8).

Sermon for the First Sunday in Advent, 1522.   WA 10/1:13

Help me, O God, to do justice, to love kindness,
and to walk humbly with you. Amen.

Resist Satan

And then the lawless one shall be revealed,
whom the Lord Jesus will destroy with the breath of his mouth,
annihilating him by the manifestation of his coming.
(2 Thessalonians 2:8)

Thus Christians, following their Lord and Master, speak even today to the devil, "Away with you, Satan! for it is written, 'Worship the Lord your God, and serve only him'" (Matthew 4:10). That is to say, the Word of God is always with them, they live in it, they study it unceasingly, reading, teaching, preaching, punishing, exhorting, comforting, and the like. By so doing they have accomplished so much among the chosen people of God that henceforth that people trusts no longer in any self-appointed work or services, however wonderful their name, however radiant their light. Henceforth they build on God's unfathomable grace and mercy alone, which are promised and revealed to us in Christ.

We all who have the mind of Christ hope that this same joyful and comforting appearance of the glory of the great God and of our Savior Jesus Christ (who is now weak, poor, and disdained, and in his followers is more and more mocked, blasphemed, spat upon, crucified, and slain) is near and at our door, and that there will be an end to the numberless horrors. In his appearing, Christ, who is our life and our hope, will manifest and reveal himself as we now preach and believe him to be. That is, he will save us from the woe and wretchedness, which we, because we confess his precious Word and holy name, must now suffer both in body and in soul, from the evil and deceitful world, and from its father, the devil, and the Antichrist, which causes nothing but sin and provokes sheer destruction.

Sermons from the year 1537. WA 45:43f.

Lord, take my hand and lead me upon life's way. Direct, protect, and feed
me from day to day. Amen. (Julie von Hausmann, 1825–1901)

Come, Let Us Meet Him

Be dressed for action and have your lamps lit.
(Luke 12:35)

When you set out on a journey, you must lay aside your long, wide garments. You must be dressed for action, for Jesus says, "Be prepared and attentive to the game, have lit candles in your hands, be cunning and skillful, for there is nothing certain. Death comes to your homestead, but that hour remains unknown to you. Work as if you were to live without end, yet be of such a mind as if you were going to die at this hour." Such is the true meaning of being "dressed for action," that we live in expectation of Christ, the bridegroom. But such teaching casts us down and calls us to repentance. For no one will be so prepared that he or she may expect the day of the Lord with a joyful heart. We love so dearly our most wicked foe, the flesh, that we do not wish to die.

If you do not yet know that you are not dressed for action, cry to your God and sigh unto him, and he will forgive you. But God will not forgive those who despise his Word and are sure of themselves; indeed, he will count their wickedness against them for evil. God can suffer weakness, but wickedness and contempt he cannot endure. Therefore, let those who find themselves not thus inclined confess to God and pray for his help, that they may become thus dressed for action, and God will forgive them and help them graciously.

Sermons from the year 1537.   WA 45:384ff.

Give me, Lord God, a proper sense of my finitude
and a firm trust in your abiding love. Amen.

The Gospel Is Preached to the Poor

Matthew 11:2-10

The blind receive their sight, the lame walk,
the lepers are cleansed, the deaf hear, the dead are raised,
and the poor have good news brought to them.
(Matthew 11:5)

We should diligently mark these words of Christ and his kingdom, and should let them peal among us, namely, that Christ has such a kingdom and is such a king that he wills to help poor, wretched people in body and in soul. We should realize that without him not all the world with all its might and means can help. For never before has there been such a doctor with such skill that he could make the lepers clean, and cause the blind to see. Just as there was never before a preacher who could preach good news to the poor, that is, who could turn and invite to himself the sad, wretched, and affrighted souls, and relieve them, give them comfort, and fill with joy their fearful hearts, which before were weighed down in heaviness and sorrow.

The good and happy news is that Christ has paid for our sin, and through his suffering has redeemed us from eternal death. It is his kingdom and his ministry to preach the gospel to the poor; this is his purpose. To the great and holy he cannot come. They do not wish to be counted sinners, and therefore do not need his good news.

Sermon for the Third Sunday in Advent, 1544.   WA 52:24ff.

Lord God, help me also to answer your call for compassion to the weak
and needy and to maintain the right of the lowly. Amen.

We Too Belong to the Kingdom

The angel said to her, "The Holy Spirit will come upon you,
and the power of the Most High will overshadow you;
therefore the child to be born will be holy; he will be called Son of God."
(Luke 1:35)

These words the angel spoke to the blessed Virgin so that she should rejoice in the babe and cast off all fear and sorrow. Yet these words do not apply to the Virgin only but also to us. Therefore, although this blessed Virgin is alone the mother of the child, we too belong under his rule and kingdom. Otherwise we should fare ill. All that is ours passes away and lasts but a short while. For what are forty years, or fifty, or even a hundred? But with a person who belongs to an everlasting kingdom, all is well, and it is fitting that such a one should dance through life forevermore.

Thus the angel's saying reminds us of our passing life, in which there are so many dangers, sin, and death, and this saying helps us to endure our earthly life in that it points to a kingdom the like of which has never been on earth, an everlasting kingdom that has no end.

Sermons from the year 1544.   WA 52:639f.

All people are grass. The grass withers, the flower fades;
but the word of our God will stand forever. (Isaiah 40:7-8)

The Whole Scripture Points to Him

We declare to you what we have seen and heard.
(1 John 1:3)

Thus, then, is Christ our Lord, true God and true man whom the Father has appointed and ordained for his mission. For he is the spring and fountain from which flow sheer grace, truth, and righteousness. From him we receive grace upon grace and truth upon truth. Of him the evangelist says that we have seen him with our eyes, heard him with our ears, touched him with our hands, and recognized by his words and works that he is the Word of Life and the indescribable fount of all truth and grace (1 John 1:1-2). Now whoever desires to partake of it, whether it be Abraham, Moses, Elijah, Isaiah, John the Baptist, or anyone else, let them come here and receive it from him, and from no other. If they fail in this, they will be lost eternally. For, says the evangelist, "from his fullness we have all received, grace upon grace" and truth upon truth (John 1:16). Thus all of Holy Scripture, from the beginning to the end, points to Christ alone and directs our minds to him, ignoring all the saints. If grace and truth are to be acquired at all, Christ's fullness must perform this. Our few morsels, drops, bits, and pieces will not do it.

Sermons on John 1.   WA 46:643

Whom have I in heaven but you? And there is nothing on earth that I desire other than you. Amen. (Psalm 73:25)

He Was Born in Human Likeness

He emptied himself, taking the form of a slave,
being born in human likeness.
(Philippians 2:7)

The soul may not and must not find contentment in any other thing but in the highest good, which created it and is the fountain of its life and blessedness. Therefore God wills to be the one to whom the soul shall cling and in whom it shall believe. There is nothing else but God alone to whom belongs the honor that all creatures should believe in him. Therefore God has come and was made a human being and has sacrificed himself for humans, has drawn them to himself and called them by his name, that they should believe in him. For God had no need in himself to come and be made human, but it was necessary and profitable for us.

God's nature is too high and incomprehensible for us. Therefore for our good he submitted himself to the nature that is best known to us, that is, our own. There he waits for us, and there he may be found, and nowhere else. Here is the throne of grace from which no one will ever be shut out, if they only come.

Sermons from the year 1526.   WA 10/1:354

He was revealed in flesh, vindicated in spirit, seen by angels, proclaimed
among Gentiles, believed in throughout the world,
taken up in glory. (1 Timothy 3:16)

A Heart That Loves Humility

Though the LORD is high, he regards the lowly.
(Psalm 138:6)

Note well the picture painted here of God, who makes known to us his true nature in that it shows him as looking *downward. Upward* he cannot look, for there is nothing above him; *beside* him he cannot look, for there is nothing like him. Therefore he can only look downward, beneath himself. Therefore, the simpler and the lowlier you are, the brighter do God's eyes see you.

In short, this verse teaches us rightly to understand God's nature in that it shows him as looking down upon the lowly and despised, and the person who truly knows God knows that God looks upon the lowly. From such knowledge springs love of God and faith in him, so that we willingly abandon ourselves to him and follow him.

The truly humble never think of the result of their humility, but with a simple heart they look at what is lowly, live gladly with it, and are never aware of their own humility. But the hypocrites wonder why their honor lingers so long on the way; and their hidden and deceitful pride is not content with humble ways, but secretly they think ever more highly of themselves. Therefore truly humble souls never know of their own humility, for if they knew, they would be proud, because they are aware of that noble virtue within them. But with their heart and mind and all their senses they cleave to the lowly things, for they have them unceasingly before their eyes. Such are the images that dwell with them, and while they keep their eyes on the lowly things, they cannot narrow their concern to themselves or be aware of themselves.

Sermons from the year 1523. WA 12:612

O Lord my God, temper my pride and help me grow in healthy relationships with those around me. Amen.

A Scandalous King of the Cross

Blessed is anyone who takes no offense at me.
(Matthew 11:6)

Yes, truly blessed! For this king and his Word, in which we should find great joy, are a stumbling block for all the world. The world takes offense and is provoked by the good news of Christ, because it will not trust in the grace of God but rather in its own works and merits. Again the world takes offense at Christ because he is so utterly poor and wretched. And again it takes offense because he carries his cross and lets himself be hanged upon it, and he admonishes his followers to take their crosses and to follow him through all manner of temptations and afflictions. To this the world is especially hostile.

Thus our dear Lord Christ everywhere in the world is an annoying preacher. The gospel will never fare otherwise. It is and it will be a message at which offense is taken, not by the lowly, but by the most saintly and most pious, the wisest and mightiest on earth, as experience teaches us. Blessed are those who know and trust that it is truly the Word of God, for they are healed, and they are comforted and fortified against all such offense.

Sermon for the Third Sunday in Advent, 1544.   WA 52:27ff.

Heavenly Father, in the life and death of your Son, Jesus,
we learn of your steadfast love, which points us to salvation. Amen.

Rejoice in the Lord

Rejoice in the Lord always; again I will say, Rejoice.
(Philippians 4:4)

Such joy is the fruit and the consequence of faith. Where there is no faith, there is sheer fright, flight, dread, and wretchedness when God is remembered or named. Yes, in such hearts are hatred and enmity against God, because they find themselves guilty in conscience, and they cannot believe that God is good and gracious unto them, because they know that he hates sin and punishes it severely. If you should talk to such a soul about great joy in the Lord, it would be like telling water to catch fire. None but the just and righteous souls can rejoice in God, the Lord. Therefore this letter is written not for sinners but for saints. Sinners must first be taught how they can be freed from sin and receive the grace of God. Then the joy will follow of its own accord as soon as they are rid of their bad conscience.

But what is the promise of the gospel other than this, that Christ is given to us in order that he might take upon him our sin? When such faith in God's Word lives truly in our hearts, God becomes to us dear and sweet, for the heart now trusts fully and feels there is nothing but grace and favor with him, and dreads his punishment no longer. But it is filled with hope and confidence that God has given in Jesus Christ such surpassing grace.

Therefore from such faith must follow love, joy, peace, singing, thanksgiving, and praise, and we must feel a great and hearty joy in God as our dearest and most gracious Father. It is of such joy that St. Paul speaks here.

Sermon for the Fourth Sunday in Advent, 1522.   WA 10/1:170f.

Restore to me, O Lord, the joy of your salvation. Amen.

The Forerunner

John 1:19-28

You, child, will be called the prophet of the Most High.
(Luke 1:76)

Because Christ was to come humbly and unassumingly, without the splendor and ostentation of which our worldly hearts are so very fond, so that the world might be won through his word and wondrous deeds, and not by muskets, swords, and earthly power, he sent not an angel but a man. This man's name was John, who was more than a prophet (as Christ testifies of him, Matthew 11:9), who came not of his own accord but was sent from God. He was sent before the Lord, that he should knock at the hearts of the Jews, and awaken them, and testify to the Lord, saying, "Open your gates and doors. Your Savior, for whom you have been waiting so long, has arrived! Awake! Behold, the light is here, which was with God from the beginning and was eternal God, and is now a human being. Take heed and let not this thing pass you by."

Therefore he has a precious name, which is John, which means "full of grace." And he could not be called by any random name like other people but by a name that signifies his message, as all other names chosen and conferred by God do. Thus also God's own beloved Son was called Jesus not without reason but because he was to save his people from their sins (Matthew 1:21). So also John was not given his name because of his person but because it signifies his testimony and ministry.

Sermons on John 1.   WA 46:573

For the men and women of faith in former times, I give you thanks,
O God. Help me to do your will in my time on this earth. Amen.

The Person of John the Baptist

He himself was not the Light, but he came to testify to the Light.
(John 1:8)

I do not spurn John the Baptist; I honor and esteem him highly. But I must distinguish him and his ministry and life from Christ, to whom he bears witness. John is a servant and not the Lord himself. He points and leads to the true light, but is not the light itself. His ministry is greater and nobler than that of all the prophets, for he not only prophesies as they did that the Lord would come sooner or later. No, he points his finger at him who is already present and says, "Behold, this is he."

For this reason I think so highly of his ministry, and I give thanks to God, our beloved Father, that he has given us so faithful a witness and a mouth that testifies to the true light, and a finger that leads us to him who illumines our hearts forever and ever. Behold the man who points with his finger to the Lord, the Lamb of God.

But as for my salvation, I will not and I cannot trust in John, nor can I cling to his holiness, his austere living, and his saintly works. For he is not God's Christ (as he himself confesses, John 3:28), who is alone the light and life for us. He is a witness to the light, and he helps us through his ministry to become children of the light. Therefore he shines like a radiant and lovely light.

Sermons on John 1.   WA 46:590

Lord God, let me proclaim the light of salvation in my community
and let me live in this light. Amen.

The Ministry of the Baptist

Prepare the way of the Lord, make his paths straight.
(Matthew 3:3)

This is the way made straight for Christ, and this is the true ministry of John, that he shall humble us and tell us that we are all sinners, lost and condemned, poor, miserable creatures, and that there is no life, nor work, nor standing so holy, great, and good that it is not under condemnation, unless Christ dwell and work and walk in it, and both is and does all things through his faith. We all need Christ Jesus and should earnestly desire to partake of his grace.

Where it is preached that all our works and all our life are counted as nothing, there sounds the true voice of John in the desert, and the pure and full truth of Christian teaching; as Paul says, "All have all sinned and fall short of the glory of God" (Romans 3:23), which means that we are completely humbled, that our pride is cut out from our hearts and altogether abolished. And this may truly be called the straightening of the path for our Lord, making the rough places plain for him, and making way for him.

Sermon for the Fourth Sunday in Advent, 1522.   WA 10/1:198

I confess to you, Lord God, my fears and failings.
Make straight my path. Amen.

With Eager Zeal Prepare Your Heart

Repent, for the kingdom of heaven has come near.
(Matthew 3:2)

If you will listen, I am the voice calling, I am the angel who is sent before the Lord to announce to you that you are to prepare and to make straight the way for him, the Lord, who is following close after me. Then lay aside all that might hinder his way. Put away the gross and open sins, but above all the sins of the spirit, which have the appearance of holiness but which most impede his coming to you. Receive him with rejoicing, obey him, and believe in him, and come to be baptized. If you do this, you will be blessed by God, will receive the forgiveness of your sins, and will truly become his people, saved and holy. But if you will not let yourselves be taught, insisting rather to abide by your old nature, all hope will be gone and your doom will be upon you before you expect it. For the ax lies not beneath the bench, neither does it hang on the wall, "but even now the ax is lying at the root of the trees" (Matthew 3:10).

Thus the man to whom I point and witness is not so weak and contemptible as you may think. Truly, I tell you, he is stronger than I am. He is so great and holy that "I am not worthy to carry his sandals" (Matthew 3:11), for he himself is God, the Lord. Know that he comes to you full of grace, that he may help you out of all your need and make you just and blessed. If you receive him, all will be well with you; if not, he will soon leave you as you are.

Sermons from the year 1540.   WA 49/114f.

Help me, Lord God, to overcome long-held patterns
that are destructive or constraining. Amen.

Behold the Lamb of God

Here is the Lamb of God, who takes away the sin of the world.
(John 1:29)

Here begins the other part of St. John's teaching, in which he turns the people away from himself toward Christ, saying, "Here is the Lamb of God, who takes away the sin of the world." Through my teaching, he says, I have first made you sinners, condemning all your works and telling you that you must despair of yourselves. But in order that you should not likewise despair of God, behold, I will now show you how you can be rid of all your sins and attain salvation.

You cannot strip yourselves free from sin; neither can you make yourselves holy through good works. That is another person's work. I cannot do it either, but I can point to him who can. He is this Jesus Christ, the Lamb of God. He, and he alone, and no one else in heaven and on earth, takes sin upon himself, so fully that you yourself cannot even atone for the smallest sin. He must take upon himself alone not only *your* sin but the *whole world's* sin; not *some* of the world's sin, but *all* the sins of the world, be they great or small, many or few. This, then, is preaching and hearing the true gospel, and beholding the finger of John, that he may show you the Lamb of God.

If you can *believe* that this voice of John is a harbinger of truth and *follow* the direction of his finger and *behold* the Lamb of God bearing your sin, you have won the victory. You have become a Christian, a master over sin and death and hell and all things. And so your conscience is gladdened, and you will love the gentle Lamb of God.

Sermon for the Fourth Sunday in Advent, 1522.   WA 10/1:206f.

Cover my failings, O God, and let me rejoice in your salvation. Amen.

God's Most High Majesty Is Now Made Flesh

Without any doubt, the mystery of our religion is great:
He was revealed in flesh,
vindicated in spirit,
seen by angels,
proclaimed among Gentiles,
believed in throughout the world,
taken up in glory.
(1 Timothy 3:16)

Oh what a ridiculous thing, that the one true God, the supreme Majesty, should be made flesh; that here they should be joined, the human being and its maker, in one person. Reason opposes this with all its might.

Here, then, those wise thoughts with which our reason soars up toward heaven to seek out God in his own majesty and to probe how he reigns there on high are taken from us. The goal is fixed elsewhere, so that I should run from all the corners of the world to Bethlehem, to that stable and that manger where the babe lies, or to the Virgin's lap. Yes, that takes precedence over reason.

Do not search what is too high for you. But here it comes down before my eyes, so that I can see the babe there in his mother's lap. There lies a human being who was born like any other child, and lives like any other child, and shows no other nature, manner, and work than any other human being, so that no heart could guess that the creature is the Creator. Where, then, are all the wise? Who could ever have conceived this or thought it out? Reason must bow, and must confess her blindness in that she wants to climb to heaven to fathom the Divine, while she cannot see what lies before her eyes.

Sermons from the year 1533. WA 37:42f.

With hearts and hands uplifted, we plead, O Lord, to see the day of
earth's redemption that brings us unto thee. Amen.
(Laurentius Laurentii, 1700)

Christmas

The Word Was Made Flesh

And she gave birth to her firstborn son, and wrapped him
in bands of cloth, and laid him in a manger,
because there was no place for them in the inn.
(Luke 2:7)

How simply these things happen on earth, and yet they are so highly esteemed in heaven! On earth it happens this way: There is a poor young wife, Mary, at Nazareth, thought nothing of and regarded as one of the lowliest women in the town. No one is aware of the great wonder that she bears. She herself keeps silent, does not pride herself, and thinks she is of the humblest folk. She goes up with Joseph. They probably have neither manservant nor maidservant. Perhaps they left their homestead to look after itself; or they may have given it into a neighbor's care.

As they approach Bethlehem, Luke presents them to us as the most wretched and disdained of all the pilgrims, being forced to give way to everyone, till at last they are turned out into a stable and made to share shelter, table, and bedchamber with the beasts, while many a wicked man sits in the inn above and is treated like a lord. Not a soul notices and knows what God is doing in that stable. He leaves empty the manors and stately chambers, and leaves the people to their eating and drinking and their good cheer. But this comfort and great treasure remains hidden from them.

Oh, what a thick, black darkness was over Bethlehem then, that she failed to apprehend so great a light! How truly God shows that he has no regard for the world and its ways, and again, how the world shows that it has no regard for God, for what God is and has and does.

Sermon for Christmas, 1522. WA 10/1:62ff.

I pray today with Mary, "My soul magnifies the Lord,
and my spirit rejoices in God my Savior, for he has looked
with favor on the lowliness of his servant." Amen. (Luke 2:46)

Luke 2:1-20

Do not be afraid, for see—I am bringing you good news of great joy
for all the people; to you is born this day in the city
of David a Savior, who is Christ the Lord.
(Luke 2:10-11)

The little word "you" should make us joyful. For to whom does the angel speak? To wood or stones? No. He speaks to human beings; and not just to one or two, but to all the people. How then shall we understand these words? Shall we continue to doubt the grace of God and say, "St. Peter and St. Paul may well rejoice that their Savior is come, but I may not—I am a wretched sinner; the dear and precious treasure is not for me"? My friend, if you would say, "He is not mine," then I shall say, "Whose is he, then? Has he come to save geese and ducks and cows? If he had come to save another creature, he would certainly have assumed the likeness of that creature. But now he has been made the Son of Man."

Who are you, and who am I? Are we not likewise human beings? Who, then, but we humans should receive this child? The angels do not need him. The devils do not want him. But we need him, and for our sake he became human. Thus we should receive him joyfully, as here the angels say: "To you is born a Savior." Is it not a great and marvelous thing that an angel should come from heaven with such good news? Is it not a wonder that afterwards so many thousands of angels are filled with overflowing joy, which makes them desire that we should also be glad, and should receive such grace with thankful hearts? And therefore we should write this little word (with flaming letters) in our hearts: "To you!" and should joyfully welcome the birth of this Savior.

Sermon for Christmas Day, 1544.   WA 52:46

We rejoice, O God, in the little words "To you!"
We thank you for the glorious joy of this night. Amen.

And the Word became flesh.
(John 1:14)

Christ has a holy birth, immaculate and pure. Our birth is sinful and accursed, and we can only be helped through the holy birth of Christ. Yet Christ's birth cannot be shared with us, but it is offered spiritually to everyone wherever the Word is preached. Those who firmly believe and receive it will not suffer harm because of their own sinful birth.

It was Christ's will and pleasure to be born as a man so that in him we might be born again. "In fulfillment of his own purpose he gave us birth by the word of truth, so that we would become a kind of first fruits of his creatures" (James 1:18). In this way Christ takes our birth away from us and immerses it in his own birth, giving us his birth, that we may be made new and clean, as if it were our own birth. Therefore shall every Christian rejoice in this birth of Christ, and glory in it, as if they too were born of Mary. The one who does not believe that, or doubts it, is no Christian.

This is the great joy of which the angel speaks. This is God's comfort and his surpassing goodness, that we (if we believe) may glory in such a treasure, that Mary be our very mother, Christ our brother, and God our father. For all these things have truly happened that we might believe in them.

See, then, that you make this birth your own, exchanging with him, so that you might be rid of your birth, and might take on his, which happens when you believe. Then you surely will rest in the virgin Mary's lap as her darling child. But you must learn to have such faith and to exercise it throughout your earthly life, for it can never be strong enough.

Sermon for Christmas Day, 1522.   WA 10/1:71

Joy comes to all the world today, to halls and cottage hasting. Come, sparrow and dove, from roof tree tall, and share our Christmas feasting.
(Bernard S. Ingemann, 1789–1862)

Do not be afraid.
(Luke 2:10)

The angel's word shows that this king is born to those who live in fear and trembling, and such alone belong to his kingdom. To them it shall be proclaimed, as the angels announced to the poor, frightened shepherd, "I am bringing you good news of great joy." Such joy is indeed offered to everyone, but only those can receive it who are frightened in their consciences and troubled in their hearts. These are they who belong to me and to my preaching, and unto them I will bring good tidings. Is it not a wonderful thing that this joy is nearest to those whose consciences are the most restless?

The world is happy and of good cheer when it has loaves and fishes, means and money, power and glory. But a sad and troubled heart desires nothing but peace and comfort, that it may know whether God is graciously inclined toward it. And this joy, wherein a troubled heart finds peace and rest, is so great that all the world's happiness is nothing in comparison. Therefore should such good tidings be preached to wretched consciences as the angel preaches here: "Listen unto me, you of a sad and troubled heart, I bring you good tidings. For he has not come down to earth and been made man that he might cast you into hell. Much less was he for that reason crucified and given over to death for you. But he has come in order that with great joy you might rejoice in him." And if you would truly understand Christ and properly describe who and what he is, mark well the angel's word, how he defines and describes him, saying that he is and is called "great joy." Blessed are those who can well understand the meaning of this word, and hold it truly in their hearts; for strength is to be found by such.

Sermon for Christmas Day, 1531.   WA 34/2:505

In my fear and troubled conscience, O Lord, I would hear again the good news of great joy for redemption. Amen.

The Heart and the Child

For a child has been born for us,
a son given to us;
authority rests upon his shoulders;
and he is named
Wonderful Counselor, Mighty God,
Everlasting Father, Prince of Peace.
(Isaiah 9:6)

This child is sent to fill your heart, and for no other reason is he born. When the heart gives itself up through faith, it finds what his name is, namely, "Dearest Jesus." Then the heart lifts itself to the Father, who in his grace has given the child into the heart. No word can say nor understand that so small a thing should hold so great a treasure. Thus the wonderful sign is repeated and the heart is made sweet and glad and fearless, for it is at peace with all the suffering that may befall it. For what should cause it woe? Where the child is, all will be well. The heart and the child cannot be parted.

But it is impossible for the heart to receive the child and experience his sweetness unless it has first cast out all earthly joy, all things that are not Christ's. We must part with all things that are good in our sight: luxury, love of property, fame, our life, and piety, and wisdom, and all our virtue. When we have thus fully abandoned all that we have, then the babe comes to us, but he brings with him everything that slays our old Adam.

Bring to the child a humble soul, and the one who can best do this is the one who is cast down under much sadness, grief, and suffering, and has nothing to be desired, in such a way that he or she still bears willingly all adversities. Never will Christ be sweet to you until you have first become bitter to yourself. If you do not feel this within your heart, you may as well keep away.

Sermon on the birth of Christ, Christmas Day, 1520.   WA 7:190f.

Lord God, I bring to you my brokenness, my failings, and my
frustrations. Heal me, I pray. Amen.

He Considers the Lowly

He has brought down the powerful from their thrones,
and lifted up the lowly.
(Luke 1:52)

How could God have revealed his loving kindness more divinely than by sinking himself deeply into our flesh and blood, by not despising human modesty, and by honoring nature most where Adam and Eve had most disgraced it?

All evil lust and all evil thoughts fall away, however strong they are, if we but turn our eyes to that nativity, seeing how the most high Majesty is creatively at work in the flesh and blood of such a lowly Virgin. As deeply as she is despised on earth, so highly, yes, a thousand times higher, is she glorified in heaven.

Behold, how very greatly God glorifies those who are despised by the world and who rejoice therein. Open your eyes and see what the Lord sees! Only downward does he gaze into the deepest lowliness, as it is written, "He is enthroned above the cherubim and gazes into the deepest depth, even into the abyss."

Neither did the angels find princes or the mighty but only untaught and lowly folk. Might they not have brought their message to the high priest, the scholars at Jerusalem who have so much to tell about God and the angels? No, not they, but the poor shepherds were found worthy of such great grace and honor from heaven, they, who on earth have no honor. Yes, truly, God casts out all that is lofty.

Sermon for Christmas, 1522.   WA 10/1:68ff.

Happy are those who consider the poor;
the LORD delivers them in the day of trouble. (Psalm 41:1)

Simeon

*Simeon took him in his arms and praised God, saying,
"Master, now you are dismissing your servant in peace . . .
for my eyes have seen your salvation."
(Luke 2:28-30)*

Simeon is old and sees death before him. He feels death in his very bones, in every limb, as death approaches day by day, and daily he grows weaker, as often happens as we age. But it does not grieve him. He desires only that death come soon, and he says that he is not frightened by his departing—indeed, that death is welcome to him, since his eyes have seen his Savior. If this were not so, there could be no joy, nor could there be happiness in dying. Therefore the godly Simeon wanted to warn everyone and to lead us to this Savior (because we must all confess that we need a Savior), that we should accept Christ Jesus, whom our fancy has not created but whom God himself has ordained. For with his help we cannot fail. For this reason alone the child is come. God, his heavenly Father, has prepared him for our help. And certainly, if anyone possesses this Savior, that person is quiet and peaceful in heart.

It all depends on this, that we with the dear old Simeon open our eyes and see the babe, take him into our arms, and kiss him, which means that he is our hope, joy, comfort, and life. Where this faith is firm and sure in our hearts—that this child is God's Savior—there, indeed, it must follow that the heart is content and is not afraid of sin or death, for it has a Savior who delivers it from it.

Sermon from the year 1544.   WA 52/157

*Lord God, I share aged Simeon's longing for the fullness of salvation.
Hasten the day when evil is a thing of the past throughout creation. Amen.*

To You I Have Given All My Grace

This is my Son, the Beloved, with whom I am well pleased.
(Matthew 3:17)

With these words he says to us nothing other than this: There I give to you all my grace, love, and blessing, which I have in my heart and my power. In order that you may not and cannot doubt it in your minds, I offer you here—not Moses, nor a prophet, nor an angel, nor a saint, nor a treasure of gold and silver, nor great earthly or heavenly gifts—but my beloved Son, that is, my very heart, the true, eternal fount of all grace and good, which no angel nor any creature in heaven and on earth can fathom. He shall be the token and pledge of my grace and love against your sin and fear. And inasmuch as he is by birth and right the true heir and Lord of all the creatures, so in him you will become my children and joint heirs, and inherit all that he possesses in his power. For, in addition to giving us his privileges and the inheritance that are his by nature, he has achieved merit and bought us through suffering and death as our priest and bishop, that we may be his chosen children, and eternally joint heirs of all his goods. What more could he have given or done for us, and what greater or better thing could the human heart desire or conceive?

Sermon on Holy Baptism, Epiphany, 1535.   EA 16:85

Lord God, I rejoice because of the ministry of your Son.
Let me learn of him how to live. Amen.

The New Year

Ascribe Greatness to Our God

I will proclaim the name of the LORD; ascribe greatness to our God!
(Deuteronomy 32:3)

These words mean that I will sing a song beginning on a high note, so high that no one on earth shall begin higher or sing better. My finest song and subject shall be God's first command, that we should worship the one true God alone, should fear and love God from the heart, and in trust build on God alone.

So in my song I ascribe to the Lord all honor and give God all praise. Our God alone is above all gods, Lord above all lords, the maker of heaven and earth and the sea and all that in is them, who holds all the kingdoms of the earth. God lifts them up and casts them down, gives the breath of life to all humankind, and shapes and guides the inmost thoughts of the hearts of all kings and of everyone on earth. God alone is the giver of all good gifts for body and soul, and without God no one can have body or life, wisdom or strength, health, power or riches, or any good, or hold them for a moment.

Learn and remember this, then, that we should give all honor to God alone, earnestly look to God for all earthly gifts and all spiritual help and comfort, give God our whole hearts, trust in God for better, for worse, for life and death, flee to God in all temptations, and seek God in all distress and grief. This is the highest and most pleasing service.

Sermon on the Song of Moses, 1532.   EA 52:404f.

You, O God, have made us for yourself, and our hearts are restless until they rest in you. Amen. (Augustine, Confessions *1.1)*

NEW YEAR'S DAY

In God Alone Will I Put My Trust

My God, my rock, in whom I take refuge,
my shield and the horn of my salvation,
my stronghold and my refuge,
my savior; you save me from violence.
(2 Samuel 22:3)

"I believe in God, the Father almighty, creator of heaven and earth." I put my trust in no one on earth, not even in myself, not in any power, skill, possession, saintliness, or whatever else may be mine. I trust in no creature, whether in heaven or on earth. I regard and put my trust in the one, true, invisible, and incomprehensible God alone, the maker of heaven and earth, who is above all creatures. I do not fear the wickedness of the devil and his band, for my God is above them all. I believe no less in God even though I am abandoned or persecuted by everyone. I believe even though I am poor, foolish, untaught, and despised, and lacking all things. I believe even though I am a sinner. For this my faith must hover above all that is and is not, above sin and virtue and above all things, so that it remains immaculate and pure in God, as the First Commandment urges.

Neither do I entreat God for a sign or token, for I would not tempt God. I trust continually in God, however long I wait, and I set no term nor time, no measure nor means, but in a true and trusting faith I leave all things to God's divine will.

Since God is almighty, what could I want that God would not give or do for me? Since God is the creator of heaven and earth, and Lord of all things, who will rob me or do me harm? Why should not all things work together for my good, since I have found favor with God, to whom all are subject? Being almighty, God is able to make all things work for my good. As Father, God desires to do so and gladly does it.

A Short Form of the Apostles' Creed, 1520.   WA 7:215f.

In this new year, almighty God and Father, I thank you for the many blessings of the past, and I trust in your steadfast love for the coming year. Amen.

We Are the Lord's

If we live, we live to the Lord, and if we die, we die to the Lord;
so then, whether we live or whether we die, we are the Lord's.
(Romans 14:8)

Yes, certainly, we are the Lord's, and this is our greatest joy and comfort, that we have as a Lord the one to whom the Father has given all power in heaven and on earth, and into whose hands God has given all things. Who, then, can and will harm us? The devil may well rage with wrath, but he cannot tear us out of his hands. Further, are not we who believe in Jesus Christ our Lord, and live under his protection, also in him and through him, ourselves made lords over the devil, sin, and death? For he was made man for our sake (that he might win for us such lordship). For our sake he entreated the Father, and so loved us that he became a curse for us and gave himself a sacrifice for us. With his dear blood he bought us and washed us clean from sin. And again he has given us in our hearts the pledge of our inheritance and salvation, the Holy Spirit, and has made us kings and priests before God. In short, he has made us children and heirs of God, and joint heirs with himself. Yes, truly, this is a faithful saying.

Sermon on Romans 14:8.   WA 48:206

O Lord, strengthen my faith in times of disappointment and trial;
keep my focus steadfast on you. Amen.

The Lord Is Our Strength

The LORD is my strength and my might;
he has become my salvation.
(Psalm 118:14)

In nothing should we trust but in the Lord, who will be our strength and will work all things in us. Therefore we should praise him and thank him, that he alone may be our song. So shall we truly be blessed in him. It follows that this Lord is Jesus Christ, true God, eternally born of the Father, and also true man, born of Mary in the fullness of time, because he is here praised as our strength and power, our Savior.

But Christ cannot be our strength until we, in our own selves, are made weak and, through much suffering, crucified. Then he becomes our praise and song and psalm. Then follows victory and salvation to eternal life.

Comment on Psalm 118:14. WA 48:65

Lord of all hopefulness, Lord of all joy,
whose trust, ever childlike, no cares can destroy;
be there at our waking, and give us we pray,
your bliss in our hearts, Lord, at the break of the day. Amen.
(Jan Struther, 1901–1953)

The Trusting Heart

You shall have no other gods before me.
(Exodus 20:2)

That is, you are to regard me alone as your God. What does this mean, and how is it to be understood? What does "to have a God" mean, or what is God?

Answer: A "god" refers to that to which we look for all good and in which we are to find refuge in all need. Therefore, to have a god is nothing else than to trust and believe that one with your whole heart. As I have often said, it is the trust and faith of the heart alone that make both God and an idol. If your faith and trust are right, then your God is the true one. Conversely, where your trust is false and wrong, there you do not have the true God. For these two, faith and God, belong together. Anything on which your heart relies and depends, I say, that is really your God.

The intention of this commandment therefore is to require true faith and confidence of the heart, which fly straight to the one true God and cling to God alone. What this means is, "See to it that you let me alone be your God; never search for another." In other words, "Whatever good thing you lack, look to me for it and seek it from me, and whenever you suffer misfortune and distress, crawl to me and cling to me. I, I myself, will give you what you need and help you out of every danger. Only do not let your heart cling to or rest in anyone else."

The Large Catechism.   *BC 386f.; WA 30/1:132f.*

O God, you are my God, I seek you, my soul thirsts for you; my flesh faints for you, as in a dry and weary land where there is no water. Amen.
(Psalm 63:1)

Kings and Priests

*You are a chosen race, a royal priesthood, a holy nation, God's own
people, in order that you may proclaim the mighty acts of him
who called you out of darkness into his marvelous light.*
(1 Peter 2:9)

The nature of this priesthood and kingship is something like this: First,
with respect to kingship, all Christians are by faith so exalted above all
things that, by virtue of spiritual power, they are lord of all things, so
that nothing can do them any harm. Indeed, all things are made subject
to them and are compelled to serve them in obtaining salvation. Our
ordinary experience in life shows us that we suffer many things and must
die. The power of which I speak is spiritual. This is a splendid privilege
and hard to attain, a spiritual dominion in which there is nothing so
good and nothing so evil but that it shall work together for good to me, if
only I believe. Yes, since faith alone suffices for salvation, I need nothing
except faith exercising the power and dominion of its own liberty. Such
are the precious freedom and power of Christians.

Not only are we the freest of kings; we are also priests forever, which is
far more excellent than being kings, for as priests we are worthy to appear
before God to pray for others and to teach one another divine things.

Who, then, can comprehend the lofty dignity of the Christian? By
virtue of their royal power, they rule over all things, death, life, and sin,
and through their priestly glory are omnipotent with God, because they
do the things that God asks and desires, as it is written, "He fulfills the
desire of all who fear him" (Psalm 145:19).

On the Freedom of a Christian, 1520.   LW 31:354; WA 7:27f.

*We know, O Lord, that all things work together for good to those
who love you. Increase in me faith, hope, and love. Amen.*

Epiphany

We Beheld His Glory

When they saw that the star had stopped, they were overwhelmed with joy.
. . . They offered him gifts of gold, frankincense, and myrrh.
(Matthew 2:10-11)

When the wise men went to search for Christ, the newborn king, they did not find him in Jerusalem. Indeed, if they were to find him at all, they had to listen to the prophet Micah. When they had received the Word, they took the road to Bethlehem. Then the star returned as soon as they had got outside Jerusalem, and it shone brightly before them right to Bethlehem, to the door where the babe was. And truly they needed such a comfort, for they found nothing there but poverty and beggary. The babe is lying in a manger; there is hardly a drink of water. Can this really be a king's abode?

But the saintly men are not misled. Heedless of the poverty and wretchedness, they fall down before the babe and worship him, and open their treasures and present them to him.

We should learn from this story also the right attitude to have toward our Lord Jesus Christ. That is, we should cast aside all offense and, together with these wise men, witness before the world to the Lord Christ, seek him from the bottom of our hearts, and adore him as our Savior. And because his reign on earth is so poor and wretched, we should with our gold, goods, and all our possessions gladly help to increase his kingdom. For on this very day we can still open to Christ our treasures and present them to him, as the wise men did. How? His answer is written for us: "Just as you did it to one of the least of these who are members of my family, you did it to me" (Matthew 25:40).

Sermon for Epiphany, 1544.   WA 52:92f.

How can I respond to your gift of grace, O God? Nothing is enough.
I can only respond in faith and praise. Amen.

JANUARY 7

The Kingdom of Herod and the Kingdom of God

When King Herod heard this, he was frightened,
and all Jerusalem with him.
(Matthew 2:3)

To all outward appearance Herod was a mighty king, fortunate in war. Wherever he struck with his sword, all went well. He was wise, keen-witted, powerful, and wealthy in trade with foreign lands. But in his house he was frail and weak, a hapless man. Thus Herod was outwardly fortunate but inwardly miserable. But Christ, our true king, was outwardly utterly poor, wretched, despised, and cast away; yet he was inwardly utterly filled with joy, comfort, and courage.

Now we must take care that Herod, who is outwardly and in the world so fortunate, not steal away from us our true and gracious king, who is Christ. Although he lies in a manger as a poor and wretched babe, we must go there to him.

Therefore, if we desire happiness and want a pure and happy conscience, we must forgo King Herod's manner of living and follow another king, who is Christ. This means that we must not be so bold as to seek justification through works, nor place our hopes in them, but that we must etch on our hearts the image of Christ alone, the gracious Lord, who comes without any show. For when the three holy kings had left all human works behind and all human help, and (trusting in the holy Word of God through Micah, the prophet, 5:2) went forth toward Bethlehem, immediately they saw the star again.

Sermon from the year 1521.   WA 7:239f.

Help us, Lord God, to set our gaze and our hope not on the might
of earthly powers but on the Prince of Peace. Amen.

57

Twofold Perceiving

We have seen his glory.
(John 1:14)

There are two kinds of sight and of hearing. The one is performed with physical eyes and ears, entirely without the Spirit. This is the way all his countrymen looked at Christ, only with their five senses, thinking that he hailed from Nazareth and was Mary's son. This is a purely natural and physical sight. But Christ cannot be recognized in this way, even if we saw him every hour before our eyes and heard him. The second is a spiritual sight, which only Christians have and which takes place by means of faith in the heart. With this—if we are Christians—we must also view and recognize one another.

You must also look at Christ this way if you want to recognize him and know who he is, not as your eyes and senses prescribe, but as his Word shows and portrays him—as born of the Virgin, as the one who died and rose again for you and now sits enthroned as Lord over all things. Then you see not only his form, as your physical eyes do, but also the power and the might of his death and resurrection. Then you do not call him a son of Mary and Joseph from Nazareth, as his countrymen did, but our one true Savior and Lord over all.

This way of looking at Christ is far different from the way all the world does and the disciples did up to this time. But now their eyes are made clear by faith; this is a new insight.

Exposition of John 14.   LW 24:34–35; WA 45:490f.

Let me know you, Lord Jesus, in following your path. Amen.

Seek God in Christ Alone

Whoever has seen me has seen the Father.
(John 14:9)

Begin your search with Christ and stay with him and cling to him, and if your own thoughts and reason, or someone else's, would lead you elsewhere, shut your eyes and say, "I should and will know of no other God than Christ, my Lord." Certainly, if he is sent by the Father, he must have something really great to say and do for us, by the Father's will, so that we should hear him as we listen to the Most High himself. And what then is the word we hear? No other than that he came to help the world and to make the Father our friend.

What is the deed? No other than that he preaches and suffers and in the end dies on the cross. Take note that the Father's heart and will and work lie open before me, and I perceive and know him fully, and this no one could ever see or reach by their own wise and penetrating thoughts, however high they might climb with their speculations.

But if you abandon this clear prospect and climb up into God's majesty on high, you must stumble, fear, and fall because you have withdrawn yourself from God's grace and have dared to stare at the majesty unveiled, which is too high and overpowering for you. For apart from Christ, nature can neither perceive nor attain the grace and love of God, and apart from him there is nothing but wrath and condemnation.

Sermons on John 1–20.   WA 28:101f.

O Lord, your steadfast love endures forever.
Let it remain with me all the days of my life. Amen.

The Gospel Is Nothing but Christ

Do not let your hearts be troubled.
Believe in God, believe also in me.
(John 14:1)

Here, then, and elsewhere I hear that all his words are designed to comfort me; indeed, all his thoughts and words and works are pure kindness and comfort.

Therefore it must be true that if anyone has a heavy, dull, and frightened heart, it cannot be from Christ. For he is not the one to make hearts fearful, sad, and heavy. He came, accomplished his work, and ascended into heaven to take away from our hearts all fear and sadness and give us instead a joyful heart and conscience and joyful thoughts. But, you say, does not Christ himself often threaten and frighten us in the Gospel, as when he says, "Repent!" and again in Luke 13:5, "No, I tell you; but unless you repent, you will all perish just as they did"?

The very meaning of such words of Christ is that a sad and heavy conscience should care for nothing but that it find him and say to him, "Say what you will, these are your own words; who can ignore them?"

Indeed, if we could understand and discern properly, both things would be true, namely, that Christ comforts those whom the devil has frightened into despair and that he frightens those whom the devil has made sure and presumptuous. For these two will always wage war against each other. What the devil spoils, Christ must build up and set right. And again, what the devil builds, Christ destroys.

Sermons on John 14. WA 45:472ff.

In the dark and troubled times of my life, O God,
let me hear and trust your words of comfort. Amen.

There Is No Other Way

I am the way, the truth, and the life.
No one comes to the Father except through me.
(John 14:6)

Seek what you will, when the hour to enter another life and leave this behind comes, you must choose this way or be lost eternally. For, says he, "I am the way by which you come to the Father, and there is no other. I am the truth and the life, I, and no other." You must hold fast to this man and remain steadfast in your faith and confession, practicing it always in suffering. And in dying, say, "I know of no other help or counsel, consolation or comfort, path or way, but alone my Lord Christ, who for my sake suffered, died, rose again, and ascended into heaven. To this I cling, and I will persevere, even if nothing but hell, death, and the devil are beneath me and before me. For this is the right way and bridge, firmer and surer than any built of iron or of stone, and heaven and earth would burst before this would fail or deceive me."

Sermons on John 14.   WA 45:493

How firm a foundation, O saints of the Lord,
is laid for your faith in Christ Jesus, the Word!

The Glory of God Shines over the Child

Luke 2:41-52

He said to them, "Why were you searching for me?
Did you not know that I must be in my Father's house?"
(Luke 2:49)

What does this mean, "I must be in my Father's house"? Are not all creatures his Father's? Yes, everything is God's. But God gave the creatures to us for our use, that we should have dominion over them in this earthly life, as we know. But one thing God has kept to himself, his holy Word. And the temple is called God's sanctuary or holy dwelling place, because God causes his Word to be heard and shows himself present there.

God does not wish to be found among our friends or acquaintances or in anything apart from the ministry of the Word. Christ will not be found in what is not his Father's—not in what you or any other person is or has. That is why such dire distress overcame Joseph and the mother of Christ. Their wisdom, thoughts, and hope failed them, and they thought that all was lost as they searched for him in pain and sorrow, wandering from place to place. For they did not seek him as they ought. They searched for him as flesh and blood would do. Here everything must be abandoned—friends, acquaintances, the whole city of Jerusalem, all skill and human wit, and what they and all others are of themselves, for all this helps nothing and gives no true comfort until he is sought in the temple, where he is about his Father's business. There he will certainly be found, and the heart will be joyful again.

Sermon on the First Sunday after the Epiphany, 1525.   WA 17/2:24f.

Even if I think, "Oh, that I knew where I might find him,
that I might come even to his dwelling" (Job 23:3),
I know, Lord God, that you will find me. Amen.

He Was Obedient to Them

Then he went down with them and came to Nazareth,
and was obedient to them.
(Luke 2:51)

In these words the evangelist gathers up all the years of our dear Lord's youth.

But what does it mean, "He was obedient to them"? Simply that he walked in those works enjoined in the Fourth Commandment ("Honor your father and mother"). Such are the works that father and mother need done in the house: he fetched water, bread, and meat; he minded the house and did other things of that kind as he was told to do, like any other child. Therefore all good and God-loving children should say, "I grieve that I am not worthy of such honor that I should be made like the child Jesus in that I do what my Lord Christ has done. He picked up shavings and did other such tasks as his parents told him, menial tasks such as need to be done in any household. Yes, and what good children we should be if we would follow his example and do as our parents tell us, however poor and lowly the task may be."

Christ is Lord above all things, and yet, as an example for us, he condescends to obey father and mother. Therefore we shall take great pains to learn this story and shall deem ourselves blessed, when we walk thus obediently, for we see that Christ himself did not find such duties irksome.

Sermons from the year 1534.   WA 37:257f.

When I become weary of well-doing, O Lord, strengthen me
and keep my eyes on the goal. Amen.

The Fourth Commandment

Children, obey your parents in everything,
for this is your acceptable duty in the Lord.
(Colossians 3:20)

To fatherhood and motherhood God has given praise above all ranks and callings that are ordained by him. Therefore God commands us not only to love our parents but to honor them also. With respect to our brothers and sisters and all our neighbors, he commands no more than love. Thus God sets father and mother apart and gives them preference to all other persons on earth, in that he places them beside himself. For to love is not so high a thing as to honor, as this comprises not only love but also obedience, humility, and awe, as toward majesty. Neither is this the only demand, that we address them kindly and with reverence, but above all that we should show by our bearing and behavior that we esteem them highly and regard them as, next to God, the highest. If we are to honor them with all our heart, we must certainly think of them as high and great. Thus it should be engraved on the heart of the young to regard their parents as representing God and as appointed by God to be their father and mother, however lowly, poor, weak, and awkward they may be. They are not without honor even if they have faults and if their ways are foolish, for it is not a case of regarding persons but of God's will that ordains it so. Before the eyes of God we are all equal, but among ourselves we cannot live without diversity and proper distinctions. Therefore it is ordained by God that I, your father, should be your master, and you should be obedient to me.

Exposition of the Fourth Commandment.   WA 30/1:147f.

As a father has compassion for his children, so the LORD
has compassion for those who fear him. (Psalm 103:13)

Nurturing Our Children

Whoever welcomes one such child in my name welcomes me.
If any of you put a stumbling block before one of these little ones who
believe in me, it would be better for you if a great millstone were fastened
around your neck and you were drowned in the depth of the sea.
(Matthew 18:5-6)

Thus it is true that parents, even if they had nothing else to do, might attain eternal blessedness through their children. And if they bring them up in the true service of God, they will have both hands full of good works to do. What else are the hungry, thirsty, naked, the prisoners, the sick, and the strangers here but the souls of your own children (Matthew 25:35-36)? It is for their sake that God makes your house a hospital and appoints you the master of it, that you may tend them, feed them, and quench their thirst with good words and works, so that they learn to trust in God, believe in him, fear him, and place their hope in him. This is in order that they will honor his name, neither swear nor curse, be diligent, worship God and hear his Word, learn to despise the kings of this world, bear misfortune meekly, not to fear death or to love this life! Oh, what a blessed home where such parents live. It is indeed like a true church, a select monastery, yes, like paradise.

And again, there is no easier way for parents to merit hell than through their own children, in their own home, when they neglect to teach them these things. What does it help them if they bring themselves to the verge of death through fasting, praying, going on pilgrimage, and doing good works? On the day of judgment God will not ask about such things but will demand of them the children he has given and committed to them.

Sermon on Good Works, 1520.   WA 9:279

I pray, Lord God, for the welfare of our children and the health of our
families. Let our homes be places of security and joy. Amen.

He Blesses the Children

He took them up in his arms, laid his hands on them, and blessed them.
(Mark 10:16)

Why does he not embrace some mighty man, or a king, or some great saint? Instead, he takes a little child, who has but little understanding, and embraces it. Thus he shows that his kingdom belongs to children, that he, the Lord, is a prince of children, and that he wills to be found among children. By this he means to say, "If you want to know who is the greatest, I will tell you; if you listen to me, you are great, for I am all in all, and whoever receives me receives the Father, the maker of heaven and earth; yes, he receives heaven and earth at the same time. He receives God, with all his heavenly gifts and glory."

So it happens that we first receive Christ, the baby, and then through him the Father in heaven, for he says, "You will not always see me with your physical eyes. Therefore I will set something else before you, which you are to value as equal to me, namely, 'Whoever receives such a child in my name receives me, and whoever receives me receives the Father.'"

Why, then, should I search far and wide or even run toward heaven to find Christ? I see here so many Christians and their children who are the mirror and dwelling place of my dear Lord Christ, and when I see them, I see the Christ; when I hear them, I hear Christ. When I give them a drink of water, I give it to Christ; when I feed them, I feed Christ; and when I clothe them, I clothe Christ, and thus I have in the Christian church the world full of God and full of Christ. Wherever I look and see Christian children, I see Christ, if only I could believe it.

Sermons on Matthew 18–24.   WA 47:243f.

As you, O Lord, received little children, let me see each person
in my midst as the brother or sister for whom you died. Amen.

The Limit of Obedience

*Jesus said to her, "O woman, what have you to do with me?
My hour has not yet come."
(John 2:4 RSV)*

He sounds bitter and hard, but I know he is sweet. Notice here how severe he is even with his own mother, thus confirming that in the things that are God's, we must know neither father nor mother. For although there is no greater authority on earth than that of father and mother, yet it ends where God's Word and work begin. For in the things that are God's, neither father nor mother, let alone a bishop or another person, shall teach and lead us, but alone God's Word. And if your father or mother should command or teach, or even beg you to do anything for God, and in God's service, which is not clearly commanded by God, you must say to them, "What have I to do with you?" For fathers and mothers are bound, and for this very purpose they are appointed by God to be father and mother, to teach and guide their children, not according to their own conceit and pious ideas, but according to God's commandment.

Sermon on the Second Sunday after the Epiphany, 1525.   WA 17/2:67

*Happy is everyone who fears the LORD, who walks in his ways. . . .
Your children will be like olive shoots around your table. (Psalm 128:1, 3)*

Change and Become like Children

Truly I tell you, unless you change and become like children,
you will never enter the kingdom of heaven.
(Matthew 18:3)

Truly, dear Lord, you deal too harshly with us. Oh, that you would deal more considerately and not exalt those little foolish children so highly! Where did you command and teach that a foolish child should be esteemed greater than a wise man? How can our Lord God assert his justice and righteousness, which St. Paul praises so highly: "God's righteousness, God's righteousness"?

Is this your righteousness, that you cast out the wise and accept fools? Here the rule is, "You shall believe in the Word of God and give yourself up a prisoner to it. Our Lord God has purer thoughts than we humans. God must therefore take away our coarseness. He must hew off rough twigs and branches before he can make such children, such little foolish ones, of us. Behold, what pure and lovely thoughts the little children have when they look heaven and death full in the face, without any doubts. They are as in paradise. And the children, who are destined to be so great, have wonderful and peculiar ways.

Oh, dear Lord God, how well you are pleased with the life and the playful ways of little children. Yes, all their sins are soon forgiven.

Miscellaneous writings.   EA 57:258f.

I pray today, O Lord, for all who teach our children.
Give them insight and understanding that they might be
examples of justice and goodness in our society. Amen.

The New Sanctity

John 2:1-11

Now standing there were six stone water jars
for the Jewish rites of purification.
(John 2:6)

The six water jars of stone out of which the Jews performed their ritual washings are the books of the Old Testament, which through law and commandments cleansed the Jewish people only outwardly.

To turn water into wine means to make lovely the understanding of the law, which is brought about as follows: Before the gospel comes, everyone understands the law as demanding works, and that we are to fulfill it with our works. From such understanding come either stubborn and arrogant hypocrites, harder than any pot of stone can be, or anxious and uneasy consciences. But the gospel transfigures the law in that it demands more than we can do, needing someone very different from us to fulfill it. That is, it calls for Christ, driving and pointing to him, that through his grace we may first by faith be made like him and other Christians, and then really do good works. So the gracious gospel comes and makes the water wine. Yes, it is now a precious thing, and has a lovely taste, for the law is at once so deep and lofty, so holy, true, and good, that it is praised and loved forever because it demands such great things. Thus it becomes sweet and easy which was previously hard and difficult, yet even impossible, for through the Spirit it is now alive within the heart.

Sermon for the Second Sunday after Epiphany, 1525.   WA 17/2:69f.

I pray, O God, that those whose lives are strangled by regret
and guilt might know the liberating power of your grace. Amen.

God's Kind and Loving Gospel

*But when the goodness and loving kindness
of God our Savior appeared, he saved us.
(Titus 3:4-5)*

Thus God has shown himself in his gospel altogether loving and kind toward us, willing to receive everyone, despising none, forgiving all our wickedness, never driving any away with severity. The gospel proclaims pure grace, with which God helps us and surrounds us in the most benevolent way, so that no one is treated according to their merits and deserts. This is the time of grace, where everyone may draw near to the throne of God with complete trust and confidence.

In the gospel God has revealed to us divine kindness not only in helping us and inviting us to be near him—but even more holds to us, seeks to be with us, and offers us unceasingly his grace and friendship. These are two sweet and comfortable words and promises of our God, namely, that God offers grace to us and does not leave us, and that God receives in a most loving way all who desire to draw near to him. What more could God do? You can see, then, why the gospel is called a comfortable and lovely message of God in Christ. What sweeter word could be spoken to a wretched, sinful conscience?

Sermons from the year 1522.   WA 10/1:(i)ff.

*How good it is to sing praises to our God; for he is gracious,
and a song of praise is fitting. (Psalm 147:1)*

The Law and the Gospel

We hold that a person is justified by faith apart
from works prescribed by the law.
(Romans 3:28)

The entire Scripture of God is divided into two parts: commandments and promises. Although the commandments teach things that are good, the things taught are not done as soon as they are taught, for the commandments show us what we ought to do but do not give us the power to do it. They are intended to teach us to know ourselves, that through them we may recognize our inability to do good and may despair of our own ability. That is why they are called the Old Testament. For example, the commandment "You shall not covet" (Exodus 20:17) proves us all to be sinners, for no one can avoid coveting no matter how much we may struggle against it. Therefore, in order not to covet and to fulfill the commandment, we are compelled to despair of ourselves, to seek the help we do not find in ourselves elsewhere and from someone else.

Now when we have learned through the commandments to recognize our helplessness and are distressed about how we might satisfy the law—since the law must be fulfilled so that not a jot or tittle shall be lost, otherwise we will be condemned without hope—then, being truly humbled and reduced to nothing in our own eyes, we find in ourselves nothing whereby we may be justified and saved. Here the second part of Scripture comes to our aid, namely, the promises of God that declare the glory of God, saying, "If you wish to fulfill the law and not covet, as the law demands, come, believe in Christ in whom grace, righteousness, peace, liberty, and all things are promised you. If you believe, you shall have all things."

On the Freedom of a Christian, 1520.   LW 31:348; WA 7:23f.

The law of the Spirit of life in Christ Jesus has set you free
from the law of sin and of death. (Romans 8:2)

The Right Use of the Law

Now we know that the law is good, if one uses it legitimately.
This means understanding that the law is laid down not
for the innocent but for the lawless and disobedient.
(1 Timothy 1:8-9)

In order to understand truly how to use the law, you must divide the human person into two parts and keep the two clearly separated, namely, the old person and the new, as St. Paul said. Leave the new person completely undisturbed by laws, but the old you must unceasingly spur on with laws, giving no rest from them. In that way you use the law well. The new person cannot be helped through works but needs something higher, namely, Christ, who is neither law nor works, but a gift and present of the sheer grace and goodness of God. When through faith he comes to dwell in your heart, God makes you saintly. But if you should ever think of becoming acceptable through some deed of your own, such as entering some order, or pursuing some vocation, you would have failed to use the law rightly and denied Christ. He wants to help you without any work of yours, but if you try to help yourself through your works, you have carried the law too high and too far. For you drive Christ out of your heart where he should reign alone, and in his place you put the law and your own works.

In this manner (I say), as new persons, we carry in our hearts Christ and all his heavenly goods and are in need of nothing, whether in heaven or on earth.

Sermon on 1 Timothy 1:8-11.   WA 17/1:122f.

Help me, my God and Father, to set right priorities in my life,
considering my debt to you and to my neighbor. Amen.

THURSDAY

Our No to the Law and Our Yes to Christ

For sin will have no dominion over you,
since you are not under law but under grace.
(Romans 6:14)

This is the main article we must learn. It gives us authority, even if we feel the lust of our flesh or fall into sin, to say, "Although it is my will to be rid of the law, neither am I still under the law or sin, but I am devout and righteous." If I cannot say this, I must despair and perish. The law says, "You are a sinner." If I say yes, then I am lost; if I say no, I must have a firm ground to stand on, to refute the law, and uphold my no. But how can I say it, when it is true and is confirmed by Holy Scripture that I was born in sin? Where then shall I find the no? I shall surely not find it in my own heart but in Christ. From him I must receive it and fling it down before the law and say, "Certainly he can say no against all law, and has the right to, for he is pure and free from sin, and he gives me the no, so that though if I look on myself I should have to say yes, because I see that I am a sinner and could not stand before the law, and feel there is nothing pure in me, and see God's wrath, yet I can say that Christ's righteousness is my righteousness, and henceforth I am free from sin." This is the goal, that we should always be able to say that we are pure and godly forever, as Christ himself can say, and this is all accomplished through faith.

Sermons from the year 1525.   WA 17/1:155f.

O Lord, I believe; help my unbelief. Amen. (Mark 9:24)

Our Sins Are Laid on the Lamb

As he watched Jesus walk by, he exclaimed,
"Look, here is the Lamb of God!"
(John 1:36)

It is extremely important that we know where our sins have been disposed of. The law deposits them on our conscience and shoves them into our heart. But God takes them from us and places them on the shoulders of the Lamb. If sin rested on me and on the world, we would be lost; for it is too strong and burdensome. God says, "I know that your sin is unbearable for you; therefore see, I will lay it on my Lamb and relieve you of it. Believe this! If you do, you are delivered of sin." There are only two abodes for sin: it either resides with you, weighing you down; or it lies on Christ, the Lamb of God. If it is loaded on your back, you are lost; but if it rests on Christ, you are free and saved. Now make your choice! According to the law, to be sure, sin should remain on you; but by grace sin was cast on Christ, the Lamb. Lacking this grace, we should be doomed in an accounting with God.

These are clear, plain, and powerful words.

Exposition of John 1.   LW 22:169; WA 46:683f.

I lay my sins on Jesus, the spotless Lamb of God; he bears them all and frees us from the accursed load. (Horatius Bonar, 1808–1889)

Seeking the Lost

The saying is sure and worthy of full acceptance,
that Christ Jesus came into the world to save sinners.
(1 Timothy 1:15)

Christ asserts, "My ministry is to save people." And he can certainly speak gloriously of his handiwork as a true master, for where people have learned every detail of their trade, they have the right to speak of their work so that everyone must acknowledge that they are master workers. Similarly, Christ is a master of his craft. He speaks most assuringly about his ministry: "I have come to help everyone who is lost; that is my craft and ministry. I have not been sent to bring a new law to burden the world." There are laws enough in the world, more than people can keep. The state, fathers and mothers, schoolmasters, and law-enforcement persons all exist to rule according to laws. But the Lord Christ says, "I have not come to judge, to bite, to grumble, and to condemn people. The world is too much condemned. Therefore I will not rule people with laws. I have come that through my ministry and my death I may give help to all who are lost and may release and set free those who are overburdened with laws, with judgments, and with condemnation."

This is a comforting saying in which the Lord Jesus portrays his dear sweet self, and it agrees with John, who says, "God did not send the Son into the world to condemn the world, but in order that the world might be saved through him" (John 3:17). Jesus says, "I have come into the world that was condemned already and has enough to do with judges and judgment; but I will take away that judgment, that all who are condemned may be saved."

Because of our desperate need, we must have such sayings.

Sermon on John 3.   WA 47:27

I thank you, Lord God, that there is forgiveness with you,
so that you may be revered. Amen.

God Is Glorified in Our Bodies

Matthew 8:5-13

When Jesus heard him, he was amazed. . . .
(Matthew 8:10)

In this example two kinds of miracles have taken place, or a twofold miracle, one that the Lord does and the other that the centurion does. For the text clearly says that Jesus himself marvelled that the centurion had such a strong faith. And what Christ regards as a miracle, we too must surely regard as such.

People deem it a great miracle that Jesus made the blind see, the deaf hear, and the lepers healed. Certainly, these are great miracles. But Christ thinks much more highly of what comes to pass within the soul than of what happens to the body. Therefore, as the soul is so much more precious than the body, so great and so much greater is the miracle that he praises here than other miracles that happen to the body.

There are two kinds of miracles here, and so it will remain to the day of judgment, that Christ daily performs miracles and will do so forever. Those regarding the body he seldom performs, as he rarely performed them while he was on earth. Those miracles were performed in order that the Christian church should be founded. But the signs that he regards as miracles happen still today and remain eternally, such as the faith of the Roman centurion at Capernaum. It is a miracle—a great miracle—that someone should have such admirable, strong faith. Therefore Christ exalts this centurion's faith as if it were a miracle above all miracles.

Sermons from the year 1535.   WA 41:18ff.

For the miracle of life and for the gift of faith I thank you, Lord God.
Give me strength to make my faith active in love. Amen.

MONDAY

God's Creature

*The Spirit of God has made me, and the breath
of the Almighty gives me life.
(Job 33:4)*

What do you mean when you say, "I believe in God, the Father almighty, creator," and so on? Answer: I hold and believe that I am God's creature, that is, that God has given me and constantly sustains my body, soul, and life, my members great and small, all my senses, my reason and understanding, and the like; my food and drink, clothing, nourishment, spouse and children, house and farm, and so forth. Besides, he makes all creation help provide the benefits and necessities of life—sun, moon, and stars in the heavens; day and night; air, fire, water, the earth and all that it yields and brings forth; birds, fish, animals, grain, and all sorts of produce. Moreover, he gives all physical and temporal blessings—good government, peace, security, and so on. All this is comprehended in the word "creator."

How much could be said if we were to describe how few people believe this article. We all pass over it; we hear it and recite it, but we neither see nor think about what the words command us to do. For if we believed it with our whole heart, we would also act accordingly, and not swagger about and boast and brag as if we had life, riches, power, honor, and such things of ourselves, as if we ourselves were to be feared and served. We ought daily to practice this article, impress it upon our minds, and remember it in everything we see and in every blessing that comes our way. Our hearts will be warmed and kindled with gratitude to God and a desire to use all these blessings to his glory and praise.

The Large Catechism.   BC 432–433; WA 30/1:183ff.

*The earth has yielded its increase; God, our God, has blessed us.
May God continue to bless us; let all the ends of the earth revere him.
(Psalm 67:6-7)*

Christi Sighs over Our Infirmities

They brought to him a deaf man who had an impediment in his speech;
and they begged him to lay his hand on him. . . . Then looking up to
heaven, he sighed and said to him, "Ephphatha," that is, "Be opened."
(Mark 7:32, 34)

He was not concerned about the tongue and ears of this poor man
alone, but this was a general sighing over all tongues and ears, yes, over
all hearts, bodies, and souls, and over all humankind from Adam till the
last human being who shall be born. So he does not sigh chiefly over the
many sins that this man will still commit. No, but best of all, the Lord
Jesus sees all humankind's flesh and blood, and how in Eden the devil
had brought it into deadly peril, making humans dumb and plunging
them into death and hellfire.

This is the vision that Christ had before his eyes, and he looked
around and saw the great evil that the devil has wrought through one
person's fall in Eden. He looks not on those two ears alone but on the
whole multitude of mortals who have been born of Adam and still are to
be born. So this Gospel paints Christ as being the one man who cares for
you and me, and for us all, as we ought to care for ourselves, as if he were
immersed in the same shame and sin as we are.

Sermons from the year 1534.   WA 37:509

Come, ye disconsolate, where'er ye languish;
*   come to the mercy seat, fervently kneel.*
Here bring your wounded hearts, here tell your anguish;
*   earth has no sorrow that heav'n cannot heal.*
(Thomas Moore, 1816)

Tongue and Ear

He took him aside in private, away from the crowd, and put his fingers into his ears, and he spat and touched his tongue.
(Mark 7:33)

He singles out these two organs, ear and tongue, because the kingdom of Christ is founded on the Word, which cannot be perceived and comprehended except with these two organs, ears and tongue. The kingdom reigns in the human heart by faith alone. The ears comprehend the Word and the heart believes it. Therefore, if tongue and ears are taken away, there remains no marked difference between the kingdom of Christ and the kingdom of the world.

In the outward life Christians go about like unbelieving persons: they build, till the ground, and plow like other persons. They do not undertake any special task, neither with regard to eating, drinking, sleeping, working, nor anything else. These two organs alone make a difference between Christians and non-Christians: a Christian speaks and hears in a different manner and has a tongue that praises God's grace and preaches Christ, declaring that he alone can make us blessed. The world does not do that. It speaks of avarice and other vices, and preaches and praises its own pomp.

Sermons from the year 1534.   WA 37:512

Let the words of my mouth and the mediation of my heart be acceptable to you, O LORD, my rock and my redeemer. Amen. (Psalm 19:14)

The Gospel Does Not Destroy Nature

Sarah died. . . . And Abraham went in to mourn for Sarah.
(Genesis 23:2)

That Abraham came to mourn and weep for Sarah is written in order to show that it is not wrong to grieve and weep and mourn when those whom we love die. Although we must all die, we are so made by love that we rejoice in each other's life, just as we are all linked in that we are poor and eat our bread in the sweat of our brow. Indeed, so long as we live we shall care for each other and be mindful of our neighbor's poverty and other sorrows.

It is not God's will that his gospel should destroy nature; rather God upholds what is natural and leads it into the right way. It is natural that a father should love his child, a wife her husband, and be happy when all is well with them. And again, a Christian is not content to stand before God as a person of faith simply when someone's world collapses, but we should interest ourselves as if it were our own trouble, and act with love. He would not have ordained it should be written that the great patriarch Abraham wept for Sarah, if it were not meant to serve us to that end. Thus God ordains that such feelings of the heart remain with us, yet it is his will that we should overcome them through faith and not despair or fall from him.

Exposition of Genesis 23.   WA 24:408f.

Sad is my heart for the blighted plants—
    Its pleasures are aye as brief—
They bloom at the young year's joyful call,
    And fade with the autumn leaf.
Ah! may the red rose live always,
    To smile upon earth and sky!
Why should the beautiful ever weep?
    Why should the beautiful die?
(Stephen Foster, 1826–1864)

Dead to Sin

But if we have died with Christ, we believe
that we will also live with him.
(Romans 6:8)

We see how in this way Paul understands the life of Christians on earth entirely in relation to the death of Christ. He pictures them as now dead and lying buried in a coffin, which means that they have died to sin and have no part in it forevermore. That is to say, sin is dead unto them and they are dead unto sin, because they are no longer found to be walking in the sinful ways of the world. Yes, now they have died twice (or in a twofold manner), once spiritually to sin, which is a blessed dying, full of grace and comfort (although to flesh and blood it is painful and bitter), and a lovely, sweet death, for it leads to an entirely heavenly, sure, perfect, and eternal life. But they have also died once physically, which is no death but rather a pure and gentle sleep laid on the flesh, because while we are here on earth the flesh never ceases to resist the spirit and life.

As long as the flesh lives here on earth, it spreads and drags sin behind it. It resists and will not die. Therefore in the end God must put it to death, that it may also die to sin. And this is again a pure and gentle death and really nothing but a sleep, for it will not remain in death (because the soul and the spirit are no longer in death) but will come forth on the day of judgment cleansed and purified, and will return to the spirit, where it will be a clean, pure, and obedient body without any sin and evil lust.

Sermon on Romans 6:3-11.   WA 22:99f.

Asleep in Jesus! Blessed sleep,
  From which none ever wakes to weep;
A calm and undisturbed repose,
  Unbroken by the last of foes.
(Margaret Markay, 1832)

Our Members Are Servants for Righteousness

*Just as you have presented your members as slaves to impurity
and to greater and greater iniquity, so now present your members
as slaves to righteousness for sanctification.*
(Romans 6:19)

Even reason teaches you that since you are no longer subject to sin and iniquity you should no longer serve them nor obey them with your bodies and members, that is, with your whole physical life and nature. Moreover, having given yourselves up to obey God and his righteousness, it is your duty to serve God with your whole body and being. This means that any person who previously did evil and lived in opposition to the will of God and their own conscience shall now live devoutly and serve God with a good conscience.

Previously, Paul says, all your members, eyes, ears, mouth, hands, feet, and the whole body, worked for uncleanness. In the same way you allowed your members to serve iniquity in life and work with all kinds of trickery and cunning. Turn this now around, according to your own judgment and understanding. Where formerly you liked to see, hear, and talk about what was lewd and obscene, or where you pursued such things and made your bodies servants of uncleanness, it should now hurt your eyes and ears to see and hear such things, and the whole body should flee from them and be chaste in words and deeds, so that all the members and the whole body shall serve righteousness.

You do this because your members and bodies become holy, that is, God's property, used alone in God's service, so that they all serve obediently to the honor of God in everything that is godly, praiseworthy, honorable, and virtuous.

Sermon on Romans 6:19-23.   WA 22:112f.

*Give me grace, Lord God, in my brief time on earth, to cultivate mercy,
compassion, and justice among all your creatures. Amen.*

God Is Glorified in Creation

Matthew 8:26-27

"Why are you afraid, you of little faith?" Then he got up
and rebuked the winds and the sea; and there was a dead calm.
(Matthew 8:26)

This is an example of trust and lack of trust. Consider what the disciples felt in their hearts. When they entered the boat with Christ, everything was calm, and they felt nothing in particular. At that moment their trust was firm. Their hearts trusted in the stillness of the waters, which shows that their faith was founded on what they could see. But when the storm arose and the waves broke over the boat, their faith collapsed, and in their souls nothing was left but despair.

And what does despair do? It perceives nothing more than it feels. It feels neither life nor safety, but only the waves breaking over the boat and the sea presenting all kinds of danger. Because they are conscious of those perils and keep their minds fixed on them and never turn away from them, their hearts become filled with anguish, fear, and trembling. Indeed, the more they feel and look at the storm, the more they tremble at the fear of death.

If there had been true faith in their hearts, it would have set up before their eyes the power and the grace of God as they are promised in his Word.

Sermons from the year 1525.   WA 17/2:104f.

When the storms of life are raging, stand by me.
When the world is tossing me like a ship upon the sea,
thou who rulest wind and water, stand by me. Amen.
(Charles Albert Tindley, 1851–1933)

Created and Upheld by the Word

*Jesus answered them, "My Father is still working,
and I also am working."*
(John 5:17)

God the Father initiated and executed the creation of all things through the Word, and now God continues to preserve the creation through the Word. God remains with his handiwork until the time comes to terminate it.

How long would the sun, the moon, and all the lights of the sky keep to the course maintained for so many thousands of years? If it were not for the divine power, it would be impossible for humankind to be fruitful and raise children. The beasts could not bring forth their young, each after its own kind, as they do every day. If God were to withdraw his hand, buildings and everything in them would collapse. The power and wisdom of all angels and humans would not be able to preserve them for a single moment. The sun would not long retain its position and shine in the heavens; no child would be born; no kernel, no blade of grass, nothing at all would grow on the earth or reproduce itself if God did not work unceasingly.

If the Creator, who continues to work forever, and his coworker were to interrupt their work, all would go to wrack and ruin in a twinkling. This truth prompts us to confess in the articles of our Christian creed, "I believe in God the Father almighty, creator of heaven and earth." If God had not preserved us whom he created, we would have died and perished long ago, yes, even in the cradle or at birth.

Sermon on John 1.   LW 22:26; WA 46:558f.

The earth is the LORD*'s and all that is in it, the world and those who live in it; for he has founded it on the seas and established it on the rivers.*
(Psalm 24:1-2)

The Creation in the Light of the Incarnation

He himself is before all things, and in him all things hold together.
(Colossians 1:17)

The article concerning creation from nothing is more difficult to believe than the article concerning the incarnation of Christ.

Through his incarnation Christ leads us back to the knowledge of the Creator in which the angels rejoice. This could not happen unless through his own person, which is the image of God, he took away our sin, which is the kingdom of death. For sin has so blinded human nature that it no longer knows the Creator, although it catches a hint of his works, especially in the order of the world. We do not even know our own sin, and we think our blindness is the highest wisdom.

If only Adam had not sinned, we would have recognized God in all creatures, and we would have loved and praised God so that even in the smallest blossom we would have seen and pondered God's power, grace, and wisdom. But who can fathom how from the barren earth God creates so many kinds of flowers of such lovely colors and such sweet scent, as no painter or alchemist could make? Yet God can bring forth from the earth green, yellow, red, blue, brown, and every kind of color. All these things would have turned the mind of Adam and his family to honor God and laud and praise him and to enjoy his creatures with gratitude.

Table Talk.   WA Tischreden 4:198

O LORD, how manifold are your works! . . .
The earth is full of your creatures. Amen. (Psalm 104:24)

All Things Have Life in Him

He sustains all things by his powerful word.
(Hebrews 1:3)

Here the author of Hebrews says that Christ sustains all things. If he sustains all things, he is not sustained himself and is above all things, which none can be but God alone. The sustaining means that he nourishes and upholds all things, so that all things were not only made by him but continue in him and are sustained by him, as Paul says: All things consist in him and through him (Colossians 1:16-17). What a fine and lovely word he uses when he says, "God sustains." God does not drive or hunt or roar; he gently sustains and lets all creatures enjoy his loving kindness, as it is written that the wisdom of God "reaches mightily from one end of the earth to the other, and she orders all things well" (*Wisdom* 8:1).

The meaning of this text is that Christ sustains all things by his powerful word, that is, by the working of his power. For by the working of his power all things are upheld, and all that has being and power has it not of itself but of the active and creative power of God. Here especially the power and the Word must not be separated, for the power and the Word are one, which means that there is one active or powerful Word, so that power is the essence and the nature of the Word that works in all things.

Sermons from the year 1522.   WA 10.1/1:158f.

By the word of the LORD the heavens were made,
and all their host by the breath of his mouth. (Psalm 33:6)

How Awesome Are Your Deeds!

How awesome are your deeds!
(Psalm 66:3)

A housewife has a set of fifteen eggs, and she places them under a hen or goose. In four or six weeks' time she has a basketful of little chickens or goslings. They eat, and drink, and grow until they are full grown. Where do they come from? The eggs open when the time has come, and inside sit the chicks or goslings. They poke their little beaks through the shell and at last creep out. The mother hen or goose does nothing but sit on the eggs and keep them warm. It is God's almighty power that is at work within those eggs, making them turn into hens and geese.

Similarly with the fish in the water and with all the plants that grow from the earth. Where do they come from? Their first beginning is the spawn that floats in the water, and from this grow, by the Word and power of God, carp, trout, pike, and all kinds of fish, so that the water is swarming with them. An oak, beech, or fir tree grows out of the earth many feet thick and many yards high. What is its first beginning? Water and earth. The root draws its sap and moisture from the soil and forces it up with all its might so that the tree grows big and strong and tall.

What is the cause of this? It is God's omnipotence and the Word that the eternal, almighty Creator spoke. "God created the great sea monsters and every living creature that moves, of every kind . . . cattle of every king and everything that creeps upon the ground" (Genesis 1:21, 25). It is the Word and omnipotence of God that bring it all about.

Sermons from the year 1544.   WA 49:436f.

O Lord, we see traces of your work in the natural world, and we see your compassion and steadfast love in the work of your Son, Jesus. Amen.

The Cross within God's Creation

We know that the whole creation
has been groaning in labor pains until now.
(Romans 8:22)

The radiant sun, the loveliest of the creatures, gives only a little of its service to the saints. While it shines on one saint it must shine on thousands of rogues, in spite of all their godlessness and evil.

It is our Lord God's good creature, and it would much rather serve devout people; but the noble creature must bear it and serve the evil world unwillingly. Yet it hopes that that service shall at long last have an end, and does it in obedience to God who has thus ordained it, that he may be known as a merciful God and Father who, as Christ teaches, "makes his sun rise on the evil and on the good" (Matthew 5:45).

But in his own time our Lord and God will find out those who have abused the noble sun and his other creatures, and God will reward the creatures abundantly. Thus St. Paul shows the holy cross in all creation, in that heaven and earth and all the creatures in it suffer with us and bear the dear, treasured cross. Therefore we must not weep and moan so piteously when we fall on evil days. We must instead wait patiently for the redemption of the body and for the glory that shall be revealed in us, the more so as we know that the whole creation groans with anxious longing, like a woman in labor pains, and sighs for the manifestation of the sons of God, for then the whole creation will also be redeemed. It will no longer be subject to futility, to serve vanity, but it will serve only the children of God, and that willingly and joyfully.

Sermons from the year 1535.   WA 41:307ff.

Lord God, I wait with eager longing for the ultimate end of evil
and the redemption of the entire cosmos. Amen.

God Is at Work in Creation

The earth is full of the steadfast love of the LORD.
(Psalm 33:5)

God's wonderful works that happen daily are lightly esteemed, not because they are of no importance but because they happen so constantly and without interruption. We have become accustomed to the miracle that God rules the world and upholds all creation. Therefore, because things daily run their appointed course, it seems insignificant, and we do not think it worth our while to meditate upon it and to regard it as God's wonderful work. And yet it is a greater wonder than that Christ fed five thousand people with five loaves and made wine from water.

I often heard my father say that he had heard from his parents, my grandparents, that there are on earth many more people eating than there could be sheaves gathered together from all the fields on earth in a year. Do the calculations and you will find that more loaves are eaten in a year than grain is cut and gathered. Where does all the bread come from? Must you not acknowledge that it is the wonderful work of God, who blesses and multiplies the grain in the fields and in the barns, the flour in the bin and the bread on the table? But there are few who think of it and notice that those are the wonderful works of God.

Sermons from the year 1544.   WA 49:435f.

I thank you, heavenly Father, for the great abundance of food in our society;
show us the way to alleviate hunger in other parts of the world. Amen.

God Is Glorified in History

Matthew 13:24-30

So when the plants came up and bore grain,
then the weeds appeared as well.
(Matthew 13:26)

With human power we cannot weed them out, neither can we change them, for they are often more clever than we. They soon make friends and gather a crowd around themselves, and in this they have the devil, the prince of this world, who has sown them among the wheat, on their side.

Moreover, they know well how to adorn their cause, pretending to great wisdom and saintliness, and thus they gain great respect among the crowd, just as the large and beautiful thistles that stand with their brown crowns among the wheat, growing taller and looking more majestic than the wheat itself. They have nice green leaves and beautiful large brown crowns; they grow and bloom and flower riotously. The precious wheat, on the other hand, has no such beautiful and striking appearance but looks a pale yellow, so that anyone who does not know both would swear that the thistles must be very good and useful plants and flowers.

We cannot eliminate the wicked, because it often happens that some who go astray return. So we must bear with them, but not in such a manner that they rule over us, just as we cannot altogether avoid sin but must not let it become our master. Therefore we must practice God's commandments and call the Lord's Prayer to our aid, until we can fully lay hold on Christ the Lord and he has become the joy of our heart.

Sermons from the year 1546. WA 51:184f.

Help me, Lord God, to see the shades of gray in human life and not look
only at the black and white. Forgive my judgmental spirit. Amen.

Satan Sows His Seed

*But while everybody was asleep, an enemy came
and sowed weeds among the wheat, and then went away.
(Matthew 13:25)*

The meaning of the parable is that no Christians, especially no preachers, should grow disheartened or despondent because they cannot bring it about that there are only saints in their churches. For the devil does not stand aloof but throws his seeds in, and this is first noticed when they burst forth and shoot up. Thus it happened with the apostles Paul and John and others. Where they hoped to have devout Christians and faithful laborers in the gospel, they got the most wicked rogues and the bitterest foes. And thus it happens with us. Those we think godly and righteous do us the greatest harm and cause us the greatest difficulties, because we sleep and fear no evil.

This is the only comfort, that Christ himself warns us that it will happen in such a way. For this reason John comforts himself in the face of such difficulties in his epistle, saying, "They went out from us, but they did not belong to us" (1 John 2:19). For it is the way of the world that what should be best turns out worst. Angels become devils. One of the apostles betrayed Christ. Christians become heretics. Out of the people of God came wicked persons who nailed Christ to the cross.

So it happens still. Therefore we must not be alarmed and must not faint in our ministry when we see weeds shooting up among the wheat. Rather we must confidently go on and admonish our people, that no one be led astray.

Sermons from the year 1544.   WA 52:132f.

You will know them by their fruits. (Matthew 7:16)

The Two Kingdoms

Do you not know that wrongdoers will not inherit the kingdom of God?
(1 Corinthians 6:9)

There are two kingdoms. The first is a kingdom of the devil. In the Gospel the Lord calls the devil a prince of this world (John 16:11), that is, of a kingdom of sin and disobedience. Now, all of us dwell in the devil's kingdom until the coming of the kingdom of God. However, there is a difference. The godly are also in the devil's kingdom, but they daily and steadfastly contend against sins and resist the lusts of the flesh and the allurements of the world. After all, no matter how godly we may be, the evil desire always wants to master us and overcome us. God's kingdom unceasingly engages in combat with the devil's kingdom. The members of the former are preserved and saved because they fight against the devil's kingdom in order to enlarge the kingdom of God.

The other kingdom is that of God, namely, a kingdom of truth and righteousness, of which Christ says, "But strive first for the kingdom of God and his righteousness" (Matthew 6:33). What is God's righteousness? It is when there is no longer any sin in us, when all our members, talents, and powers are subject to God and are employed in his service, enabling us to say with Paul, "It is no longer I who live, but it is Christ who lives in me" (Galatians 2:20). That happens when we are ruled not by sin but only by Christ and his grace. Thus God's kingdom consists only of peace, discipline, humility, purity, love, and every kind of virtue and is devoid of wrath, hatred, bitterness, unchastity, and the like.

Therefore let all persons test themselves to see whether they are inclined in this or in that direction, and they will know to which kingdom they belong.

Sermons on the Lord's Prayer. LW 42:38; WA 2:96f.

Whom have I in heaven but you? And there is nothing on earth that I desire other than you. Amen. (Psalm 73:25)

God's Hour

Then they tried to arrest him, but no one laid hands on him,
because his hour had not yet come.
(John 7:30)

Who is Christ's protector? Who fends off his enemies? No one. But the text declares: "His hour had not yet come." Listen! The text mentions only an hour. This seems a poor and feeble protector. Nothing is said about many thousands of mounted soldiers or about thirty thousand foot soldiers who defended him. No, his entire armor is a little hour granted him until his crucifixion. That hour was not yet at hand, and since it was not, all the designs of his enemies against him were futile.

For God has so ordered and measured everything that he controls all thoughts and deeds, and nothing can come to pass until the hour strikes that he has assigned to it.

God has so arranged it that everything in the world has its time and season. He has fixed a free hour for everything. The whole world may be the enemy of this certain hour and assail it. The devil, too, may shoot and throw at the poor little hour hand—but in vain, for every event is assigned to its own proper hour. Before the hand of time points to that hour, the devil and the world will accomplish nothing.

To sum up, whatever we may set our minds on, it shall not come to pass, or rather it shall come to nothing, if it is not commanded and ordained by God; or if it does come to pass, it will do ten times as much harm. It is all gathered up in one hour. Our planning will not bring it about; God must ordain the hour.

This is a glorious comfort.

Sermons on John 6–8.   LW 23:254; WA 33:404ff.

Our times are in your hands, O God.
Keep me in your care all the days of my life. Amen.

Your Will Be Done

Your will be done, on earth as it is in heaven.
(Matthew 6:10)

People say, "Yes, certainly, God has given us a free will." To this I reply, "To be sure, God has given us a *free* will; why then will you not let it remain free but make it your *own* will?" If you do with it what you will, it is not a free will. It is your own will. But God has given neither you nor anyone your own will, for your own will comes from the devil and from Adam. They changed the free will that they received from God into their own will. For a free will desires nothing of its own. It only cares for the will of God, and so it remains free, clinging to nothing.

Hence you see that in this prayer God commands us to pray against ourselves, and so teaches us that we have no greater enemy than ourselves. For our will is the greatest power within us, and we must pray against it: "O Father, do not let me get to the point where my will is done. Break my will; resist it. No matter what happens, let my life be governed not by my will, but by yours. As no one's own will prevails in heaven, so may it also be here on earth." Such a prayer, if it is offered, hurts our nature, for self-will is the deepest and mightiest evil in the world, and there is nothing we love more than our own will.

Sermons on the Lord's Prayer.   LW 42:48; WA 2:104f.

Take my will and make it thine; it shall be no longer mine. Amen.
(Frances R. Havergal, 1874)

Out of the Mouths of Babes

Out of the mouth of babes and infants you have founded a bulwark because of your foes, to silence the enemy and the avenger.
(Psalm 8:2)

Why does Christ found such a kingdom? Why does he not send the heavenly spirits and princes, Gabriel, Michael, and other angels who could offer strong resistance to the enemy and break his power? For the enemy and avenger is a strong and powerful spirit.

Answer: The Lord our Master does not will to use Gabriel or Michael for this purpose but wills instead to ordain strength out of the mouth of babes and infants. Because the enemy's wickedness is great and his wrath fierce, it pleases the Maker to despise this wicked, vain, and furious spirit and to mock him. Therefore, because he wills to ordain such strength, he lowers himself, is made a human being, and even makes himself subject to all persons. He goes about in poverty, as he himself says in Matthew 8:20. With such a weak body and humble appearance he attacks the enemy, allows himself to be crucified and slain, and through his cross and death overcomes the enemy and avenger.

Thus our Lord God lays aside the great and mighty power of the angels in heaven and takes the most unlearned, simplest, and weakest people on earth and sets them over against the wisdom and power of the devil and the world. Such are the works of God. For our God gives life to the dead, and calls that which is not, and it is. It is God's nature to show his divine majesty and power through weakness. That is the way in which the Lord our God founds his kingdom. It is carried on in weakness, but out of that weakness strength shall come.

Sermons from the year 1537.   LW 12:110; WA 45:218ff.

Lord God, you have chosen the humble over the proud and the weak over the strong to reveal our redemption. I give you thanks. Amen.

You Command Him and Never Come Too Late

He got up and rebuked the winds and the sea; and there was a dead calm.
(Matthew 8:26)

Thus we should come to know our Lord and Savior and to believe that he is the Lord who can control the roaring winds and raging waves of the devil, and stay their power, if he wills. In this we should take comfort and consolation against all the might of the wicked and scornful enemies of the poor church, that for all their storming against this little ship, they will not prevail. The reason: Christ, the Lord, who has for more than five thousand years calmed and stilled those winds and waves, still knows how to command and stay them. For five thousand years they have failed, and in the future, even in the last hour, they will still fail and not succeed in their designs. This man who is lying here in the ship and is asleep will through our prayer wake up when the hour is come and will reveal himself and show that he can command the winds and the waves, and then everything that has fought and stormed against the ship must come to nothing.

Sermons from the year 1546.   WA 51:155

When the storms of life are raging, O Lord,
let me put my trust in you. Amen.

The Glory of Christ

Luke 18:31-34

Then he took the twelve aside and said to them, "See, we are going up
to Jerusalem, and everything that is written about the Son of Man
by the prophets will be accomplished."
(Luke 18:31)

The right way to reach a true knowledge of Christ's sufferings is to
perceive and understand not only what he suffered but how it was his
heart and will to suffer. For whoever considers Christ's sufferings without
seeing in them his heart and will must be filled with fear rather than joy.
But if we can truly see his heart and will in them, they give true comfort,
trust, and joy in Christ.

Here in the Gospel he reveals this will to suffer, when he declares
that he will go up to Jerusalem in order to be crucified, as if he said,
"Consider and see that I endure my suffering freely and gladly in
obedience to my Father's will. You must not be afraid or terrified when
you witness my sufferings and think that I bear them unwillingly, that I
am compelled to endure them and am forsaken, and that the powerful
are able to do this to me."

But the disciples did not understand his meaning, and the Word was
hidden from them. Reason, flesh, and blood cannot grasp that the Gospel
should tell us that the Son of Man must be crucified. Much less can they
perceive that such should be his will and that he did it joyfully. It is a
great and wonderful thing that the Son of Man is crucified willingly and
joyfully in order that the Scriptures should be fulfilled, which is for our
good. It is and it remains a mystery.

Sermons from the year 1525.   WA 17/2:173f.

Have mercy, Lord God, on your suffering people in this world.
Show us the way to wholeness and peace. Amen.

On Him God the Father Has Set His Seal

It is on him that God the Father has set his seal.
(John 6:27)

There is a special accent in these words, as if Jesus were saying, "My Father is not a common man, not a plain fellow. I will tell you who he is: he is God. The Father is the one who is known as God. And this Father has his eyes on his Son. God has made everything dependent on him, so that one is saved by eating his body and drinking his blood. Otherwise all will be damned. God has chosen only his Son, Christ, for this mission. God has put his seal on him and has placed his will and all his mercy on Christ, and on none other."

God has only one seal, and this he has set on Christ. On him alone God has bestowed the Holy Spirit, so that all people should look only to him. All of Holy Scripture points solely to him, attesting that he alone possesses seal and letter; for he is the exemplar, made, given, and offered to be our sole help. Thus God himself spoke from heaven: "This is my Son, the Beloved; with him I am well pleased; listen to him!" (Matthew 17:5). Since God has put his seal exclusively on him, we must listen to him and accept him alone.

Sermons on John 6–8.   LW 23:16; WA 33:79f.

O Christ, our hope, our hearts' desire, creation's mighty Lord,
let your mighty love prevail to purge us of our pride. Amen.
(Latin hymn, eighth century)

He Testifies to the Father

He testifies to what he has seen and heard.
(John 3:21)

People wondered, "What is this Christ to do? Of what use is the Messiah? What sort of a Messiah is he? Is this the way he comes on the scene?" He bears witness. "Is he so impotent that he does nothing but bear witness? Can't he do anything but preach and speak? He wields no sword, possesses not a foot of land, and rules no nation. What is his function?" To preach. "Should we be expected to accept such a Messiah?" Well, do as you like! Today we hear similar talk.

But what if it is not God's plan that the Messiah should come like an emperor? The fact that he comes so destitute and engages in nothing but preaching displays inexpressible wisdom and strength, namely, that whoever believes in him shall live eternally. Christ's kingdom is to consist in his message. Now whoever wishes to be justified before God must hear this witness—the preacher. His is a sermon that bears witness solely of things not seen and heard in law books or anywhere else in the world. A judge does not pass sentence on a matter that he himself observed; no, he needs witnesses. The problem here is to preach and to speak about something not seen. Now the Lord Christ becomes the Father's witness from heaven. He is to do nothing else than open his lips. His sermon is to be a testimony of the Father's attitude, of his plan for humankind's salvation and redemption from sin, death, and the power of the devil. He submits to becoming human and to dying. He rises again from the dead and says, "My words bear witness to this. If you believe this testimony and these works, then you believe the witness of God."

Sermons on John 3.   LW 22:465; WA 47:177f.

For faithful men and women of the past, and for those
who showed me the path of faith, I thank you, Lord God. Amen.

Cast Your Lot with Christ

*I am not ashamed of the gospel; it is the power of God
for salvation to everyone who has faith.*
(Romans 1:16)

Christ has no money or purse, nor any worldly kingdom, for he has
given all such things to the kings and princes. One thing, however, he
has kept to himself that is the work neither of humans nor of angels,
namely, that he is a victor over sin, death, the devil, and hell and is able
to save and uphold in the midst of death all those who believe in him
through his Word.

Amen! We have cast in our lot with that man, the Lord Christ, the
Son of God, and he will certainly not abandon us. Our life and soul
are bound to him; where he abides there we too shall abide. Apart from
him I know of nothing by which to defy the world. Therefore, if Christ
lives, he knows that we do and suffer everything for his sake, as regards
preaching, teaching, and writing. As the world knows and we know too,
if we rely on him, he will help us. Yet all things must be broken. Things
cannot remain as they are.

Table Talk. WA Tischreden 6:73

Lord, to whom can we go? You have the words of eternal life. Amen.
(John 6:68)

In Christ We Have Our Glory

He has put all things under his feet and has made him the head
over all things for the church.
(Ephesians 1:22)

Our greatest honor, glory, and praise is that we have Christ, the Son of God, flesh of our flesh, yet born without sin, seated at the right hand of God the Father, the Lord over all creatures in heaven, on earth, and in hell. But whoever wants him as Lord will have the devil as his enemy.

Of what concern is the whole world to God, or what concern would ten or more worlds be? He has set up Christ, as it is written in the second psalm (verse 6). Even if we refuse to accept him, God has enthroned him so firmly that God will never let him be overthrown or cast down from his seat. If the world dares to attempt that, he throws everything into a heap; for once with a glorious voice resounding from heaven he gave the command "Listen to him" (Mark 9:7).

Table Talk.   WA Tischreden 1:469

Eternal God, the source of life and blessing, you have exalted
the Lord Jesus, who humbled himself and lived among us. Amen.

On the Cross He Is Glorified

After Jesus had spoken these words, he looked up to heaven and said, "Father, the hour has come; glorify your Son so that the Son may glorify you."
(John 17:1)

With these words Jesus indicates how it fares with him, and what is the sorrow that drives him to such a prayer. The time is drawing near (he says) when I must die the most shameful death, and it will darken all my purest light, and swallow up my honor and my name. Until that hour he had done great things, had preached with wonderful words, done wonderful works, and given proof of his mighty power, so that all the world should eagerly praise and honor and adore him. Then adversity befalls him. He is covered with disgrace and shame, and must hang on the awful tree between two murderers, and die as if he were the wickedest criminal this earth has ever borne, for no murderer has been treated with so much shame and spite.

That really is casting out the faithful, wondrous man into utter darkness. This is in Christ's mind when he says that his hour is near or has come, for he prays with such earnestness as if in that moment he were hanging on the cross—as if he said, "Now I am shrouded in shame and death; now I lie in deepest darkness. Yet it is now the time when you will bring me forth and lift me up, and bring me to honor, for my light is gone out, and the world is trampling me underfoot."

How did such glorification come to pass? In no other way than that the Father raised him again from death, threw the devil under his feet, and made him King and Lord over all creation.

Sermons on John 16–20.   WA 28:79f.

In a world of shallow values, O God,
let me glory in the cross of Christ. Amen.

Be Christlike

Let the same mind be in you that was in Christ Jesus.
(Philippians 2:5)

Oh, dear brothers and sisters, your attitude should be like that of Christ, who did not exalt himself in the form of God, even though he could be equal with the Father, but emptied himself and utterly lowered himself and took on the form of a servant and was found in every degree and way a human being, like us even in that he died for the sake of obedience to his Father. Note, dear friends of Christ, what a choice, profound saying that is. We should all be equal. For he speaks, not as a mere man, but as one in whom is the form of God, the very presence of power, honor, righteousness, wisdom, piety, and purity, who never did evil, who is full of every virtue even in his humanity, who desired to be equal with us, not with God, not like Lucifer who desired to snatch the image of God, nor like the proud, who so look down on their neighbors that they can scarcely recognize them as grasshoppers. This Christ did not do; he put off the form of God and was found in the form of a human being, in sinful flesh, though he never sinned; nor could he ever sin. So he became a fool, the object of mockery, reproach, and derision by all the people; he bore our misfortune, and in him were found all the titles of our poverty. This he did in order that we might freely follow him.

Sermons from the year 1518.   LW 51:37; WA 1:268f.

All who exalt themselves will be humbled, and all
who humble themselves will be exalted. (Matthew 23:12)

Being Called and Being Chosen

Matthew 20:1-16

So the last will be first, and the first will be last:
for many are called but few are chosen.
(Matthew 20:16, variant reading)

Because this Gospel speaks of those who think themselves first before God, it aims high and strikes the most excellent people; indeed, it frightens the greatest saints. For it sometimes happens that a person appears weak and poor and despised before the world, yet secretly within her heart well pleased with herself, so that she thinks herself the first before God; and even for this reason is she the last. On the other hand, there may be a person so fearful and fainthearted that despite his gold and honor, he thinks himself the least before God; and even for this reason is he the first.

It is also well known that the greatest saints have been moved with fear in this connection, and that many who hold high spiritual office have fallen. Consider how Saul fell! How God let David fall! How Peter had to fall, and likewise some disciples of Paul!

No one is so high or can rise so high that they need no longer fear that they may be made the lowest. Again, no one has fallen so low or can fall so low that there is no hope of their becoming the highest, for by this all merit is reduced to nothing and God's mercy alone is praised, and it is firmly decreed that "the last shall be first and the first last." In saying, "The first shall be last," he takes away all your pride. But in saying, "The last shall be first," he takes from you all despair.

Sermons from the year 1525.   WA 17/2:139f.

Deliver me, O Lord, from vaunting pride,
and help me value the gifts of those around me. Amen.

God Has Given Each Person the Measure of Faith

*For by the grace given to me I say to everyone among you not to think
of yourself more highly than you ought to think, but to think with sober
judgment, each according to the measure of faith that God has assigned.
(Romans 12:3)*

Jesus often does through little saints what he does not do through great
saints. When he was twelve years old, he hid himself from his mother
and let her go about in search of him. He appeared to Mary Magdalene
on Easter Day before he revealed himself to his mother and the apostles.
He spoke more kindly to the Samaritan woman and to the woman taken
in adultery than he ever spoke to his own mother. While Peter fell and
betrayed him, the thief on the cross was full of faith.

With such wonders he shows us that he will not have us know
the measure of grace he gives to his saints, and that we shall not judge
according to the person. He gives his gifts freely, as he pleases, and not
as we think. He even says that whoever believes in him shall do greater
works than he himself did (John 14:12). And all this is said in order that
we do not exalt ourselves above others or place one saint higher than
another, but we regard them all as equal in his grace, however different
they may be with regard to the gifts he bestows. Through St. Stephen
he wills to do what he does not do through St. Peter, and again through
Peter what he does not do through his mother; so that he alone is the one
who does everything according to his will, without respect of persons.

God may give to a great saint small faith and to a small saint great
faith, in order that the one shall always esteem the other higher than
oneself.

Sermons from the year 1525.   WA 17/2:77f.

*The LORD does not see as mortals see; they look on the outward
appearance, but the LORD looks on the heart. (1 Samuel 16:7)*

He Has Chosen Us

You did not choose me but I chose you. (John 15:16)

This cuts off and condemns at a stroke all the presumption of spurious saints who want to do and deserve so much even to reconciling God and making him their friend. For what do they do but make the choice and seek to be first, in that their merits precede and God's grace toddles on behind? It is not he who chooses us, but we seek him and make him our friend that we may glory in that he has received much good from us. That is what all the world does in seeking to merit God's grace by previous works. But the Gospel says, "You did not choose me." That is, you are my friends not because of what you do but because of what I do. If it were because of what you do, I should have to regard your merit, but it is because of me and through me, because I draw you to myself and give you all that I possess, so that your glory is in nothing but my grace and love, and not your own nor all the world's work or merit. For I have not let myself be found by you; rather I have had to seek you and bring you to myself, when you were far off, without knowledge of God, and were held in the grip of error and condemnation like the rest. But now I have come, and I have called you out of the darkness before you prayed or did anything about it. Thus you are my friends in that you have received all good from me, and know that you have received it all for nothing and out of sheer grace.

Sermon on John 15.   LW 24:259; WA 45:697f.

I thank you, Lord God, that your grace operates in us even during our emotional lows and that it does not depend on our mental state. Amen.

In the Hands of God

They were yours, and you gave them to me.
(John 17:6)

No one on earth can help but fear and tremble and desire to escape if they think of God. As soon as they hear God mentioned, they are quiet and subdued. I do not speak of irreligious people, but of those whose hearts are pierced, who feel their sin. (It is only to such that we preach.) For the conscience is awake, feeling and knowing that God is hostile to sinners and will condemn them, and that they cannot escape or flee from God's wrath. Therefore their conscience flinches and trembles and quakes, faints and grows pale and chilled as before lightning and thunder. Therefore Christ must deal mightily with such fear and graft into the heart such sweet and kind and comforting words that those grievous, bitter, and horrible thoughts are removed, and must present the Father in as sweet a way as ever a heart could wish. Therefore let us heartily receive these words, and let them sink into our hearts, as the only comfort and salvation of our souls.

If you cling to your Lord Christ, you are certainly one of those whom God has chosen from the beginning to be his own. Otherwise you would not come to him nor listen to such a revelation and accept it. Therefore let those be troubled who have not the gospel and do not want to listen to Christ. But you may know that there is no greater comfort on earth than that which he himself reveals and gives you here, namely, that you are God's own beloved child because his Word pleases you and your heart is graciously inclined toward him. For if Christ is kind and gracious to you and comforts you, God the Father himself comforts you. For God revealed himself in this way so that you would not need to search and wonder what he may have decided concerning you; rather you may know from his Word all that concerns his will and your salvation.

Sermons on John 1–20.   WA 28:120ff.

I thank you, heavenly Father, for your grace
that operates in advance of my faith. Amen.

Hold Fast the Faith

Having faith and a good conscience . . .
(1 Timothy 1:19)

If we reflect on the diversity of sins that remain in the saints in this life, we must not inquire into the secret election, or Providence, or predestination, as it is called, for such reflection causes nothing but doubt. Is it certainty or is it despair? If you are chosen, no fall can harm you; you are always in grace and cannot perish. If you are not chosen, nothing can help you. Such words are dreadful, and it is a sin to lead the heart to such thoughts. The gospel points us straight to the plain Word of God, wherein God has revealed his will, and through which God wills to work and to be known. It is plain that God's Word punishes sins and reveals diversity of sins and points to our Savior, Jesus Christ. We should look at this plain Word of God and judge according to it whether we are in grace.

For where there is the faith by which we are made righteous, there must be a pure conscience. It is quite impossible for these two things to live side by side—faith that trusts in God, and an evil will or, as it is called, a bad conscience. Faith in God and prayer to him are delicate things, and a little wound of conscience can drive out faith and prayer, as every advanced Christian must often experience.

But where there is faith and a pure conscience, there the Holy Spirit certainly dwells. Yet such a trust is based not on our good conscience or worthiness, but on Christ alone. Therefore we are in grace for Christ's sake because of his promise, and true prayer can be offered. As St. John says, "If our hearts do not condemn us, we have boldness before God; and we receive from him whatever we ask" (1 John 3:21-22).

Questions with Regard to Sin in Believers.   EA 55:161ff.

Create in me a clean heart, O God, and put a new
and right spirit within me. Amen. (Psalm 51:10)

The Sacrifices of God Are a Broken Spirit

Say to those who are of a fearful heart, "Be strong, do not fear!"
(Isaiah 35:4)

If we are anxiously afraid that we are not among those who are chosen, or if we are tempted concerning our election, we should give thanks and rejoice that we are anxious, because we may confidently know that God cannot lie. And God said, "The sacrifice acceptable to God is a broken spirit," that is to say, a despairing spirit. "A broken and a contrite heart, O God, you will not despise" (Psalm 51:17). A person who is "broken" is fully aware of it. Therefore we should throw ourselves with all our hearts onto the truthfulness of God who gave his promise, and we should turn ourselves away from what we know of the wrath of God, and we will be chosen and saved.

Lectures on Romans.   LW 25:337

Your steadfast love, O God, undergirds the universe;
let me trust in your faithfulness. Amen.

Built on the Rock of God's Good Pleasure

Without faith it is impossible to please God.
(Hebrews 11:6)

Even if it were possible, I should not wish to have free choice given to me, or to have anything left in my own hands by which I might strive toward salvation. For, on the one hand, I should be unable to stand firm and keep hold of it amid so many adversities and perils and so many assaults of demons; on the other hand, even if there were no perils or adversities or demons, I should nevertheless have to labor under perpetual uncertainty and to fight as one beating the air, since even if I lived and worked to eternity, my conscience would never be assured and certain how much it ought to do to satisfy God. For whatever work might be accomplished, there would always remain an anxious doubt whether it pleased God or whether he required something more, as the experience of all self-justifiers proves, and as I myself learned to my bitter cost through so many years. But now, since God has taken my salvation out of my hands into his, making it depend on his choice and not mine, and has promised to save me, not by my own work or exertion but by his grace and mercy, I am assured and certain both that he is faithful and will not lie to me, and also that he is too great and powerful for any demons or any adversities to be able to break him or to snatch me from him. Therefore some and indeed many are saved, whereas by the power of free choice none at all would be saved, but all would perish together.

Moreover, we are also certain and sure that we please God, not by the merit of our own working, but by the favor of his mercy promised to us, and that if we do less than we should or do it badly, he does not hold this against us, but in a fatherly way pardons and corrects us.

On the Bondage of the Will.   LW 33:288

I am free to choose many things each day, but can I choose to believe?
Lord, help my unbelief. Amen.

What Happens to the Divine Word

Luke 8:5-15

But as for that in the good soil, these are the ones who,
when they hear the word, hold it fast in an honest
and good heart, and bear fruit with patient endurance.
(Luke 8:15)

Christ says, "in an honest and good heart." Like a field that is large and level, with no thorns or thistles, so pure and wide and open is the heart that is free from anxiety and greed about temporal food, and the Word of God finds room in it.

Thus we may see that it is no marvel that there are so few true Christians, for not all the seed falls on good ground, but only a fourth part, and that those should not be trusted who boast of being Christians and praise the teaching of the gospel. Christ himself here cries and says, "Let anyone with ears to hear listen" (verse 8), as if he meant to say, "Oh, how few true Christians there are." Indeed, one cannot trust all who are called Christians and who listen to the gospel. Much more is needed.

Why should we be troubled that many respond with disdain? Is it not ordained that many are called and few are chosen? For the sake of the good soil, which brings forth fruit with patience, some of the seed must fall by the wayside, some upon the rocky places, and some among thorns. We do know that the Word of God certainly does not remain fruitless but that it always finds some good ground, as he says here, that some of the sower's seed fell upon good ground. For where the gospel is, there are Christians: "My word shall not return to me void."

Sermons from the year 1525.   WA 17/2:156f.

O Lord, give me ears to hear the Word
that can guide my path through life. Amen.

Listen to His Word

Anyone who resolves to do the will of God will know whether
the teaching is from God or whether I am speaking on my own.
(John 7:17)

It is the Father's will that we should listen to what the man Jesus says and give ear to his Word. You are not to try to be clever in connection with his Word, to master it or to argue about it, but simply to hear it. Then the Holy Spirit will come and dispose your heart so that you will believe and say from the bottom of your heart concerning the preaching of the divine Word, "That is God's Word and it is the pure truth," and you will risk your life on it. But if you yourself want to be heard, and to obliterate the Word of Christ with your own reason, if you attempt to subject the Word to your own ideas, kneading false teaching into it, probing and prying how to understand, to measure, and to distort it so that his Word must sound as you want it to do, and if you ponder it as though you were in doubt about it, wanting to judge it according to your own mind, that is not listening to it, or being a disciple, but being a master.

In that way you can never be able to say, "This is the Word of God." Therefore, lock up your reason, tread your wisdom underfoot, and do not let them grope about or feel or think in matters that concern your salvation, but simply and solely listen to what the Son of God says, to what is his Word, and stop there. "Listen, listen!" is the command. That is truly and honestly doing our Lord God's will, and he has promised that all who listen to the Son will receive the Holy Spirit, to enlighten and kindle them so that they will rightly understand that it is the Word of God. God will change them into persons after his own heart.

Sermons on John 6–8.   LW 23:229; WA 33:362f.

With my whole heart and mind, Lord God, I praise you. Amen.

The Word Took on the Form of a Servant

At that time Jesus said, "I thank you, Father, Lord of heaven and earth, because you have hidden these things from the wise and intelligent, and have revealed them to infants."
(Matthew 11:25)

I beg and I faithfully admonish all devout Christians that they not be offended or stumble over the simple stories related in the Bible, nor doubt them. However poor they may appear, they are certainly the words, history, and judgments of the high divine majesty, power, and wisdom. For this is the book that makes all wise and clever people fools, and can only be understood by simple people, as Christ says (Matthew 11:25). Therefore let go of your own thoughts and feelings and esteem this book as the best and purest treasure, as a mine full of great wealth, which can never be exhausted or sufficiently excavated. Thus you will find the divine wisdom that God presents in the Bible in a manner so simple that it damps the pride of clever people and brings it to nothing. In this book you find the swaddling clothes and the manger in which Christ lies, and to which the angel directs the shepherds. Those swaddling clothes are shabby and poor, yet precious is the treasure wrapped in them, for it is Christ.

Table Talk.   WA Tischreden 6:16

We have this treasure in clay jars, so that it may be made clear that this extraordinary power belongs to God and does not come from us.
(2 Corinthians 4:7)

The Devil Hates the Word of God

The ones on the path are those who have heard;
then the devil comes and takes away the word from their hearts,
so that they may not believe and be saved.
(Luke 8:12)

This is the true black—or rather the white—appearance of the devil. For he is a bright and brilliant devil, who does not tempt us with gross sins but with unbelief. For when he has our faith he has won. We must have God's Word and cling to it by faith. As soon as we allow ourselves to be separated from the Word, we are lost and there is no help for us.

Therefore mark how the devil works, for he attacks nothing but faith. Pagans, the unbelieving, the non-Christians he does not tempt. They cling to him like scales to a fish. But when he sees those who have the Word of God, faith, and the Holy Spirit, he cannot get at them. He well knows that he can never win the victory over them, though they may stumble. He well perceives that even if one falls into gross sin, that person is not lost thereby but can always rise again. Therefore he realizes that he must try a different method and take away their greatest good. If he can prevail on the soul and make it doubt whether it is the Word of God, the game is won. For God can work all things for good, however often we may stumble, only if we abide by the pure, true Word of God, which says: This is right and this is wrong. The devil knows this; therefore he first sneaks in at this point. Once faith is torn away, no one can of oneself resist the devil. He or she inevitably falls into all kinds of vice.

Sermon on Genesis 3.   WA 24:86

God of steadfast love, we experience the evil of this world in both national and personal life. Deliver us from evil, we pray. Amen.

God's Silence Is God's Wrath

The time is surely coming, says the Lord GOD,
when I will send a famine on the land;
not a famine of bread, or a thirst for water,
but of hearing the words of the LORD.
They shall wander from sea to sea,
and from north to east;
they shall run to and fro, seeking the word of the LORD,
but they shall not find it.
(Amos 8:11-12)

God's wrath is never greater than when he is silent and does not speak to us, but leaves us to follow our own minds and wills and do as we please.

Oh, dear Lord God, punish us with pestilence and with any foul diseases rather than by your silence. God speaks, "I have stretched out my hand and cried, 'Come hear and listen!' But you answer, 'No, we won't!' I send my servants to you, the prophets Isaiah, Jeremiah, and others, and I say to you, 'Listen unto them!' 'Yes,' you say, 'we will strike them dead!' 'There, you have my Son.' 'Yes, we will crucify him!'"

We still act in the same way, as can easily be seen. We are weary and tired of the Word of God. We do not want to hear devout and faithful teachers who chastise us and preach to us the pure and unadulterated Word of God, who keep a careful watch, earnestly condemning false teaching and faithfully warning us against it. Therefore God will surely chastise us.

Oh, heavenly Father, keep us forever by this radiant sun, and do not let us fall from your Word and stumble into false teaching.

Table Talk.   WA Tischreden 5:237f.

Oh, that I knew where I might find him,
that I might come even to his dwelling! (Job 23:3)

The Divine Word Is Despised

*The one who rejects me and does not receive my word has a judge;
on the last day the word that I have spoken will serve as judge.
(John 12:48)*

The dear Lord sees what poor and wretched people we are. Unless we
have the treasure of the holy gospel, one error always tumbles over
another.

Again, when we have the gospel, a far more dreadful calamity
occurs, namely, that everyone despises it, and the few accept it for their
good. We are thoroughly poor and wretched people. If God withholds his
Word from us, we cannot live without suffering detriment to our souls.
On the other hand, if God grants it, nobody wants it. Therefore there
is nothing better than that the Lord God should hasten the last day, to
smite everything into a heap, for the ungrateful world will not be helped
either by grace or by punishment.

Therefore God admonishes us again and appoints another day,
saying, "Today, if you will hear his voice, do not harden your hearts"
(Hebrews 4:7). Behold, every day is "Today!" and God calls and appeals
to us not to miss the opportunity.

It is right for us to thank God most deeply for such grace, that he
comes so near to us, abides with us in our homes, at our table, at our
bedside and wherever we want him, offering and presenting us all his
help, and all things that we may ask of him. Yes, we ought to treasure and
honor this dear guest because he stays with us.

Sermon on Ephesians 5:15-21.   WA 22:329

*Lord, take my hand and lead me upon life's way. Direct, protect, and feed
me from day to day. Amen. (Julie von Hausmann, 1825–1901)*

Redeem the Time

Then he opened their eyes to understand the scriptures.
(Luke 24:45)

Luke, in his last chapter, says that Christ opened the minds of the apostles to understand the Scriptures. And Christ, in John 10:3, 9, declares that he is the gate by which one must enter, and whoever enters by him, to him the gatekeeper (the Holy Spirit) opens in order that he might find pasture and blessedness. Thus it is ultimately true that the gospel itself is our guide and instructor in the Scriptures.

But what a fine lot of tender and pious children we are! In order that we might not have to study in the Scriptures and learn Christ there, we simply regard the entire Old Testament as of no account, as done for and no longer valid. Yet it alone bears the name of Holy Scripture. And the gospel should really not be something written, but a spoken word that brings forth the Scriptures, as Christ and the apostles have done. This is why Christ himself did not write anything but only spoke. He called his teaching not Scripture but gospel, meaning good news or a proclamation that is spread not by pen but by word of mouth. So we go on and make the gospel into a law book, a teaching of commandments, changing Christ into a Moses, the one who would help us into simply an instructor.

A Brief Instruction on What to Look For in the Gospels, 1521.   LW 35:122f.

For all the prophets and apostles, for all martyrs and pious teachers, for the faithful of all generations, I thank you, Lord God. Amen.

The Transfiguration

Matthew 17:1-9

This is my Son, the Beloved; with him I am well pleased; listen to him!
(Matthew 17:5)

Be on your guard against ideas that disregard the Word and separate and tear Christ from God. For he did not bid you soar to heaven on your own to gape to see what God is doing with the angels. No, this is his command: "This is my Son, the Beloved; listen to him. There I descend to you on earth, so that you can see, hear, and touch me. There and nowhere else is the place for those to encounter and find me who desire me and who would like to be delivered from their sin and be saved." We should quickly assent and say, "God himself says this, and I will follow God and give ear to no other word or message; nor do I want to know anything else about God." For as St. Paul declares, in his person "the whole fullness of deity dwells bodily" (Colossians 2:9), and there is no God apart from him where I could come to him or find him—although God is everywhere else, of course. Now wherever one hears this man's Word and sees his work, there one surely hears and sees God's Word and work.

Sermon on John 14.   WA 45:520f.

Lord God, as the disciples saw the glory of Christ on the mountain,
so let your face shine on my life. Amen.

Carry Your Cross within Your Heart

Rejoice insofar as you are sharing Christ's sufferings.
(1 Peter 4:13)

Illness, poverty, pain, and the like must not be called a cross; they are not worthy of that name. But if we suffer persecution for our faith, that may rightly be called a cross. But how can it be found? Not in cloisters, but in the gospel and in the true understanding of it. This is finding the cross: to know your own self, or to know the cross. Where do you find that? In your heart. Unless you find it there, the finding of it outwardly is of no avail. "If any want to become my followers, let them deny themselves and take up their cross and follow me" (Mark 8:34). You must come to the point when you say, "My Lord and my God, would that I were worthy of it." You must be as joyful about it as were the dear saints.

The honor of the cross must be inward, within the heart, so that I thank God that I must suffer, and that must spring from a joyful will toward the cross or death. Is it not a wonder to have a ready will toward death, while everyone dreads it? Thus is the cross sanctified.

Sermons from the year 1527.   WA 17/2:425f.

Lord God, I rejoice in the blessings of the here and now.
Give me strength also to face my final hour. Amen.

TUESDAY

Suffering Has to Be

Whoever does not carry the cross and follow me cannot be my disciple.
(Luke 14:27)

Though our suffering and cross should never be so exalted that we think we can be saved by it or earn the least merit through it, nevertheless we should suffer after Christ, that we may be conformed to him. For God has appointed that we should not only believe in the crucified Christ, but also be crucified with him, as he clearly shows in the Gospels, for example, "Whoever does not take up the cross and follow me is not worthy of me" (Matthew 10:38).

Therefore each one must bear a part of the holy cross; nor can it be otherwise. St. Paul too says, "In my flesh I am completing what is lacking in Christ's afflictions" (Colossians 1:24). It is as if he were saying that his whole Christendom is not fully completed. We too must follow after, in order that none of the suffering of Christ may be lacking or lost, but all brought together into one. Therefore every Christian must be aware that suffering will not fail to come.

It should be, however, and must be the kind of suffering that is worthy of the name and honestly grips and hurts, such as some great danger of property, honor, body, and life. Such suffering as we really feel, which weighs us down; otherwise, if it did not hurt us badly, it would not be suffering.

When one knows this it is easier and more bearable, and one can comfort oneself by saying, "Very well, if I want to be a Christian, I must also wear the colors of the court; the dear Christ issues no others in his court. Suffering there must be."

Sermon on suffering and the cross.   LW 51:199; WA 32:29

The sufferings of this present time are not worthy comparing with the glory about to be revealed to us. (Romans 8:18)

Lent

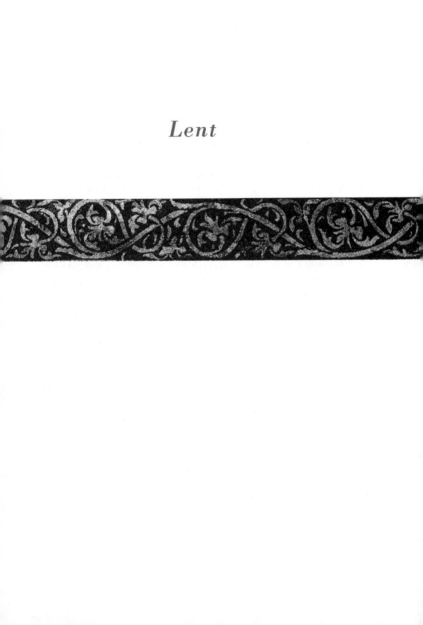

The Necessity of Suffering

Happy are those whom you discipline, O LORD,
and whom you teach out of your law.
(Psalm 94:12)

It is highly necessary that we should suffer, not only that God may thereby prove his honor, might, and strength against the devil, but also because the great and precious treasure that we have, if it were given to us without such suffering and affliction, would make us snore in our security. And we can see—unfortunately it is a general thing—that many abuse the holy gospel, behaving as if they were freed from all obligations through the gospel and that there is nothing more they need do or give or suffer. This is a sin and a shame.

The only way our God can check such evil is through the cross. God must so discipline us that our faith increases and grows stronger, and we thus draw the Savior all the deeper into our soul. For we can no more grow strong without suffering and temptation than we can without eating and drinking.

Therefore, since it is better that we should be given a cross than that we should be spared a cross, no one must falter and take fright at it. Have you not a good, strong promise in which you can take comfort? Nor can the gospel advance except through us as we suffer willingly and bear our cross.

Sermon on suffering and the cross.   LW 51:207; WA 32:37f.

On this Ash Wednesday, Lord God, I reflect on my life
during the past year and on my relationship with others
and with you. Keep me steadfast on your path. Amen.

Our Deliverance Is in the Cross

Nevertheless I am continually with you.
(Psalm 73:23)

If for the sake of God's Word hardship, sorrow, and persecution come to us, all of which follow in the train of the holy cross, the following thought should, with God's help, comfort and console us, and should make us determine to be of good cheer, full of courage and confidence, and lead us to surrender the cause trustingly into God's gracious and fatherly will.

Our cause is in the hands of the one who says so clearly, "No one will snatch them out of my hand" (John 10:28). It would not be wise to take our cause into our own hands, for we could and should lose it by our loose ways. Likewise all the comfortable words are true and do not lie, which say, "God is our refuge and strength" (Psalm 46:1). Has anyone who trusts in God ever been put to shame? All who trust in God will be saved, and again, "You, O Lord, have not forsaken those who seek you" (Psalm 9:10). Thus it is really true that God gave his only Son for our salvation. If God gave his own Son for us, how could God ever bring himself to desert us in small things?

God is much stronger, mightier, and more powerful than the devil. Thus says St. John, "The one who is in you is greater than the one who is in the world" (1 John 4:4). If we fall, Christ, the almighty king of this world, must suffer with us, and even if his cause should fall, we should wish rather to fall with Christ than to stand with the highest power on earth.

Comforting words.   WA 48:327f.

My times are in your hand, O God. Give me the will and the strength to live confidently in the pursuit of justice. Amen.

The Suffering of the Saints Is a Holy Thing

All who want to live a godly life in Christ Jesus will be persecuted.
(2 Timothy 3:12)

Our teaching is this, that we should not dictate or choose our own cross and suffering, but rather, when it comes, patiently bear and suffer it. We also say that we earn nothing by our suffering. It is enough that we know that it pleases God that we suffer in order that we may be conformed to Christ.

So we see that the very ones who boast and teach so much about cross and suffering know the least either about the cross or of Christ, because they make their own suffering meritorious. Dear friends, it isn't that kind of thing at all; nor is anybody forced or compelled to it. If you don't want to do it for nothing and without any merit, then you can let it lie and so deny Christ. The way is at hand, but you must know that if you refuse to suffer, you will also not become a servant of Christ. So you may do either one of these two, either suffer or deny Christ.

Finally, Christian suffering is nobler and precious above all other human suffering because, since Christ himself suffered, he also hallowed the suffering of all his Christians. Through the suffering of Christ, the suffering of all his saints has become utterly holy, for it has been touched with Christ's suffering. Therefore we should accept all suffering as a holy thing, for it is truly holiness.

Sermon on suffering and the cross.   LW 51:199, 308; WA 32:30ff.

God of compassion, help me to overcome the evils
that come into my life, and give me strength to work
toward alleviating the suffering of others. Amen.

In the Cross Is Peace

Peace I leave with you; my peace I give to you. I do not give to you as the world gives. Do not let your hearts be troubled, and do not let them be afraid.
(John 14:27)

Thus we see that the office of the Holy Spirit is given only to those who are sunk in suffering and misery. For this is the meaning of the words he speaks: Do not think that the peace I give you is like that which the world gives. The world calls it peace when suffering is ended and leaves a person. For example, when a man is poor he thinks that he has much bitterness because of poverty, and he ponders how to get rid of poverty, thinking that if he can get rid of that, his person will be able to live in peace and wealth. Again, if someone is about to die, she thinks, "If I could but throw off death, I should live and have peace." But that is not the peace that Christ gives. Rather he allows the evil that is laid on us to lie upon us still and to continue oppressing us, and he does not take it away, but he uses another device: he changes us and removes us from the evil, and not the evil from us.

This is how it is done: You are held in the grip of suffering. He turns you away from it and gives you such courage that you would think you were sitting in a rose garden. Thus there is life in the midst of dying, and peace and joy in the midst of adversity, and that is why it is a peace that, as St. Paul says to the Philippians (4:7), surpasses all understanding.

Sermons from the year 1523.   WA 12:576f.

There are some who remain at peace with themselves and with others. And some neither have peace in themselves nor allow others to have peace. And there are some who are at peace with themselves, and who try to guide others into peace. The person who knows the secret of endurance will enjoy the greatest peace. Such a one is conqueror of self, master of the world, a friend of Christ, and an heir of heaven.
(Thomas à Kempis, The Imitation of Christ *2.3)*

Trial and Temptation

Matthew 4:1-11

Jesus said to him, "Away with you, Satan! for it is written,
'Worship the Lord your God,
and serve only him.'"
(Matthew 4:10)

There is a twofold armor with which the devil is slain and which he fears:
(1) to listen unceasingly to the Word of God, to instruct oneself in it, and
to be comforted and strengthened by it; (2) then, when temptation and
struggle come upon us, to lift up our hearts to that same Word and cry to
God, invoking him for help. Thus one of the two things is always present,
continuing as an eternal conversation between God and the soul. Either
God speaks to us and we are still, listening to God, or he listens to us as
we speak to him, praying for what we need.

Whatever way it may be, the devil cannot endure it, and he cannot
hold his own against it. Therefore Christians must be armed with both,
so that their hearts may be everlastingly turned toward God, keeping
his Word and with unceasing sighs eternally praying, "Our Father . . ."
This perseverance Christians will be taught by temptation and calamity
with which they are constantly oppressed by the devil, the world, and the
flesh, so that they must ever keep their heads up, watching for the assault
of the enemy who neither sleeps for a moment nor takes his ease.

Sermons from the year 1539.   WA 47:758

Almighty God, I know that evil is a horrendous reality in our world.
Give me strength to oppose the forces of evil and to work
for the spread of justice and mercy. Amen.

MONDAY

Beset by Trials

And lead us not into temptation.
(Matthew 6:13 RSV)

Since God himself has called our life a trial, and since it is inevitable that we are assailed in our body, our goods, and our honor, and since injustice is bound to face us, we must view this kindly and accept it wisely, saying, "Well, this is a part of life. What can I do? It is a trial and remains a trial. It is unavoidable. May God aid me so that it does not alarm me or bring me to fall."

So you see that no one is free from trials. However, we can defend ourselves against them and check them by entreating God's help in prayer. Thus we read in the book of hermits how a young brother longed to rid himself of his thoughts. The aged hermit said to him, "Dear brother, you cannot prevent the birds from flying over your head, but you can certainly keep them from building a nest in your hair." Thus, as St. Augustine declares, we cannot prevent trials and temptations from overtaking us, but with our prayer and our invocation of God's assistance, we can stave off their victory over us.

But why does God let us be thus assailed by sin? Answer: So that we may learn to know ourselves and God; to know oneself is to learn that we all are capable of sinning and doing evil; to know God is to learn that God's grace is stronger than all creatures. Thus we learn to despise ourselves and to laud and praise God's mercy.

Exposition of the Lord's Prayer.   LW 42:73f.; WA 2:124ff.

Many are the afflictions of the righteous, but the LORD rescues them from them all. (Psalm 34:19)

Overcoming Temptation

*For we do not have a high priest who is unable to sympathize
with our weaknesses, but we have one who in every respect
has been tested as we are, yet without sin.*
(Hebrews 4:15)

When the devil tempts me, my heart is comforted and my faith is
strengthened, because I know him who for my sake has overcome the
devil, and that he comes to me to be my help and my comfort. Thus
faith overcomes the devil. Therefore, first, God teaches me faith, that I
may know that for my sake Christ has overcome the devil. Then, since I
now know that the devil has no power over me but is overcome by faith,
I must be ready to be tempted. The purpose of this is that my faith may
be strengthened, and that my neighbor may be given an example by my
victory over temptation and may be comforted.

And mark this: whenever faith begins, temptation soon follows. The
Holy Spirit does not leave you to rest in quietness, but soon throws you
into temptation. Why? In order that your faith may be confirmed, for
otherwise the devil would blow us about like chaff. But if God comes and
hangs a weight on us, making us weighty and heavy, then it is manifest to
the devil and to all humankind that the power of God is at work. Thus
God manifests his glory and majesty in our weakness; therefore he casts
us out into the desert—that is, he casts us down, so that we are deserted
of all creatures and can see no help. We even think that God himself has
utterly forsaken us. For as he acts toward Christ, even so he acts toward
us. It does not run smoothly. Our heart must faint within us.

Sermon from the year 1523.   WA 11:22f.

*In times of despair and trial, Lord God,
give me confidence in your steadfast love. Amen.*

Severe Temptations

The snares of death encompassed me;
the pangs of Sheol laid hold on me;
I suffered distress and anguish.
Then I called on the name of the LORD:
"O LORD, I pray, save my life!"
(Psalm 116:3-4)

When God has given us true faith so that we walk in firm trust, having no doubt that he, through Christ, is gracious to us, then we are in paradise. But before we do anything wrong, all that may be changed and God may allow our hearts to faint, so that we think it is his will to snatch the Savior from our hearts. Then is Christ so veiled that we can have no comfort in him, and the devil pours into our hearts the most terrible thoughts about him, so that our conscience feels it has lost him and is cast down and disquieted as if there were nothing but God's wrath toward us, which we by our sins have well deserved.

Yes, even if we know of no open sins, yet the devil has the power to make sin out of what is no sin, and thus he frightens our hearts and makes us anxious so that we are tormented by such questions as: Who knows whether God will have you and give Christ to you?

This is the direst and deepest temptation and suffering with which God now and again attacks and tests even his greatest saints, so that the heart feels that God has taken his grace away from us, that he no longer wills to be our God, and wherever we turn we see nothing but wrath and terror. Yet not every soul is sorely tempted, nor does anyone know what it is like unless they have experienced it. Only the strongest spirits could endure such blows.

Sermons from the year 1525.   WA 17/2:20f.

O Lord, when I feel like praying with Job, "Why do you hide
your face and count me as your enemy?" (Job 13:24),
give me a clear vision of your shining presence. Amen.

Our Victory Is in Christ

Thanks be to God, who gives us the victory through our Lord Jesus Christ.
(1 Corinthians 15:57)

Here Christians learn how to grasp and use the gospel message when the time of battle is come and the law attacks and accuses them. Then their own conscience tells them, "This wrong you have done, and you are a sinner, and what you deserve is punishment." At such a time we may with true confidence reply, "Alas, I am a sinner and I have well deserved death. You are right, but condemn and kill me on that account you shall not. There is one who will hinder you, who is called my Lord Christ, whom you have accused and murdered, although he was innocent. But do you not know how you were burned and bruised by him, thus losing all your rights over me and all other Christians? For he bore sin and death not for his own sake but for me. Therefore I grant you no right over me; instead I have a right over you, because you attack me although I am innocent, you who were before conquered and condemned by him, so that you should leave me in peace. For I am no longer merely a child of humans; I have become the child of God; for I have been baptized in his blood and his victory, and arrayed in all the riches of his bounty."

In this way all Christians must arm themselves with the victory of Christ and repel the devil with it.

Sermons from the year 1532. LW 28:211; WA 36:693f.

In our time of narcissism and self-indulgence, heavenly Father,
lead me to an honest self-appraisal. Amen.

Beholding Jesus

*Looking to Jesus the pioneer and perfecter of our faith,
who for the sake of the joy that was set before him
endured the cross, disregarding its shame.
(Hebrews 12:2)*

In all temptations we should keep our gaze fixed on the image of Christ and keep close to it. For Christ goes on, however much it hurts, and he is full of courage. Therefore we must pray that he will also give us his courage and spirit that we too may learn to be strong in the midst of weakness and to overcome in the days of affliction. In this way Christ comes to us not as an image. He implants in us all his courage, so that we too can endure. Therefore, whatever may come upon us, however much shame and blame, people will see that Christ, our prince, perceives and overcomes it triumphantly. Therefore we must beseech him for courage that, in the midst of adversities, we may be made strong and be given power to overcome death.

In this same way Paul sets Christ before us in all his letters, first as an example that we are to follow, then as he gives us the spirit and the courage that he himself possesses. This is the true Christian teaching.

Similarly, no one knows how to use the passion of Christ, and no one rightly experiences it unless they have endured adversities and been brought near to Christ, and have suffered and come through because they received from Christ the power to endure. In this spirit one must come right to the center and learn how to use Christ.

Sermons from the year 1522.   WA 10/3:77

*Lord God, let me learn to follow the example of Jesus,
the pioneer and perfecter of our faith. Amen.*

The Deep and Hidden Yes

She said, "Yes, Lord, yet even the dogs eat the crumbs
that fall from their masters' table." Then Jesus answered her,
"Woman, great is your faith! Let it be done for you as you wish."
(Matthew 15:27-28)

Is this not masterly? She catches Christ by means of his own words. He compares her to a dog, which she admits, and she asks no more than that he let her be like a dog as he himself judges. How could he respond? He was caught. No dog is denied the bread crumbs under the table. They are its rightful share. Therefore he listens to her and submits to her will, so that she is no longer a dog but has become a child of Israel.

This was written in order that we might be comforted, and that it may be made manifest to us all how deeply God hides his grace from us, and that we should not judge him according to our feeling and thinking about him but in accordance with his Word. For here you see that Christ, although he showed himself hard, pronounced no final judgment by saying "No" to her; but all his answers, though they sound like "No," are not "No" but indefinite.

This shows how our heart should stand firm in the midst of temptations, for as hard as we feel him, so Christ feigns to be. Our heart hears and understands nothing but "No," and yet it is not "No." Therefore sweep your heart clean of such feelings and trust firmly in God's Word and grasp from above or from underneath the "No" the deeply hidden "Yes," and hold on to it as this woman did and keep a firm belief in God's justice. Then you have won and caught him with his own words.

Sermons from the year 1525.   WA 17/2:203

Lord of all life, in my hour of need let me hear your "Yes."
Let my life be filled with praise until the last day. Amen.

He Was Obedient unto Death

Philippians 2:5-11

My food is to do the will of him who sent me and to complete his work.
(John 4:34)

The will of God that Christ came to do can be nothing else but Christ's own obedience. As Paul says, he "became obedient to the point of death" (Philippians 2:8). By that will we are all sanctified: "By the one man's obedience the many will be made righteous" (Romans 5:19). "He humbled himself and became obedient to the point of death."

But all this he did, not because we have merited it or are worthy of it (for who is the one to be worthy of such a service from such a person?), but because he obeyed his Father. By this saying St. Paul with one word flings open the gates of heaven, thus letting us behold the unspeakable, gracious will and love of the Father's heart toward us, so that we feel how from the beginning of time Christ's sacrifice for us has been well-pleasing to God.

What heart should not melt with joy at this? Who should not love and praise and thank? Who should not joyfully become the servant of all the world, and even less than nothing, when they perceive that God holds them to be so dear and precious, and that he proves and pours out his Fatherly will so abundantly in his own Son's obedience?

Sermons from the year 1525.   WA 17/2:244

What wondrous love is this, O my soul, that caused the Lord of bliss
to bear the dreadful curse for my soul? (American folk hymn)

Not What I Want but What You Want

Your will be done.
(Matthew 26:42)

Who can fulfill this lofty command to the extent that he surrenders all things and has no will of his own? This is my reply: You must learn how important and necessary this petition is, why we must pray it ardently and earnestly, and why it is important that our will be mortified and God's will alone be done. Thus you must confess that you are a sinner who cannot do God's will, who must petition God to give you help and mercy, to forgive your shortcomings, and to aid you in doing his will. It is imperative that if God's will is to prevail, our will must be submerged, for these two are at war with each other. We can take an example from Christ our Lord. When he asked his Father in the garden to remove the cup, he also added, "Not what I want but what you want" (Matthew 26:39). If Christ had to surrender his will, which after all was good, yes, undoubtedly and always the best, in order that God's will be carried out, why should we poor little worms make such a fuss about our will, which is never free of evil and always deserves to be thwarted?

Exposition of the Lord's Prayer.   LW 42:45; WA 2:102

Lead on, O King eternal; we follow, not with fears, for gladness
breaks like morning where'er your face appears. Amen.
(Ernest W. Shurtleff, 1862–1917)

The Right Attitude in Prayer

*This is the boldness we have in him, that
if we ask anything according to his will, he hears us.
(1 John 5:14)*

The affliction that caused the Lord in this instance to pray was a temporal, physical affliction. Now in all things that have to do with the body, we ought to give our will to God, for as St. Paul says, we know not how to pray (Romans 8:26). Thus it is often necessary for us that God should leave us under the cross, overwhelmed by calamities. And as God alone knows what is good and needful, it is right for us to place his will before our will and to prove our obedience in patience.

But where the eternal and not the temporal good is concerned, namely, that God keeps us by his Word, sanctifies us, forgives our sins, and bestows upon us the Holy Spirit and eternal life, there God's will is certain and manifest. He desires that all be saved. God wills that all should see and acknowledge their sins and that they all, through Christ, should believe in the forgiveness of sins. Therefore in such a case it is not necessary to say, "Not what I want but what you want." We ought to know and believe that God delights to do such things, and that he will undoubtedly do them. Note well that here we have his Word before our eyes that reveals his will in such things.

Sermons for the year 1545.   WA 52:741f.

*I thank you, Lord of heaven and earth, that you are merciful,
abounding in steadfast love and faithfulness. Amen.*

Growing More Perfect in Obedience

Now may God . . . make you complete in everything good so that you may do his will, working among us that which is pleasing in his sight, through Jesus Christ, to whom be the glory forever and ever. Amen.
(Hebrews 13:20-21)

If you want to convert the whole world, raise the dead, lead yourself and all others to heaven, and perform every miracle, you should still not want to do any of this unless you had first consulted God's will and subordinated your will wholly to his, and said, "My dear God, this or that seems good to me; if you approve, let it be done, but if you disapprove, let it remain undone."

God very often breaks this goodwill in his saints to prevent a false, malicious, and evil good will from establishing itself through the semblance of good, and also to help us learn that no matter how good our will may be, it is still immeasurably inferior to God's will. Therefore our inferior goodwill must necessarily give way to the infinitely better will of God; it must submit to being destroyed by it.

Moreover, this goodwill in us must be hindered for its own improvement. God's only purpose in thwarting our goodwill is to make of it a better will. This is done when it subordinates itself to and conforms to the divine will (by which it is hindered), until the point is reached when we are entirely unfettered by our own will, delivered from our own will, and know nothing except that we wait on the will of God. Now that is what is meant by genuine obedience.

Exposition of the Lord's Prayer.   LW 42:47; WA 2:103f.

God our Savior . . . desires everyone to be saved and to come to the knowledge of the truth. (1 Timothy 2:3-4)

Obedient—For Us

Although he was a Son, he learned obedience through what he suffered;
and having been made perfect, he became the source
of eternal salvation for all who obey him.
(Hebrews 5:8-9)

Christ loves the sinner at the command of the Father, who sent him for our comfort. So the Father wills that we should look to Christ's humanity and love him in return, but yet in such a way as to remember that he did all this at the bidding of Father's supreme good pleasure. Otherwise it is terrifying to think of Christ. For to the Father is ascribed power, to the Son wisdom, and to the Holy Spirit goodness, which we can never attain and of which we must despair.

But when we know and consider that Christ came down from heaven and loved sinners in obedience to the Father, then there springs up in us a bold approach to and a firm hope in Christ. We learn that Christ is the real epistle, the golden book, in which we read and learn how he always kept before him the will of the Father. For then it will be impossible that we should have a miserable, frightened, dejected conscience; in Christ it will be heartened and refreshed.

This tastes sweet to the faithful soul and it gives all the glory, praise, and honor to the Father through the Son, Christ Jesus. So God has nothing but the best and he offers it to us, guides us, sustains us, and cares for us through his Son. That's the way our hearts are changed to follow Christ.

How kindly, sweetly, and lovingly Christ has dealt with people. For the Father commanded him to do so.

Lenten sermon from the year 1518.   LW 51:46f.; WA 1:274f.

Father, Son, and Holy Spirit, sustain me
and guide me in my path through life. Amen.

That the Scriptures May Be Fulfilled

*Do you think that I cannot appeal to my Father, and he will at once
send me more than twelve legions of angels? But how then would
the scriptures be fulfilled, which say it must happen in this way?*
(Matthew 26:53-54)

One angel would have been enough to defend Christ against those who
called for his death, but Christ said that he might have had twelve legions
of angels, that is, more than seventy thousand angels. One angel would
have been enough to defend Christ even against the whole world.

But Christ says, "Put your sword back into its place. . . . How then
would the scriptures be fulfilled?" (verses 52, 54)—as if he said, "The
scriptures will not be fulfilled unless I suffer." But the scriptures must be
fulfilled; therefore these things must all come to pass. This is the reason
why Christ suffered. He did not suffer because he was compelled to do
so or because God could not find any other way to manifest his honor
and glory, but that God should be found truthful in keeping his Word,
which he had spoken through the prophets. It was God's will to act
according to his good pleasure. God could have acted otherwise, but that
was not his will.

Sermons from the year 1534.   WA 37:324f.

*No drops of grief can e'er repay the debt of love I owe;
Here, Lord, I give myself away; 'tis all that I can do. Amen.
(Isaac Watts, 1707)*

He Has Left Us an Example

Christ also suffered for you, leaving you an example,
so that you should follow in his steps.
(1 Peter 2:21)

When your heart is confirmed in Christ and is opposed to sin out of love, not out of fear of punishment, then the suffering of Christ should become an example for your whole life, and you should regard suffering in a different manner. If pain or illness afflicts you, think of how little this is compared with the nails and the crown of thorns of Christ. If you have to do or leave something that you do not wish to do or leave, think of how Christ was caught and bound and led here and there. If pride tempts you, remember that your Lord was mocked and despised with the thieves. If lust and unchastity kindle you, think of how bitterly Christ's tender flesh was scourged, pierced, and lashed. If hate and envy tempt you, or if you seek revenge, think of how Christ, with uncountable tears and sighs, has prayed for you and all his enemies, he who might well have taken revenge. And if affliction or any other adversity, physical or spiritual, grieve you, fortify your heart, saying, "Why then should I not suffer some small woe when my Lord in the garden sweated blood, with fear and anguish?" A wretched and slothful servant would be the man who lies comfortably in his bed while his master struggles with the pains of death.

A Meditation on Christ's Passion.   LW 42:13; WA 2:141

If you, O LORD, should mark iniquities, Lord, who could stand?
But there is forgiveness with you, so that you may be revered. Amen.
(Psalm 130:3-4)

The Son of Man Has Come to Serve

John 13:1-5

*Jesus, knowing that the Father had given all things into his hands, . . .
tied a towel around himself . . . and began to wash the disciples' feet.
(John 13:3-5)*

St. John writes these truly great words to indicate what thoughts were
in the mind of the Lord Jesus before he rose and washed their feet. He
did not think of his sufferings; neither was his mind heavy with the
sorrow that followed soon afterwards. He thought about his glory, which
he shared with his Father from eternity, to whom he was to return and
remain there forever.

But just then, when he was meditating on eternal glory, he rose
from supper, laid aside his garments, wrapped himself in a towel, and
poured water into a vessel. See how his thoughts and his work agree.
His thoughts are, "I am God and Lord over all things; in less than a day
the devil will have done his worst. Then he and all my enemies will lie
at my feet and leave my Christians in peace." But what is his work? He,
the greatest of Lords, does what slaves and servants do. He washes his
disciples' feet.

In this way he gave us an example. As he laid aside his glory and
forgot it and never misused it for his own pride, power, and splendor but
used it for the good of his servants, we should do the same. We should
never exalt ourselves because of our gifts, never abuse them as an occasion
of pride, but we should serve our neighbor with them to the very limit of
our power.

Sermon on Maundy Thursday, 1544. WA 52:218f.

*O divine Master, grant that I may not so much seek to be consoled,
as to console; to be loved, as to love. Amen.
(Francis of Assisi, 1181–1226)*

The Son of God, Our Servant

The Son of Man came not to be served but to serve,
and to give his life a ransom for many.
(Matthew 20:28)

Look at this picture and love it. There is no greater bondage or form of service than that the Son of God should be the servant and should bear the sin of everyone, however poor and wretched or despised. What an amazing thing it would be if some great king's son should go into a beggar's hut to nurse him in his illness, wash off his filth, and do all the things that otherwise the beggar would have to do. All the world would gape with open mouths, noses, ears, and eyes, and could never think and talk enough about it. Would that not be a wonderful humility?

Therefore it would be well to sing, talk, and preach of this forever, and on our part to love and praise God for so gracious a gift. But what does it mean? The Son of God becomes my servant and humbles himself so much that he carries even my afflictions and my sin—yes, the whole world's sin and death he takes on himself, saying to me, "You are no longer a sinner, but I, I myself, step into your place. You have not sinned; I have. The whole world lies in sin, but you are not in sin, but I am. All your sin shall be upon me, and not on you."

No one can comprehend it. In the life hereafter we shall have a knowledge of the love of God and gaze upon it in eternal blessedness.

Sermon on John 1. LW 22:166; WA 46:680f.

O love that will not let me go, I rest my weary soul in you;
I give you back the life I owe, that in your ocean depths
its flow may richer, fuller be. Amen.
(George Matheson, 1852, alt.)

Our Savior Must Be Both Divine and Human

Though he was in the form of God, [he] did not regard equality with God as something to be exploited, but emptied himself, taking the form of a slave, being born in human likeness. And being found in human form . . .
(Philippians 2:6-8)

On the one hand, we need a Savior who can save us from the god and prince of this world, the devil, and likewise from sin and death, that is, a Savior who is eternal God, through whom all who believe in him are justified and blessed. For if he is no more and no higher than Moses, Elijah, Isaiah, or John the Baptist, he is not our Redeemer. But if he, as the Son of God, sheds his blood for us in order to redeem us and cleanse us from sin, and if we believe it and hold it under the devil's nose whenever he frightens and plagues us with our sin, the devil will soon be beaten so that he must give way and leave us in peace.

On the other hand, we need a Savior who is also our brother, of our flesh and blood, made in all things like us, yet without sin, as we are taught to say and sing as little children, so that I can say with a joyful heart, "I believe in Jesus Christ, the only Son of God, who sits at the right hand of the Father and intercedes for me, who is also my flesh and blood, yes, my brother. Because for us humans and for our salvation he came down from heaven and was made man and died for our sin."

Sermon on John 1.   WA 46:556f.

I believe that Jesus Christ, begotten of the Father in eternity, and also a true human being, born of the virgin Mary, is my Lord.
(Martin Luther, Small Catechism)

The Bondage of Sin

Who gave himself for our sins to set us free from this present evil age,
according to the will of our God and Father.
(Galatians 1:4)

Friend, take these words, "who gave himself" to heart and seriously meditate on them. Then you will come to see that the word "sin" comprises the eternal wrath of God and all of Satan's hellish might and power. Because he inflicts so much misery and woe on earth that our lives are not for a moment safe from him, we must always be prepared for many dire afflictions. All this is because of sin. Therefore it is not so trifling a matter as blind and confident reason dreams.

Therefore this passage ends most emphatically, saying that all humanity is in the bondage of sin, or as St. Paul says elsewhere, "They are sold into slavery under sin" (Romans 7:14). Further, it asserts that sin is a powerful and cruel master and tyrant over all humankind on the whole earth, and that no one can resist it, however wise, high, learned, and mighty he may be. Yes, even if all persons under the sky would unite, even with all their power, they could not overcome this tyrant but would all have to submit and be slain and devoured by him. Jesus Christ alone is the hero who can thwart that cruel, unconquerable foe. But it costs our Lord very dearly, for he must lose his life in doing it.

Lectures on Galatians.   LW 26:33; WA 40/1:82ff.

Oh, let your mighty love prevail to purge us of our pride, that we may
stand before your throne by mercy purified. Amen.
(Latin hymn, eighth century)

He Has Atoned for Us

He has rescued us from the power of darkness
and transferred us into the kingdom of his beloved Son,
in whom we have redemption, the forgiveness of sins.
(Colossians 1:13-14)

Because sin was under an eternal, unchangeable condemnation (for God cannot and will not be gracious to sin, and his wrath therefore remains eternal and irrevocable against it), this redemption could not take place unless something precious and valuable should compensate for sin, taking the wrath upon itself and paying the price, so taking away sin and blotting it out utterly. No creature could do this, nor was there any other way to help except that God's own Son should come to our aid and be made a human being, should draw eternal wrath upon himself and give his own life and blood as a sacrifice.

This he has done, in his great and immeasurable mercy and love toward us. He gave himself and bore the condemnation of eternal wrath and death. This costly sacrifice is so dear and precious to God because it is the deed of his own beloved Son, who is one with him in Godhead and majesty, that he is reconciled through it and forgives the sins of and receives in grace all who believe in his Son.

For this reason alone we enjoy the fruits and merits of the precious redemptive deed, won and given to us out of unfathomable and unspeakable love, and thus we have nothing of our own to boast about, but we can only give thanks and praise him who gave such a price to redeem us lost and condemned sinners.

Sermon on Colossians 1:3-14.   WA 22:389

Have mercy on me, O God, according to your steadfast love; according to
your abundant mercy blot out my transgressions. Amen. (Psalm 51:1)

The Image of Grace

So Moses made a serpent of bronze, and put it upon a pole,
and whenever a serpent bit someone, that person would look
at the serpent of bronze and live.
(Numbers 21:9)

You must think only of Christ's death, and you will find life. Look not on the sin that is in the sinner, or in your own conscience, or in those who remain in their sins and are damned. You would surely follow them and be overcome. You must turn your thoughts away and not look upon sin except in the image of grace. Form this image in your mind with all your strength and keep it before your eyes.

The image of grace is nothing other than Christ crucified, and all his dear saints. How is that to be understood? That Christ on the cross takes away your sin and carries it for you and destroys it. That is grace and mercy. Believe firmly in it, have it before your eyes, and do not doubt it. That is to behold the image of grace and to form it in yourself.

Note well the wonder: sin is no longer sin. It is bound and consumed in Christ. Thus Christ is the image of life and of grace in contrast to the picture of death. He is our bliss and beatitude.

A Sermon on Preparing to Die.   LW 42:105; WA 2:689f.

On my heart imprint your image, blessed Jesus, king of grace,
that life's troubles nor its pleasures ever may your work erase. Amen.
(Thomas H. Kingo, 1634–1703)

Follow Him

Remember the word that I said to you, "Servants are not greater than their master." If they persecuted me, they will persecute you.
(John 15:20)

As I have said, servants should impress it on their hearts and be moved to do and suffer willingly what they must, because Christ did so much for them. They must think as follows: "Since my Lord served me even though he was not obliged to do so, and since he sacrificed life and limb for me, why would I refuse to serve him in return? He was completely pure and without sin. Yet he humbled himself so deeply, shed his blood for me, and died to blot out my sins. Should I then not also suffer something because it pleases him?" Now he who contemplates this would surely have to be a stone if it did not move him. For if the master takes the lead and steps into the mire, it stands to reason that the servant will follow.

Therefore St. Peter says, "To this you have been called" (1 Peter 2:21). To what? To suffer wrong, as Christ did. It is as if he were saying, "If you want to follow Christ, you dare not argue and complain much when you are wronged; but you must suffer it and be forgiving, since Christ suffered everything without any guilt on his part."

You should praise and thank God for being worthy of becoming like Christ. You should not murmur or be impatient when you are wronged, since the Lord neither reviled nor threatened but even prayed for his enemies.

Sermon on 1 Peter.   LW 30:85; WA 12:339f.

Lord God, I pray today for those unjustly accused. Vindicate them and let your justice prevail over the earth. Amen.

Christ's Sacrifice

Romans 5:1-11

God proves his love for us in that while we still were sinners
Christ died for us.
(Romans 5:8)

He sacrifices himself on the cross, becomes a sinner and a curse, and yet he alone is the blessed seed through whom all the world will be blessed, that is, redeemed from sin and death. He hangs on the cross between two malefactors, being counted equal to them, and he dies a shameful death, all for the benefit of the whole human race, to redeem it from the eternal curse. Thus he is both the greatest and the only sinner on earth, for he bears all the world's sin; and the only righteous and holy one, for no one can be made righteous and holy before God but through him alone.

All who believe that their sin and the sin of the world are laid on our dear Lord, who was baptized and nailed to the cross for our sin, and shed his precious blood in order that he, the only sin-bearer, should thus cleanse us from sin, and make us holy and blessed—those persons receive forgiveness of sins and eternal life. Christ's baptism, cross, and blood become their own.

Sermons from the year 1540.   WA 49:121

O sacred head, what glory, what bliss till now was thine!
Yet, though despised and gory, I joy to call thee mine. Amen.
(Paul Gerhardt, 1607–1676)

Gethsemane

In the days of his flesh, Jesus offered up prayers and supplications,
with loud cries and tears, to the one who was able to save him
from death, and he was heard because of his reverent submission.
(Hebrews 5:7)

Merciful Father, why is my Lord Christ Jesus in dread? Why does the Son of God shrink from what lies ahead? What is his agony? He asks that the cup be taken from him. What kind of cup is it? It is the bitter death on the cross. But why should he suffer death? He is without sin; he is holy and just. It is for the sin of the world that God has laid on him. That presses on him and alarms him.

Is it not true that if God has laid my sin on him (for St. John called him the Lamb of God who takes away the sin of the world), I am free and rid of my sin? Why then should I accuse myself and my Lord Christ Jesus? I am a sinner. Alas, it is true. Sin frightens me. That, alas, I feel deeply and my heart ever faints within me. I fear before God and his severe judgment. And yet of what shall I accuse myself, and of what shall I accuse my Lord Christ Jesus? There, on the Mount of Olives, he shivers and quakes and is in such dread and alarm that he sweats blood. And my intolerable sin brings him to this, my sin that he has taken upon himself and that is so hard to carry. Therefore I will let it lie there and confidently hope that whenever I come before God and his judgment, he will find no sin in me.

The Mount of Olives is a comfort to you, showing that you may be certain that Christ has taken your sin on himself and paid the price for it. If, then, your sins are laid on Christ, be content. They lie in the right place; it is where they belong.

Sermons from the year 1545.   WA 52:738

Why are you so far from helping me, from the words of my groaning? . . .
O LORD, do not be far away! O my help, come quickly to my aid! Amen.
(Psalm 22:1, 19)

He Has Borne Our Griefs

Surely he has borne our griefs and carried our sorrows.
(Isaiah 53:4 RSV)

These are clear and powerful words. The sufferings of this king are our griefs and sorrows. He carries the burden that ought to be ours forever. The stripes and bruises that we have merited—that we should suffer thirst and hunger, and die eternally—all this is laid on him. His suffering avails for me and for you and for us all; for it was undertaken for our good. But we esteemed him to be the one who was afflicted and smitten of God.

And that is true. For Moses himself says, "Anyone hung on a tree is under God's curse" (Deuteronomy 21:23). That is why he was railed at as one condemned and cursed. He cannot even help himself; how then can he heal others? But they did not see properly. For, note well, he is carrying our sorrows. According to outward appearance he seems to be cursed, but according to the spirit he carries my sorrows and yours, and the sorrows of us all. "Upon him was the chastisement that made us whole, and with his stripes we are healed" (Isaiah 53:5 RSV). He is chastised, and we are made whole. I and you and we all have called forth God's wrath. He has atoned, that we, redeemed from sin, may rest in peace. He must suffer; we are set free.

We ought not so shamefully to forget such great love and mercy.

Sermons from the year 1531.   WA 34/1:264f.

Bend your boughs, O tree of glory, your relaxing sinews bend;
for a while the ancient rigor that your birth bestowed, suspend;
and the Lord of heavenly beauty gently on your arms extend. Amen.
(Fortunatus, 530–609 B.C.)

Forsaken by God

I am a worm and not human;
  scorned by others, and despised by the people.
(Psalm 22:6)

St. Paul speaks of it this way in Philippians 2:6-7: Jesus Christ, "who, though he was in the form of God, did not regard equality with God as something to be exploited, but emptied himself, taking the form of a slave." He says that Christ emptied himself of the divine form; that is, he did not use his divine might nor let his almighty power be seen, but withdrew it when he suffered. In this emptying and humiliation the devil tried all his hellish might. The man, the Son of Man, stands there and bears the sins of the world (John 1:29), and because he does not give the appearance of having divine consolation and power, the devil set his teeth over the innocent Lamb and wanted to devour him. Thus the righteous and innocent man must shiver and quake like a poor, condemned sinner and feel God's wrath and judgment against sin in his tender, innocent heart, taste eternal death and damnation for us—in short, he must suffer everything that a condemned sinner has deserved and must suffer eternally.

By this the kingdom of heaven, eternal life, and salvation were secured for us, as Isaiah also says, "He shall see the fruit of the travail of his soul and be satisfied" (53:11 RSV). His body and soul, he says, endure deep and difficult suffering. But he does this for our great benefit and for his own great joy. For he conquers his enemies and triumphs, and by his knowledge he makes many righteous.

Sermons from the year 1537.   WA 45:240f.

O Lord, in times of despair, when my lifeblood seems drained,
let me glimpse your shining face, restoring my hope. Amen.

The Guiltless One Suffers for the Guilty

But he was wounded for our transgressions,
crushed for our iniquities;
upon him was the punishment that made us whole;
and by his bruises we are healed.
(Isaiah 53:5)

Accept this, and take comfort from it, believing that it was done for your sake and for your good. For here you hear it, not once, or twice, but many times: what he suffers, he suffers innocently.

Why does God allow this? Why does God ordain it and bring it to pass? In order that you should be comforted by it. He did not suffer for his own sake. He suffered for your sake and for the whole world's sake. That is why it is so full of contradiction. He is the Son of God, entirely holy and without sin, and therefore he should have no part in death nor the curse. We are sinners, under God's curse and wrath, and therefore we should bear death and condemnation. But God reverses it; he who has no sin, in whom there is nothing but grace, must be made the curse and bear the chastisement, and through him we are in a state of grace, and the children of God. Therefore we should hold fast to this comfort and especially treasure this testimony of Christ's innocence. For our guilt and sin were the occasion of what Christ innocently suffered. That is why we can take comfort against sin and every ill, through his innocence. For such innocence is a sure and certain testimony that we enjoy the fruit of his sufferings, and that our devoted Lord and gracious Redeemer has suffered for us and paid our debt.

Sermons from the year 1545. WA 52:786f.

O Lord, we who are mere mortals need redemption—freedom from all
that constricts life. Restore to me the joy of your salvation. Amen.

By the Sacrifice of Himself

He has appeared once for all at the end of the age
to remove sin by the sacrifice of himself.
(Hebrews 9:26)

Such knowledge and faith produce a joyful heart, which is certain and can say, "I know of no more sins, for they are all lying on Christ s back. Now they can never lie both upon him and upon us." Therefore none of us can say that we make satisfaction for sin through our own righteousness or discipline; for atonement and redemption of sin belong to Christ alone. But Christ is neither my work nor yours nor anyone's works. Nor are they his body and blood, which he sacrificed for our sins; he is true God, true man, who bears the sins of the whole world. But he takes them and drowns and smothers them in baptism and the cross, and lets you proclaim that he has given his body for you and poured out his blood for the forgiveness of your sins. If you believe this, then they are forgiven, you are good and righteous, you receive the Holy Spirit, in order that henceforth you may be able to resist sin. And when through weakness you are overtaken by it, it shall not be imputed to you, as long as you otherwise remain in this faith.

This is what the forgiveness of sins means.

Sermon on the Friday after Easter, 1540.   LW 51:317; WA 49:125

Wide open are your arms, a fallen world to embrace.
Give me the soul-transforming joy for which I seek your face. Amen.
(Bernard of Clairvaux, 1091–1153)

We Are Set Free by His Death

For freedom Christ has set us free. Stand firm, therefore,
and do not submit again to a yoke of slavery.
(Galatians 5:1)

Christ has not freed us from human duties but from eternal wrath.
Where? In the conscience. That is the limit of our freedom, and it must
go no further. For Christ has set us spiritually free; that is, he has set us
free in the sense that our conscience is free and joyful and no longer fears
the coming wrath of God. That is true freedom, and no one can value it
highly enough. For who can express what a great thing it is that a man
or woman is certain that God is no longer angry with them and will
never be angry again, but for the sake of Christ is now, and ever will be,
a gracious and merciful Father? Truly, it is a wonderful freedom, above all
understanding, that God's high majesty is gracious to us.

From this there follows another freedom, that we, through Christ,
are set free from the law, sin, death, hell, and the power of the devil. For,
as the wrath of God can no longer frighten us, because Christ has set us
free from it, so the law and sin can no longer accuse or condemn us.

The Prophet Joel, with Commentary.   *EA (Latin) 25:288f.*

Eternal God, we pray for those who are oppressed by the power
of evil and for freedom for those who suffer from poverty,
oppression, and discrimination. Amen.

A High Priest Forever

Hebrews 9:11-15

You are a priest forever, according to the order of Melchizedek.
(Hebrews 5:6)

"Priest" is a strong and lovely word. There is no lovelier or sweeter name on earth. It is much better to hear that Christ is called "priest" than "Lord" or any other name. Priesthood is a spiritual power that means nothing else than that the priest steps forth and takes all the iniquities of the people upon himself as though they were his very own. He intercedes with God for them and receives from God the Word by which he can comfort and help the people. It is lovelier and more comforting than "Father" and "Mother," for this name brings us everything else. For by being a priest he makes God our Father and himself our Lord. When I believe in his priesthood, then I know that his work is none other than to be seated in heaven as our mediator, and that he makes intercession for us before the Father, without ceasing, and all the time speaks on our behalf. This is the highest comfort that can be given to anyone, and no sweeter sermon can be preached to our hearts.

He offered himself once for all, so that he is himself both priest and sacrifice, and the altar is the cross. No more precious sacrifice could he offer to God than to give himself to be slain and consumed in the fire of love. That is the true sacrifice.

Exposition of Genesis 14.   WA 24:280

Heavenly Father, as Jesus is my mediator, let me act as intercessor
for those whom I love. Amen.

His Flesh and Blood Are a Spiritual Sacrifice

*How much more will the blood of Christ, who through the eternal Spirit
offered himself without blemish to God, purify our conscience
from dead works to worship the living God?*
(Hebrews 9:14)

[St. Paul] refers to two kinds of priesthood. The old priesthood was of
the body, with bodily adornments, offerings, forgiveness, and all that
belongs to it. The new priesthood is spiritual, with spiritual adornments,
offerings, and all that belongs to it! For Christ did not go about wearing
precious stones and gold and silk when he fulfilled his priesthood and
sacrificed himself on the cross, but in godly love, wisdom, patience,
obedience, and all the virtues, which no one saw but God, and such as
the Spirit enlightened.

Therefore, although the body and blood of Christ were seen like
any other bodily thing, it was not in the same way seen that they were
an offering and that he sacrificed them. It was not as when Aaron made
offerings and the people clearly saw that he had made a sacrifice. But
Christ offered himself before God, and this no one saw or noticed;
therefore his bodily flesh and blood are a spiritual offering.

Similarly, the tabernacle and churches of Christ are spiritual. They
are in heaven, or in the presence of God. For on the cross he hung not
in a temple but in the presence of God, where he still is. Again, the altar
is in a spiritual sense the cross, for anyone could see the wood but no
one knew that it was the altar of Christ. Thus his prayer, the shedding of
his blood, his incense, were all spiritual, for it all took place through his
Spirit. And so the fruit and the benefit of his sacrifice and ministry—the
forgiveness of sins and our justification—were spiritual.

Sermons from the year 1525.   WA 17/2:227f.

*I thank you, Lord God, for the many blessings of my life, both physical
and spiritual. Let my life be a blessing for others. Amen.*

He Made a Sacrifice for Our Sins

The LORD has laid on him the iniquity of us all.
(Isaiah 53:6)

This high priest is both priest and offering, for he offers his body and life upon the cross. It looks very unpriestly that he hangs there on the cross, stripped and naked, bruised and covered with blood, having a crown of thorns pressed down on his head. Yet he is the true priest and bishop who offers himself, and out of his great love gives his own body to be consumed, as through fire, for the redemption of all the world. The old priesthood was endowed with great splendor, but about this high priest there is no splendor. His altar is the cross and the gallows. That is a shameful, ghastly, and unusual altar. That is why he is in the eyes of the world such a mean, disdained high priest. He has such an offensive and dishonorable altar and is such a sacrifice as makes people shudder.

There, then, we have this high priest, Jesus Christ, with his altar and offering, most shamefully treated by the Jewish leaders and the soldiers. And yet he carries on his shoulders the sin of us all. There we lie, you and I and all humanity, from the first human beings, Adam and Eve, until the end of the world.

Sermon for Good Friday, 1534.   WA 37:353f.

Lord God, let the cross of Jesus stimulate in me compassion for all those who suffer—from famine, from poverty, from the terrors of violence. Amen.

He Has Become a Curse for Us

Christ redeemed us from the curse of the law by becoming a curse for us—for it is written, "Cursed is everyone who hangs on a tree."
(Galatians 3:13)

Who, then, will take offense at the cross? Who will think such a death shameful? Who will not give thanks to God that his Son hangs on the tree and takes upon himself the curse that belongs to us because of our sin? There he hangs like a cursed man, who is hateful to God, whom God allows to fall into shame, distress, and anguish. All this takes place (says St. Paul) for me and for you in order that we may attain to salvation. Learn this difference so that you do not judge by what your eyes see but according to what the Word of God tells you. From outward appearance, the death of our Lord Christ is a shameful death; God himself calls such a death a cursed death. The tree on which he dies is damned and accursed. But why? Because the sin of us all hangs on it. The tree is accursed, and the man who hangs on it is accursed. The cause of his hanging on it is also accursed. For the curse follows sin, and the more sin lies upon the Lord, the greater is the curse. But it is a death for our salvation, which takes away the curse from us and wins for us the blessing of God.

Sermons from the year 1545.   WA 52:807

Take away from me, O Lord, the curse of sin and finitude,
and lead me at last to your eternal home. Amen.

He Went to His Father

But now I am going to him who sent me.
(John 16:5)

These words "I am going to the Father" comprise the whole work of our redemption and salvation for which God's Son was sent down from heaven, which he has done for us and goes on doing until the end of time. This work is his suffering death and resurrection, and his whole kingdom in the church. For this going to the Father means nothing else than that he gives himself as a sacrifice through the shedding of his blood and through his dying in order to pay for our sin. After that, through his resurrection, he overcomes sin, death, and hell and brings them under his power, and, as the living one, seats himself at the right hand of the Father, where he reigns unseen over all things in heaven and on earth. From there he gathers his church and causes it to grow, and as an eternal mediator and high priest, he represents and intercedes before the Father for those who believe, because they are still beset by weakness and sin. Moreover, he gives the power and the strength of the Holy Spirit, in order that sin, death, and devil may be overcome.

This then is the Christian's justification before God, that Christ goes to the Father—that is, he suffers for us and rises again, and so reconciles us to the Father—so that for his sake we receive forgiveness of sins and grace. There is nothing of our work or merit, but it is all because of his going to the Father, which he did for our sake. That means another person's righteousness is given to us and made our own, so that it becomes our righteousness through which we become well-pleasing to God and his heirs, God's dear children.

Sermon on John 16:5-15.   WA 21:363

O Lord, let me live each day in the light of resurrection. Amen.

FRIDAY

His Priesthood Saves Us from the Wrath of God

He entered once for all into the Holy Place . . .
with his own blood, thus obtaining eternal redemption.
(Hebrews 9:12)

By his kingdom and reign he protects us from all evil in all things, but
by his priesthood he protects us from all sins and from the wrath of God.
He steps into our place, offering himself in order that he may reconcile
God to us, so that through him we can put our trust in God, and our
consciences need not fear his wrath nor stand in dread of his judgment,
as St. Paul says, "Through [him] we have obtained access to this grace in
which we stand" (Romans 5:2).

He makes us confident toward God and at peace in our own
consciences, so that God is not against us and we are not against
ourselves. And this is a far greater thing than that he takes away all harm
that the creatures might do to us. For guilt is much greater than pain,
and sin than death. For it is sin that brings death, and without sin there
would be no death, or death would do us no harm.

It is a mighty defiance that we can set this high priest over against our
sin, over against our bad conscience, over against God's terrible wrath and
judgment, and in sure faith can confess, "You are a high priest forever."

Sermons from the year 1522.   WA 10/1(i):717ff.

*Lord God, I thank you for the redemption accomplished in Jesus, for
freedom from the terror of death, and for the hope of resurrection. Amen.*

His Offering Is Valid Forever

For it was fitting that we should have such a high priest, holy, blameless, undefiled, separated from sinners, and exalted above the heavens. Unlike the other high priests, he has no need to offer sacrifices day after day, first for his own sins, and then for those of the people; this he did once for all when he offered himself.
(Hebrews 7:26-27)

The sacrifice of Christ, which was offered once for all, avails forever. Christ is himself the sacrifice that he offered in his death, to cleanse us from sin eternally. Therefore, where his suffering is ended and the offering is perfected, his honor begins. On the cross his honor falls to the ground along with his reputation and his mighty deeds. People begin to doubt whether he helped people by the power of God or of the devil. There, at that moment, his own conscience fails and the might of death prevails over him. Therefore, if it is to be a sacrifice, his own blood must be taken; the little Lamb must be stabbed; the sacrifice costs blood. Yet the struggle of Christ endures but a while. And Christ cries out with priestly voice, "My Father, though they have done this against me, pardon them, and forgive."

What does Christ do after that? He sits at the judgment seat of God. When all the world has deserted him and thinks he is finished, he begins his eternal reign and represents us before the Father, interceding for us when we are accused of sin. Judgment is spoken over us; the alarmed conscience feels God's anger at sin. There is then no help for us except in the sacrifice of Christ, who prays to the Father for us, saying, "My Father, the sinner is weak and is gripped by great anxieties. Give him to me; I have atoned for him. He trusts in my eternal sacrifice."

Sermon on Hebrews 7.   WA 45:398

Merciful God, in a world of callousness and self-seeking, give me an honest heart and a willing spirit. Amen.

The Crucified Christ

Matthew 21:1-9

Pilate asked him, "So you are a king?" Jesus answered, "You say that I am a king. For this I was born, and for this I came into the world, to testify to the truth. Everyone who belongs to the truth listens to my voice."
(John 18:37)

See how Christ the king abandons possessions, body, and life. Learn from this that his kingdom is not of this world. To enjoy the Christian faith here on earth does not mean to have all things in abundance and lack nothing. Look at your king, the Lord Jesus. Of what does he boast? What comfort has he in life? How highly is he praised? He has nothing but suffering, scorn, and disdain, and he dies in shame. One little thing he has with which to rule. It is his testimony to the truth, the holy gospel. Through this he pours the Holy Spirit into our hearts, forgives sin, and bestows the hope of eternal life. But all these things remain in faith and in the Word. They are not seen, nor are they handled. They exist in hope.

All those who know the way of this king and his kingdom willingly bear the cross. For they not only know that Christ, the eternal king, fared in the same way and is thus himself willing and ready to suffer (because a servant should not fare better than his Lord), but they also take comfort in the knowledge that life in the eternal kingdom is full of joy and splendor, even though suffering must be endured on earth. That makes Christians joyful even in the midst of sorrows and trials.

Sermons from the year 1545.   WA 52:768

Jesus Christ . . . though he was rich, yet for your sakes he became poor, so that by his poverty you might become rich. (2 Corinthians 8:9)

Judas and Peter

For godly grief produces a repentance that leads to salvation and brings no regret, but worldly grief produces death.
(2 Corinthians 7:10)

Judas had a heavier load on his back than Peter. Therefore he fell into despair, thinking there would never be any help or consolation. So out of woe and sorrow he went away and hanged himself, poor man! But why? Because he had been slothful in hearing the Word of God. He despised it and never bettered himself by it. Thus when he needed consolation and had the Word no longer, it was impossible for him to find help.

Peter also wept bitterly. He was anxious and worried because of his sins, but he had been more diligent in listening to the Word of his Lord Christ, and had engraved it on his mind. Therefore now, in the hour of his need, he seized on it and held fast to it, comforted himself with it, and hoped that God would be gracious to him. That is the one true help in such a need, and the hapless Judas lacked it. But that Peter held firmly to the Word and grace of God, the Lord himself testifies when he says, "I have prayed for you, that your own faith may not fail" (Luke 22:32).

Therefore learn here what is true repentance. Peter weeps bitterly; that is the beginning of repentance, that the heart acknowledges sin and is grieved for it, that it has no love for it or desire to continue in it, but is saddened that it has not kept God's will and has fallen into sin. But we cannot do that by ourselves; the Lord must look upon us as he looked upon Peter.

Sermons from the year 1545.   WA 52:768

In the hour of trial, O Lord, plead for me. Amen.

Judged by Public Authority

Those who had arrested Jesus took him to Caiaphas the high priest,
in whose house the scribes and the elders had gathered.
(Matthew 26:57)

Thus our dear Lord Christ Jesus suffered, not secretly at the hands of those who had no authority, but publicly and at the hands of those holding public authority, so that we should not take offense when we see that both spiritual and worldly authority are against God. Christ suffered, as we testify in the Christian creed when we say, "I believe in Jesus Christ, . . . who suffered under Pontius Pilate." In all ages—and still today—Christians and true martyrs are put to death by public authority, both spiritual and worldly.

No prophet has ever been treacherously murdered, but they have all been put to death by those in true official power. All blood that is shed in the name of Christ is shed by those who are kings, princes, judges, or counselors in worldly jurisdiction, or bishops and preachers and the like in spiritual jurisdiction. Prophets die by the judgment of humans.

But what will happen when the tide turns? Then what God will do will grieve them and leave undone what they desire. They stormed against God and would not let him remain, although he would have let them remain. Because they would not let God remain, they must perish.

Sermons from the year 1534.   WA 37:322f.

We mourn, O God, over all the victims of religious war and for those
persecuted for their beliefs. When will we ever learn? Amen.

Weep Not for Me

But Jesus turned to them and said, "Daughters of Jerusalem,
do not weep for me, but weep for yourselves and for your children."
(Luke 23:28)

He suffers for our sake. For this reason it grieves the Lord that his
suffering should make us weep. He wants us to be happy, to praise God
and give thanks for his grace, and to glorify him and bear our witness,
for it is through his passion that we received God's grace, and were freed
from sin and death, and became God's dear children. But we are as slow
to the one as to the other, for by nature we are contrary. When we should
weep over our sins, we laugh; when we should laugh and our hearts be
joyful because Christ, through his death, has won eternal life for us, we
weep. For either we have no regard for such joy, because our hearts are
bewitched by the merriment of this world, or we weep, lament, and pine
as if Christ had never died, never paid for our sin, never stilled the wrath
of God, and never redeemed us from death.

Therefore prayer is needed for both: first, that God through the
Holy Spirit may touch our hearts, that he may make us shun sin, draw
us away from it, and take away our trust in ourselves. Second, we need
prayer that God may kindle in our hearts his comfort in the midst of sin,
and give us a firm confidence in our Lord's sacrifice and satisfaction.

Sermons from the year 1545.   WA 52:798ff.

We weep, O Lord, for victims of violence in our time. We weep for those
who are threatened with death by starvation. We weep for those
unjustly accused. We pray for justice. Amen.

At the Mount of Olives

I am deeply grieved, even to death.
(Matthew 26:38)

Our dear Lord Christ stands here for our sake as a poor sinful man. The divine nature constrains itself, and the comfort and assurance that up to now have belonged to Christ have deserted him. So the tempter, the devil, is able to draw closer to him, and to assault him harder than before. That is why he speaks here as a man in the midst of the struggle, wrestling with death, seeking comfort from his disciples, whom until now he had comforted. He trembled and quaked, and his heart was filled with sadness, for he despaired of life and felt death, and saw that he must die. That is why he laments before his disciples. Such great fear and anguish break upon him that he turns to his disciples, although they are so much weaker than he.

No one has words to tell the sufferings of our dear Lord Jesus in the garden. It is above all human thought and understanding, what had befallen that divine and godly man.

More deeply has this man been distressed than anyone else on earth. More sorely has he dreaded death than anyone else. And this was done for our sake.

Sermons from the year 1534.   WA 37:326

In the days of his flesh, Jesus offered up prayers and supplications, with loud cries and tears, to the one who was able to save him from death, and he was heard because of his reverent submission. (Hebrews 5:7)

How to Receive the Sacrament

*As often as you eat this bread and drink the cup, you proclaim
the Lord's death until he comes. . . . Examine yourselves,
and only then eat of the bread and drink of the cup.*
(1 Corinthians 11:26, 28)

Anyone who wishes to receive the Holy Sacrament must offer to God Almighty an empty, single, and hungry soul. Therefore it is most fitting when the soul is least fit; that is, when the soul feels altogether wretched, poor, and devoid of grace, it is most receptive for God's grace and least fitted to receive it.

But then the soul must intend to come to the sacrament with perfect faith, or with all the faith possible, and most firmly believing that he will receive grace. For we receive as much as we believe we will receive. Therefore faith alone is the best and highest preparation.

Your hungry heart must build on these words and you must trust in the promise of the divine truth, and in this spirit go to the sacrament, imploring God and saying, "Lord, it is true that I am not worthy that you should come under my roof, yet I am needy and eager for your help and grace, that I too may be made godly. Thus I come with no plea but that I have heard sweet words, namely, that you invite me to your table. Dear Lord, your Word is true; I do not doubt it. In that faith I eat and I drink with you. May it be done to me according to your will and words. Amen."

That is how to come worthily to the sacrament.

Sermon on the Worthy Reception of the Sacrament. LW 42:174; WA 7:695f.

*Lord, I am not worthy, but only speak the word
and let your servant be healed. Amen. (See Luke 7:6-7.)*

The Thief on the Cross

Then he said, "Jesus, remember me when you come into your kingdom."
He replied, "Truly I tell you, today you will be with me in Paradise."
(Luke 23:42-43)

As comfort came in the garden from an angel (Luke 22:43), so here on the cross it came from a murderer who hung beside him. It is a wonderful God who allows his Son to be comforted by a murderer. The robber must have seen through the veil of Christ's body—through shame, disdain, and suffering. Otherwise he could not have believed and testified that Christ was Lord of a mighty kingdom. Thus, then, Christ had passed through hell, and comfort begins to reach him through the robber. God does not allow his church to perish. Therefore it is well said that the faith which had died in Peter rose again in the robber. For this word must stand: "Rule in the midst of your foes" (Psalm 110:2). Then Christ thinks, "After all, I have a gracious God who has prepared for me a kingdom, and he permits the sinner to enjoy the fruit of my sufferings." Therefore he says to him, "Today you will be with me in Paradise." The robber, perceiving his guilt and Christ's innocence, thinks, "Christ's innocence will help me." And he sees right into the heart of Christ, as though through a solid wall. The malefactor is one of us, and we are like him; therefore let us cry unto Christ, and he will say unto us, "Yes, truly!" as he did to the robber.

Comment on Luke 23:42-43.   WA 45:371

Lord, remember me when you come into your kingdom. Amen.

Christ Dies

When Jesus had received the wine, he said, "It is finished."
Then he bowed his head and gave up his spirit.
(John 19:30)

Here he reminds himself of the divine will that he had to suffer in this way. He can think of nothing else that remains to be done, for all that was written in Holy Scripture was finished. Therefore he gives himself up to God, saying, "Into your hand I commit my spirit" (Psalm 31:5). That is Christ's farewell, which he speaks for our sake, so that we may know the Father's heart. For what Christ suffered in the body we ought to have suffered in the soul before the eyes of God, and the severity that God here manifests in his Son, we deserved. If God were to act justly, he would do the same to us. Therefore we should repent; then forgiveness of sins follows, so that as God saved his Son, Christ, our model, from death and the devil, he will save us too. That is our comfort and our salvation. Because we perceive this in Christ, we should not turn away from God but should remember the words about Christ, "Rule in the midst of your foes" (Psalm 110:2), and no suffering will be too hard for us. If we are burdened with sins, let us carry them to Christ. He has nailed them to the cross and will forgive us and subdue death and the devil. Thus we are made partakers even of the death of Christ.

Comment on John 19:30.   WA 45:372

Dear God, at the moment of utter devastation,
I put my life in your hands. Amen.

He Descended into Hell

*He disarmed the rulers and authorities and made a public example
of them, triumphing over them in it.
(Colossians 2:15)*

There are two ways of speaking of our Lord's descent into hell. First,
simply, with childlike and simple words and pictures. This is the best
and the surest way. Or one may talk about it critically, how it could have
happened that Christ descended into hell and yet his body was lying
in the grave until the third day. But what is the good of long and keen
disputes about it? Our thinking will never fathom it. I must let it remain
in faith and in the Word, for my words and thoughts will never reach it.

Therefore my counsel is that you let it remain at those simple words
and childlike pictures and do not let yourself be troubled by those keen
and clever spirits who think about it without any picture, and seek to
fathom it with their clever reason.

When I say that Christ is Lord over the devil and hell, and that the
devil has no power and might over him and over those who belong to
him, that is spoken without the use of pictures and flowery speech. If I
can believe it and understand it in such a way of speaking, that is good.
If I portray it with flowers and images, so that those who cannot grasp it
otherwise may likewise understand, grasp, and believe, that too is good.
Thus, in whichever way we may comprehend it, both are right and good,
so long as this article remains firm and unshaken, which says that our
Lord Jesus Christ descended into hell, broke it into pieces, overcame the
devil, and redeemed those who were held prisoner by him.

Sermon on Easter Day, 1532.   WA 36:159

*Out of the depths I cry to you, O LORD. Lord, hear my voice!
Amen. (Psalm 130:1)*

His Rest Will Be Full of Glory

*Now there was a garden in the place where he was crucified,
and in the garden there was a new tomb in which no one
had ever been laid. And so, because it was the Jewish day
of Preparation, and the tomb was nearby, they laid Jesus there.
(John 19:41-42)*

It is a good ministry that they take care of the body of Jesus and do not fear Pilate's power. They go and close the tomb: Christ is at rest; God must work. Thus the burial takes place.

Our Lord God approves when we honor the dead and do not cast them out like dogs. For if a soul has passed away by the Word of God, the body must rise again; for we do not live by bread alone, but by every word of God. This is the ground of the resurrection.

Yet we must remember that all the women, and even the apostles, doubted the words of Christ, and no one believed that he would rise from the dead, as the two said when they were on the way to Emmaus. For if they had had any hope, they would not have embalmed him and laid him in a grave. And if it had been the doing of humans, God would not have been the doer of it, and this day would not have been called in the Scriptures the great day. This is a much greater article than the first, that God created heaven and earth, for no one can be saved unless he believes that God raised Christ from the dead. Such faith is no human work but is wrought by God, as St. Paul and the Scriptures say in many places.

Comment on John 19:38ff.   WA 45:375f.

*It was a strange and dreadful sight when life and death contended.
The victory remained with life, the reign of death was ended.
(Martin Luther, 1483–1546)*

Easter

Christ Is Risen

Matthew 28:1-10

"Death has been swallowed up in victory."
"Where, O death, is your victory?
Where, O death, is your sting?"
. . . But thanks be to God, who gives us the victory
through our Lord Jesus Christ.
(1 Corinthians 15:54-55, 57)

This is a strange message, such as reason cannot comprehend. It must be accepted in faith: Christ is alive and yet dead, and dead in such a way that in him death itself has had to die and lose all its power.

As the Lord Christ has conquered death, he has also conquered sin. For in his own person he is pure and just; but because he takes upon himself the sins of others, he becomes a sinner. That is why sin can assault him. And he, the Lord Christ, is very ready to be thus assaulted and nailed to the cross in order that he may die, as if he had himself sinned and brought his death upon himself. But there, hidden under the sin of others, his holiness is so great that death cannot overcome him. Thus sin, like death, attacked the wrong person and so grew weak and died in his body.

Likewise the devil wanted to prove his power over Christ and used all his might against him, trying to bring him down. But he met with a higher power that he could not overcome. All this has been done in order that our Lord Christ might be glorified, because by being cast down he was lifted up on high, and these three mighty foes, sin, the devil, and death, must lie low under his feet. This great victory we celebrate today. Now all power consists in this, that we take it well to heart and firmly believe in it.

Sermon for Easter Day, 1544.   WA 52:249f.

This is the day that the LORD has made; let us rejoice and be glad in it.
(Psalm 118:24)

He Is Not Here

But the angel said to the women,
"Do not be afraid; . . .he has been raised."
(Matthew 28:5-6)

The dear angels preach very well, and they have good reason to do so. The substance of their preaching is this: "You seek Jesus in the tomb. But he has become a different person. You believe that he was crucified, but we will tell you where he is now. He has been raised from the dead and is not here. You will not find him in this life. On earth, which is the realm of death, you must not seek Christ. Different eyes, fingers, or feet are needed to see Christ, to take hold of him or to walk toward him. We will show you the place where he lay, but he is no longer there." His name is now "He is not here," as St. Paul writes, "If you have been raised with Christ, seek the things that are above" (Colossians 3:1).

Christ is not here. Hence a Christian must not be here. No one can tie down Christ or a Christian with certain special rules. It says, "He is not here." He has left the husks down here, such as earthly justice, piety, wisdom, the law, and whatever else belongs to earth; of all those he has stripped himself entirely. Christ has in himself overcome all things and left them behind. And in that we believe this: we too are called "Not here," even as he is. As St. Paul says, "Set your minds on things that are above, not on things that are on earth" (Colossians 3:2). What a wonderful saying it is. Your life is hidden, not in a chest, for there it might be found, but in him who is nowhere. Our life shall be above all human wisdom, justice, and piety. As long as you abide in yourself, you are not devout, which means that our life is hidden high above our eyes and high above all that we can feel.

Sermons from the year 1530.   WA 32:49f.

So it is with the resurrection of the dead. . . . It is sown a physical body,
it is raised a spiritual body. (1 Corinthians 15:42, 44)

He Was Raised for Our Justification

[Christ] was handed over to death for our trespasses
and was raised for our justification.
(Romans 4:25)

When I look at my sins, they slay me. Therefore I must look upon Christ, who drew my sins upon himself and has become a blessing. Now they lie no longer on my conscience but on Christ, and they seek to slay him. Let us see, then, how they get on with him. They cast him down and kill him. O Lord God, where is now my Christ and my Redeemer? Then God comes and brings Christ forth and makes him alive, and not only alive but God sets him in heaven and lets him rule over all things. Now where is sin? It is on the cross. When I hold on to this and believe it, I have a joyful conscience, like Christ, for I am without sin. Now I dare death, the devil, sin, and hell to do me harm. Inasmuch as I am a descendant of Adam they can harm me; I must shortly die. But now that Christ has laid on himself my sin and has died for it and been slain for it, they can do me no harm, for Christ is too strong for them. They cannot hold him. He breaks forth and smites them to the ground, and ascends into heaven, binds and fetters sin and sorrow, and rules over them eternally. Therefore I have a good conscience; I am joyful and blessed, and fear those tyrants no longer, for Christ has taken my sin away from me and laid it on himself. But they cannot remain on him.

On the Power of the Resurrection of Christ.   WA 10/1(ii):221.

Easter morrow stills our sorrow, stills our sorrow forevermore. Light ever glowing, life overflowing, stream from that dawn on benighted shore.
(Nicolai F. S. Gruntvig, 1783–1872)

If Christ Is Not Raised, We Are Yet in Our Sins

*If Christ has not been raised, your faith
is futile and you are still in your sins.
(1 Corinthians 15:17)*

Firmly believe that Christ has taken upon himself your sin and death. For that is how the virtue of the resurrection is given to me and to you and to all humankind who believe in Christ. For if I do not make use of it in this way, I do my Lord Christ great injustice, for I let his triumph and victory remain barren. It should not remain barren, for he wills that it shall bear great fruit, namely, that in all affliction, sin, and fear, I should see nothing but Christ triumphant rising from the dead.

All who can picture this victory in their hearts are already saved. But those who have no Good Friday and no Easter Day have no good day in the year. That is, those who do not believe that Jesus suffered and rose for them are without hope. For we are called Christians because we can look to Christ and say, "Dear Lord, you have taken upon yourself my sin and have become Martin, Peter, and Paul, and have trodden my sin underfoot and consumed it! There I look for my sin as you have directed me. On Good Friday I still see my sin before my eyes, but on Easter Day a new person has been born. My hand has been made new and sin is seen no more. All this you have given to me freely, and have said that you have overcome my devil, my sin, and my death."

Sermons from the year 1530.   WA 32:44

*O sing to the LORD a new song, for he has done marvelous things. His
right hand and his holy arm have gotten him victory. (Psalm 98:1)*

The Risen Christ Is Our Brother

Jesus said to her, "Do not hold on to me, because I have not yet ascended to the Father. But go to my brothers and say to them, 'I am ascending to my Father and your Father, to my God and your God.'"
(John 20:17)

If Christ is our brother, what could we lack? For as with brothers in the flesh, so it applies here. Brothers in the flesh possess common goods. They have *one* father, *one* inheritance, which does not decrease by sharing, as other inheritances do. Rather it grows more and more because it is a spiritual inheritance.

And what is Christ's inheritance? His is life and death, sin and grace, and all things that are in heaven and on earth—eternal truth, might, wisdom, and justice. He rules over all things, over hunger and thirst, over joy and sorrow, over all things that can be conceived, whether in heaven or on earth, and not only spiritual things but material things as well. In a word, he holds everything in his hand, whether it be temporal or eternal. When I believe in him, I, along with him, have a share in them all, and not in one thing or merely a part of the whole. Like him, I rule as lord over all things, such as eternal righteousness, eternal wisdom, and eternal power.

On the Power of the Resurrection of Christ.   WA 10/1(ii):214f.

We are children of God, and if children, then heirs, heirs of God and joint heirs with Christ. (Romans 8:16-17)

The Risen Christ Is Our Comfort

When it was evening on that day, the first day of the week, and the doors of the house where the disciples had met were locked for fear of the Jews, Jesus came and stood among them and said, "Peace be with you."
(John 20:19)

What did the disciples fear? They feared death. Yes, they were in the midst of death. But why did they fear death? Because of sin, for if they had not sinned, they would not have been afraid. Death could not have harmed them, for the sting of death, by which it kills, is sin. Yet they lacked—as we all lack—the right knowledge of God. For if they had known God to be God, they would have been confident and without fear. But anyone who does not believe in God must be afraid of death. Such a one can never have a glad and sure conscience.

Whenever in such fear we cry to God, God cannot refrain from helping us. Just as Christ did not stay long outside, away from his frightened disciples, but soon was there comforting them and saying, "Peace be with you, I have come, be of good cheer and do not be afraid," so it is still. When we are afraid, God lifts us up and causes the gospel to be preached to us and thus restores to us a glad and sure conscience.

Where Christ is, yes, most certainly, the Father and the Holy Spirit surely come. Then there is pure grace and no law, pure mercy and no sin, pure life and no death, pure heaven and no hell, and there I take comfort in the works of Christ as if I had done them myself.

Sermon for the First Sunday after Easter, 1526.   WA 10/1(ii):234ff.

O give thanks to the LORD, for he is good;
his steadfast love endures forever! (Psalm 118:1)

Christ's Resurrection Is Our Own Resurrection

*For since we believe that Jesus died and rose again, even so,
through Jesus, God will bring with him those who have died.
(1 Thessalonians 4:14)*

As in his resurrection he has taken all things with him, so that both heaven and earth, sun and moon, and all creatures must rise with him and be made new, even so will he bring us with him. The same God who raised Christ from the dead will give life again to our mortal bodies, and with us all creatures, which are now subject to futility, and which with earnest expectation await our glorification and desire to be set free from this transient existence and to be made glorious. For us more than half of our resurrection is already accomplished, because our heart and head are already above, and only the smallest part remains to be done, namely, that the body be buried in order that it too may be made new.

No one will deny that the corpse of a dead man is a wretched thing. But I possess an understanding higher than the eyes can see, or the senses perceive, which faith teaches me. For there stands the text saying, "He has been raised." He is no longer in the grave and buried under the earth but has been raised from the dead, and this not for his own sake but for our sake, that his resurrection be made ours so that we too may rise in him and not remain in the grave and in death, but that our bodies may celebrate with him an everlasting Easter Day.

Sermons from the year 1532.   WA 36:161f.

*Death has been swallowed up in victory. Where, O death, is your victory?
Where, O death, is your sting? (1 Corinthians 15:54-55)*

Reborn

1 John 5:15

Blessed be the God and Father of our Lord Jesus Christ!
By his great mercy he has given us a new birth into a lively hope
through the resurrection of Jesus Christ from the dead.
(1 Peter 1:3)

How, or by what means, has such rebirth come to pass? St. Peter says, "through the resurrection of Jesus Christ from the dead." It is as if he would say, "God the Father has begotten us again, not of corruptible seed but of incorruptible seed, that is, of the word of truth, which is a power of God that re-creates and enlivens and saves all who believe in it." What sort of word is that? It is the Word of Jesus Christ that is preached to us, namely, that he died for your sin and for the sin of the whole world, and rose again on the third day, that through his resurrection he might win for us justification, life, and blessedness. Whoever believes in this message, namely, that Christ died and is risen for us, with that person the resurrection has proved its power. Such a one is reborn through it, which means that he or she is created anew after the image of God. That person receives the Holy Spirit and knows the gracious will of God, and has such a heart, mind, courage, will, and thoughts as no hypocrite ever had or anyone who believes in salvation through works. For we know that no works of the law and no righteousness of our own, but Christ alone in his suffering and resurrection can make us righteous and blessed.

This is rightly called apostolic preaching.

Sermon on 1 Peter.   EA 52:11

My hope is built on nothing less than Jesus' blood and righteousness.
All other ground is sinking sand. (Edward Mote, 1836)

Reborn of Water and the Spirit

Jesus answered, "Very truly I tell you, no one can enter the kingdom of God without being born of water and of the Spirit."
(John 3:5)

Do not think that you will enter the kingdom of God unless you are first born anew of water and the Spirit. That we must be born anew is a strong and hard saying. It means that we must come out of the birth of sin to the birth of justification or else we shall never enter the kingdom of heaven. Upon this birth or justification, good works must follow.

Of these things the Lord Christ speaks much with Nicodemus, but Nicodemus cannot understand, nor can these words be understood unless we experience them and have been born of the Spirit.

Sermon on John 3.   WA 47:10

Lord God, you have given me new life in baptism. You have enlivened me with your grace. Now keep me faithful in good works on behalf of those around me. Amen.

Reborn through the Word of Truth

In fulfillment of his own purpose he gave us birth by the word of truth,
so that we would become a kind of first fruits of his creatures.
(James 1:18)

The first thing and greatest thing he has done for us from above is that he has given us birth and made us his children and heirs so that we have become and are called "children born of God." How, or by what means, did that happen? Through the word of truth.

Thus have we become firstborn of his creation, which is a newly begun creature and work of God. Thus he separates his new creation from the world and human creatures.

God has made for himself a new creature, made without any human help and skill. In virtue of this a Christian is called a new creature of God, which God himself alone makes, above and besides all other creatures and works, yet in such a way that in this temporal life there is made but a beginning, and he works daily at it until it is perfected, when it will be a godly creature, pure and bright like the sun, without any sin and frailty, and all on fire with godly love.

Sermons from the year 1536. WA 41:585ff.

How firm a foundation, you saints of the Lord, is laid for your faith
in his excellent Word! What more can he say than to you he has said,
to you who for refuge to Jesus have fled? (J. Rippon, 1787)

Reborn to an Everlasting Life

Whoever believes in the Son has eternal life.
(John 3:36)

We should preach on these words for a hundred thousand years and proclaim them again and again. In fact, we can never preach enough about them, for Christ promises eternal life immediately to the one who believes. He does not say, "Whoever believes will receive eternal life," but "Immediately, when you believe in me, you already *have* eternal life." He does not speak of some future gift but of a present grace, namely, "If you can believe in me, you are already saved and you have already received the gift of eternal life."

Eternal life is already mine. Unless I receive it here on earth, I shall not win it thereafter. Here in this mortal body I must obtain it and attain to it. How then is it attained? God makes the beginning and becomes your Master, preaching to you. God works the beginning of eternal life in that he preaches to you the oral and outward word. He then gives the heart that receives the Word and believes it. Such is the beginning. And those same words that you hear and believe lead you to Jesus Christ alone; you cannot go further. If you can believe in him and cling to him, you are redeemed from physical and spiritual death, and you already have eternal life.

Sermons on John 6–8.   LW 23:105; WA 33:160f.

Lord God, I look for freshness and newness each day of my life.
Restore to me the joy of your salvation. Amen.

There Must Be a New Birth

*Now that you have purified your souls by your obedience to the truth . . .
you have been born anew, not of perishable but of imperishable seed,
through the living and enduring word of God.*
(1 Peter 1:22-23)

You are not what you were before. You are new persons. That has not
come about through works but through a new birth. For you cannot
create the new self; it must grow or be born, as a joiner cannot make a
tree but it must itself grow out of the earth.

The apostle here wants to say that since you are now new creatures,
should you not now bear yourselves differently and lead a new life? As
you used to live in hate you must now walk in love, doing the opposite in
all things.

How then does that happen? In this way: God lets the Word, the
gospel, go forth and lets the seed fall into the hearts of men and women.
Wherever that takes root in the heart, the Holy Spirit is at work making
a new self, who really does become another person, with other thoughts
and words and works. Thus you are wholly transformed. All things from
which you previously have fled you now seek, and what you previously
sought you now flee. For in this way you begin to be all on fire with
godly love, and you become a different person, completely reborn, and
everything that is you is changed. Now you are as eager to be chaste as
you were before to be unchaste, and the same applies to all your desires
and inclinations.

Sermons from the year 1522.   WA 10/3:88

*Almighty God, your Word is cast like seed into the ground; now let the
dew of heaven descend and righteous fruit abound. Amen.*
(John Cawood, 1775–1852)

The Water of Rebirth

*He saved us . . . according to his mercy through the water
of rebirth and renewal by the Holy Spirit.
(Titus 3:5)*

He calls the washing a rebirth, a renewing in the Holy Spirit, in order
that the greatness and the might of grace may be perfectly expressed. So
great is this thing that no creature can do it, but the Holy Spirit alone.
Indeed, how you, St. Paul, do spurn the free will, the good works and the
great merits of the proud saints! How high you place our blessedness, and
yet you bring it so near to us, even within us! How purely and clearly you
preach grace! Therefore, however you may work to renew us and change
us, it is only possible through the water of rebirth through the Holy
Spirit.

This is truly preaching freely and fully of the grace of God. No
patching with works avails, only the complete changing of the nature.
Those who truly believe must endure much affliction and must die in
order that grace may demonstrate its nature and its presence.

God's grace is a great, strong, mighty, and active thing. It upholds,
leads, drives, draws, changes, and works all things in a person and is
really felt and experienced. It remains hidden, but its works are manifest.
Works and words point to where it is, just as the fruit and the leaves show
the kind and nature of the tree.

Sermons from the year 1522.   WA 10/1(i):116ff.

*Through many dangers, toils, and snares, I have already come;
'tis grace has brought me safe thus far, and grace will lead me home.
(John Newton, 1725–1807)*

On Victorious Living

Whatever is born of God conquers the world.
(1 John 5:4)

With these words St. John admonishes Christians that those who believe should remember that they should give proof of the power and practice of their faith in life and deed. For he wrote this epistle mainly in order to punish the false Christians, who like to listen when we teach that we are saved through Christ alone, and that our works and deeds merit no salvation, and then think when they have heard it that they too are now Christians and that they need not work or join in the fight. They do not perceive that through and out of such faith new persons should be born, persons who overcome the world and the devil.

The words here spoken do not mean that you are born of God and yet remain in the old, dead, worldly nature, and live on in sins, to the delight of the devil just as you were before, but that you resist the devil and all his works. Thus, if you do not overcome the world but are overcome by it, you may well glory in your faith and in Christ, but your own deeds witness against you that you are not a child of God.

Sermon on 1 John 5:4-12.   WA 21:280

The earth and all that is in it are yours, almighty God.
Help me to appreciate the beauty of nature and to work
to protect it for those who come after me. Amen.

The Good Shepherd

John 10

I am the good shepherd.
(John 10:14)

These are comforting words. They set before our eyes a gracious picture of our Lord Jesus Christ, and teach us what sort of a person he is, what sort of work he does, and how he is disposed toward us.

If you ask me whether Christ is saintly, I answer without hesitation, "Yes," and I place him like a shield before my own saintliness, and I trust in him with my whole heart. For I was baptized in him and have received in the gospel a letter and seal, that I am his dear lamb, and that he is my good shepherd, who seeks his lost lamb and deals with me in no legalistic way. He demands nothing of me, nor does he drive me on. He does not threaten, nor does he frighten me, but he shows me his sweet grace, and lowers himself to me, even beneath me, and takes me upon himself, so that I now lie on his back and am carried by him. Why then should I be afraid at the quaking and thundering of Moses or even of the devil? I am under the protection of the man who has given me his saintliness and all that he has, who supports me and upholds me that I cannot be lost so long as I remain his lamb and do not doubt him or willfully fall away from him.

Sermons from the year 1532.   WA 36:296

The Lord's my shepherd; I'll not want. He makes me down to lie.
In pastures green he leadeth me, the quiet waters by.
(Edinburgh Psalter, 1650)

Christk Ever Upholds Us

When he has found [the lost sheep],
he lays it on his shoulders and rejoices.
(Luke 15:5)

There is scarcely any more precious illustration in the whole Gospel than when the Lord Christ compares himself to a shepherd carrying back to the flock, on his shoulders, the sheep that was lost. He is still carrying to this day.

Therefore the sum of the gospel is this: The kingdom of Christ is a kingdom of grace and mercy, in which there is never anything but carrying. Christ bears our griefs and infirmities. He takes our sins upon himself and is patient when we fall. We always rest on his shoulders, and he never tires of carrying us, which should be the greatest comfort to us when we are tempted to sin. Preachers in this kingdom should comfort the consciences, and deal kindly with them, and feed them with the gospel. They should carry the weak, heal the sick, and know just how to minister the Word to each person according to their need.

Sermon on Luke 10:23-27.   WA 10/1(ii):366.

Today, O Lord God, I pray for the lost souls in our materialistic culture.
Let your Word prevail to bring hope and direction. Amen.

To Seek and to Save What Is Lost

All we like sheep have gone astray;
we have all turned to our own way,
and the LORD has laid on him
the iniquity of us all.
(Isaiah 53:6)

Dear friend, if we can feed and rule ourselves, protect ourselves against error, gain grace and forgiveness of sins through our own merit, resist the devil and all misfortune, conquer sin and death—then we do not need a Christ either as a shepherd who would seek, gather, and direct us, bind up our wounds, watch over us, and strengthen us against the devil. Then he has also given his life for us in vain. For as long as we can do and gain all these things through our own powers and piety, we do not need the help of Christ at all.

But here you hear the opposite, namely, that you lost sheep cannot find your way to the shepherd yourself but can only roam around in the wilderness. If Christ, your shepherd, did not seek you and bring you back, you would simply have to fall prey to the wolf. But now he comes, seeks you, and finds you. He takes you into his flock, that is, into the Christian church, through the Word and the sacrament. He gives his life for you, keeps you always on the right path, so that you may not fall into error. You hear nothing at all about your powers, good works, and merits. No, Christ alone is active here and manifests his power. He seeks, carries, and directs you. He earns life for you through his death. He alone is strong and keeps you from perishing, from being snatched out of his hand (John 10:28). For all of this you can do nothing at all but only lend your ears, hear, and with thanksgiving receive the inexpressible treasure, and learn to know well the voice of your shepherd, follow him, and avoid the voice of the stranger.

Exposition of Psalm 23.   LW 12:156; WA 51:275f.

I have heard your voice, Lord Jesus, saying in your grace divine:
"Have no fear, I have redeemed you; I have called you, you are mine."
(Edith G. Cherry, alt.)

He Alone Is the Good Shepherd

*The hired hand, who is not the shepherd and does not own the sheep,
sees the wolf coming and leaves the sheep and runs away—
and the wolf snatches them and scatters them.
(John 10:12)*

There are many—alas, all too many—who are called shepherds and who
dare to take it upon themselves to govern souls, to feed them, and to
direct them. But I am the only one who is called the Good Shepherd.
Apart from me the shepherds are not good. All the others are merciless
and cruel, because they leave the poor sheep to the jaws of the wolf.
But you should learn to know me as your dear, faithful, saintly, kind,
gracious, and comforting shepherd, toward whom your hearts should be
joyful and full of trust because through me you are redeemed from all
your burdens, fears, sorrows, and dangers. He will not and cannot suffer
you to be lost. This I prove (he says) in that I lay down my life for the
sheep.

Therefore hold on to me with a cheerful heart, and let no other rule
over your conscience, but listen to me when I speak such comforting
words to you and show you in very deed that it is not my will to force
you forward, to plague and burden you, like Moses and others, but with
loving kindness to lead you and direct you, protect you and help you.

Exposition of John 10:12-16.   WA 21:331

*Be to me, O Lord, a sure guide through times of trouble
and let me trust in your steadfast love. Amen.*

The Shepherd Fears for Our Sake

*You were going astray like sheep, but now you have returned
to the shepherd and guardian of your souls.*
(1 Peter 2:25)

If we want to grow in confidence and to be strengthened and comforted, we must learn to recognize the voice of our shepherd and to ignore all other voices that lead us into error, chasing us and driving us here and there. And we must listen to and comprehend this article alone that sets Christ before us more kindly and helpfully than anyone could paint him. Hence we can say with full confidence, "My Lord Jesus Christ is the one and only shepherd, and I am, alas, the lost sheep that has gone astray." I languish in fear and fright, and would so like to be saintly, and to have a gracious God, and peace in my conscience. Then I hear that he longs as sorrowfully for me as I for him. My soul is anxious and troubled about how I can come to him for help. And he is anxious and troubled and only wants to bring me back to himself.

If we could so portray our Lord and imprint his heart on our heart, with his overflowing longing, concern, and desire for us, it would be impossible for us to be afraid of him. Rather we should joyfully run toward him and stay with him and listen to no other word nor master.

Sermons from the year 1532.   WA 36:292

*Imprint your image, O Lord, on my heart, and let it be
with me all the days of my life. Amen.*

I Know My Sheep

I am the good shepherd. I know my own, and my own know me,
just as the Father knows me and I know the Father.
And I lay down my life for the sheep.
(John 10:14-15)

Who is it who knows and recognizes the sheep while they are so deeply covered with shame, suffering, death, disgrace, and scandal that they do not even know themselves? Certainly, none but Christ. And he speaks to them these comforting words, that in spite of all the things that lead the world and our own flesh and blood astray, he will know his lambs and will not forget them or desert them.

To implant this knowledge more firmly in our hearts, he uses an analogy, "just as the Father knows me." That is indeed penetrating knowledge, that God the Father knows his beloved only Son while he lies in a manger, unknown and even disdained and cast out by his own people. And while he hung most shamefully and ignominiously in the air, naked, between two murderers, as the most wicked blasphemer and agitator of the people, accursed of God and all the world, he was moved to cry in great distress, "My God, my God, why have you forsaken me?"

Yet he says here, "My Father knows me" (even in such shame, suffering, and disgrace) "as his beloved Son, sent forth by God to be made the sacrifice and to surrender my soul to save and to redeem my sheep. In the same way, I know the Father and know that he will not forget me or forsake me, but that through shame and cross and death, he will lead me to life and to eternal glory.

"Likewise, my lambs, when they are in sorrow, shame, distress, and death, will learn to know me as their faithful Savior, who has suffered like themselves, and has even sacrificed my life for them. They will trust in me and look to me for help."

Sermon on John 10:12-16. WA 21:335f.

Your life was given for me. What, O Lord, have I given for you? Amen.

Feed My Sheep

A second time he said to him, "Simon, son of John, do you love me?"
He said to him, "Yes, Lord, you know that I love you."
Jesus said to him, "Tend my sheep."
(John 21:16)

Lord God, are we so blind that we do not take such great love to heart?
Who could have discovered that God lowers himself to such a depth that
he looks on all the deeds we do to the poor as if they had been done to
him? Thus the world is full of God. In every lane you meet Christ. You
find him at your door. Do not stand gaping into heaven, saying, "If only I
could see our Lord God, how eager I should be to render him every service
possible." You are a liar, says St. John, if you say you love God, and hate
your neighbor whom you see suffering before your eyes (1 John 4:20).
Listen, wretched one, do you wish to serve God? You have him in your
house, in the persons of your servants and your children. Teach them to
fear God, to love him, and to trust in him alone. Go and comfort your
sad, sick neighbors; help them with your possessions, wisdom, and skill.
Behold, I will be very close to you in every poor brother who needs your
help and teaching. There am I, right in the midst. Whether you help little
or much, you do it to me. A cup of cold water will not be given in vain;
you will receive back a thousandfold, not because of the work you have
done, but because of the promise that I have given.

Sermons from the year 1526.   WA 20:514f.

Open my eyes, Lord God, to the neighbor in need. Open my heart
to speak a word of comfort. Amen.

SUNDAY/FOURTH WEEK OF EASTER

The Heart Shall Rejoice in the Holy Spirit
John 16:16-23

So you have pain now; but I will see you again, and your hearts
will rejoice, and no one will take your joy from you.
(John 16:22)

The one thing needful is that we trust in our Lord Jesus Christ and
believe in his Word, which means that when we are cast down under
sorrow and temptation, it is but for a little while, so that we may find
comfort in our suffering. For it is impossible for us to attain to happiness
unless we have previously suffered pain and sorrow.

But what comfort! The Lord informs his disciples what joy awaits
them. He says, "I will see you again." This happened on holy Easter
Day when they saw him again in a new and everlasting life. Similarly
Christ also sees us, and our hearts see that for our sake he has overcome
sin, death, and the devil, that we too through him should live eternally.
That is everlasting and eternal joy, which overcomes all sorrow and
shall never be taken from us. Therefore we must not lose patience nor
be fainthearted under the cross. For Christ is risen and is seated at the
right hand of the Father, that he may shield us from the devil and from
all misery, and make us blessed forevermore. May our faithful God and
Father grant us this through his Son, our Redeemer, Jesus Christ. Amen.

Sermon on John 16:16-23.   WA 52:288f.

O Lord, not only in good times but even through days of sorrow
let me rely on your steadfast love. Amen.

The Secret of Joy

*Very truly, I tell you, you will weep and mourn, but the world will
rejoice; you will have pain, but your pain will turn into joy.*
(John 16:20)

There are many kinds of sorrow on earth, but the deepest of all sorrows
is when the heart loses Christ, and he is no longer seen, and there is no
hope of comfort from him. Only a few are so sorely tempted. All comfort
has gone, all joy is ended, there is no help from heaven or sun or moon,
from angel or any creature. There is even no help from God. But the
world rejoices.

Such joy Christ here gives to the world and, on the other hand, deep
sorrow to his Christians. And yet at the same time, he paints the world as
a place of horror and a child of the devil, for it has no greater joy than to
see Christ perish and his Christians shamefully condemned and lost.

That is why Christ tells us here, "You have heard both how the
world will rejoice and how you will be sorrowful. Therefore hear it and
remember it so that when sorrows abound you may have patience and
receive true comfort from such sufferings. I must tempt you thus and
let you taste what it means to have lost your Savior and to have died in
your hearts, so that you may be given a little knowledge of this mystery.
Otherwise you cannot be given knowledge of my nature. It is too high
for you to understand aright, this lofty work, that the Son of God returns
to his Father, that is, he dies for you and rises again, that he may bring
you likewise into heaven."

Sermon on John 16:16ff.   WA 49:258ff.

*Lord, save me from despair; lift me up and let me stand
by faith on heaven's tableland. Amen.*

TUESDAY

A Parable of Joy

When a woman is in labor, she has pain, because her hour has come.
But when her child is born, she no longer remembers the anguish because
of the joy of having brought a human being into the world.
(John 16:21)

We must look carefully at this image. For it is the same in all temptations as it is here, and most of all in the anguish of death. See how God deals with a woman when she is in travail. She is left by all lying helpless in her pain. No one can help her. The whole creation cannot save her from this hour. It stands alone in the power of God. The midwife and others who are with her can give her some comfort, but they cannot save her life in it. She may die, or she may recover, with the child. She is right in the travail of death, completely surrounded by death.

It is the same with us when our conscience is alarmed or when we are in anguish of death. There is no comfort. Reason cannot help, or any creature, or anything we have done. You think that God and all creatures have abandoned you, and even that God and all creatures have turned against you. Then you must be still and cling to God alone. He must deliver you; nothing else can, whether in heaven or on earth. He will help you when he thinks it right and good, as he helps the woman, giving her something that makes her so happy that she forgets her pains. As earlier she was filled with death and anguish, she is now full of joy and life. So it is with us. When we are beset with temptation or when we are struggling with death, God alone can gladden our hearts and give us peace and joy where there was nothing but fear and sorrow.

Sermon on the Third Sunday after Easter.   WA 22:429

When I am nearly overcome by sorrow, O God, gladden my heart
and give me peace and joy. Amen.

Perfect Joy

I have said these things to you so that my joy may be in you,
and that your joy may be complete.
(John 15:11)

We must cling to the Word with our whole hearts and find strength in his precious promise that he will be with us in union with the Father, shielding us so that no calamity shall harm us and no power of the world or the devil shall oppress us or snatch us from his hands. Thus we always find joy and comfort, growing happier and happier, letting no suffering or opposition dismay us or make us despair. It is a lovely thing to bear all suffering for the love of Jesus. There is no other joy for a Christian on earth, which is perfect. For if you had all the world's happiness gathered up in one heap, it would not help you at all against sorrow and calamity, for the world's joy is based only on uncertain temporal goods—honor, lust, and so forth—and it cannot last longer than they do, but it withers and perishes when a slight chill wind blows on it and it suffers a small discomfort. But this is a joy without end (as it is grounded in the eternal), and in the midst of outward calamity it stands and grows, so that with a joyful heart we can despise the world's happiness and lightly give it up.

Sermons on John 16–20. WA 28:156f.

Lord God, your Word is a lamp to my feet and a light to my path.
Let me follow that light all the days of my life. Amen.

The Fruit of the Spirit Is Joy

The fruit of the Spirit is . . . joy.
(Galatians 5:22)

By this we should learn that God does not want people to be sad and that he hates sad thoughts and sayings and doctrines that oppress us. God makes our hearts joyful. For he did not send his Son to make us sad but to make us glad. That is why the prophets and apostles and the Lord Christ himself admonish us and even command us at all times to be joyful and of good cheer:

"Rejoice greatly, O daughter Zion! Shout aloud, O daughter Jerusalem!" (Zechariah 9:9).

Many times in the Psalms: "Let us rejoice in the Lord."

"Rejoice in the Lord always" (Philippians 4:4).

And Christ says, "Rejoice that your names are written in heaven" (Luke 10:20).

Where there is this joy of the Spirit, there is a dear joy in the heart through faith in Christ, and we know of a certainty that he is our Savior and high priest, and this joy is seen in the things we say and do.

Commentary on the prophet Jonah.   EA (Latin) 26:50

Each day, I pray, restore to me the unmatched joy
of your salvation. Amen.

Joy under the Cross

I myself will show him how much he must suffer for the sake of my name.
(Acts 9:16)

If you would be a joint heir with your Lord Jesus Christ, but will
not suffer with him and be his brother and be made like him, he will
certainly not accept you as his brother and joint heir at the last day. But
he will ask you where your crown of thorns, your cross, your nails and
scourging are, and whether you too have been an abomination to the
world, as he and all his members have been from the beginning of the
world. If you cannot give proof of this, he will not be able to accept you
as his brother. In a word, we must suffer with him, and must all be made
like the Son of God, or else we cannot be exalted to his glory.

The marks, nails, crown of thorns, and scourgings I must bear, and
so must all Christians, and not just painted on the wall, but stamped in
our flesh and blood.

Here St. Paul admonishes every Christian to bear the marks of
Christ our Lord. And he comforts them that they should not be afraid
even if all human suffering should be laid on them, as now for some years
has been the lot of our brothers and sisters. But it will become even worse
when the hour of our foe and the might of the darkness comes. But let it
be. We must suffer or we shall not come to glory.

Sermons from the year 1535.   WA 41:304f.

Let your will be done in my life, O Lord.
Give me strength to face the morrow. Amen.

That Our Joy May Be Full

Ask and you will receive, so that your joy may be complete.
(John 16:13)

Joy cannot be perfect until we see the name of God perfectly hallowed. That will not be done in this life but in the life to come, where there will be perfect joy and no sorrow at all. In this life we can have it only in part, a little drop, in faith, which is the beginning or foretaste of it, laying hold on the consolation that Christ has redeemed us and that we, through him, have entered the kingdom of God. But we are weak and slow to follow him and claim his power. We will not follow and cannot remain pure in faith and life, for we fall again and again and are weighed down by sadness and a heavy conscience, so that our joy cannot be pure, or there is so little joy that we can scarcely feel it.

Therefore this word must be added, which calls for prayer for help and strength that we may at last be given a pure, whole, and perfect joy. You must not seek it in yourself or within this world, for its joy is impure and in the end death takes it all away. But seek it in prayer, says Christ, asking in my name that that for which I came into the world and called you and ordained you may come to pass, namely, that God's name and kingdom and will may be glorified in all the world, and that the opposition that the world, the flesh, and the devil wage without ceasing may be hindered and brought to an end.

Exposition of John 16.   *WA 46:91f.*

Eternal God, I look for the day when suffering and sorrow shall have passed away and true joy fills all creation. Amen.

The Church's Song of Praise

John 16:5-15

And when he comes, he will prove the world wrong about sin and righteousness and judgment; about sin, because they do not believe in me. (John 16:8-9)

Everyone is in danger because of their own deeds, and if someone is lost, it is because of their own guilt. They deserve condemnation not because they are descendants of Adam or because of their former unbelief but because they refuse to accept this Savior, Christ, who abolishes our sin and condemnation. If I do not believe, sin and condemnation must remain upon me, because I do not lay hold of him who alone can save me from them. Indeed, the sin and condemnation become twice as great and heavy because I will not accept the redemption accomplished through this precious Savior, nor believe in him who seeks to help me.

Thus our salvation or our condemnation depends on whether we will or will not believe in Christ. Unbelief retains all sin, so that it cannot find forgiveness, while faith destroys all sin. Therefore, apart from such faith, all things are sinful and remain sinful, even the noblest living and the best works we can do, for though they are in themselves praiseworthy and even commanded by God, they are corrupted by unbelief and therefore cannot please, while all the works and ways of a Christian please him because they are done in faith. To sum up, apart from Christ all is lost and condemned; with Christ all is good and blessed, so that even sin (which remains still in flesh and blood born of Adam) cannot bring us to harm and condemnation.

Sermon on John 16.   LW 24:344; WA 46:41f.

Lord God, give me faith to cling to your promises. Amen.

He Will Prove the World Wrong about Righteousness

*And when he comes, he will prove the world wrong about sin
and righteousness and judgment; . . . about righteousness,
because I am going to the Father and you will see me no more.
(John 16:8, 10)*

Christians should know of no other righteousness with which to stand
before God and be justified and to receive the forgiveness of sins and
eternal life, than this going of Christ to his Father, which means that he
took upon himself our sin and for our sakes suffered death upon the cross
and was buried and descended into hell. But he did not remain under sin
and death and in hell, but passed through them in his resurrection and
ascension, and now he is seated at the right hand of the Father, a mighty
Lord over all creatures.

This righteousness is hidden not only from the world and reason
but also from the saints. For it is not a thought, word, or deed within
ourselves, but it is right outside us and above us. It is this going of Christ
to his Father, and this is not within the range of our eyes or senses, so that
we can neither see it nor feel it. It can be perceived only through faith in
the Word that is preached about it, that he himself is our righteousness,
so that we do not glory in ourselves but in Christ the Lord alone.

Sermon on John 16.   LW 24:346; WA 46:43f.

*My hope is built on nothing less
    than Jesus' blood and righteousness.
No merit of my own I claim,
    but wholly lean on Jesus' name. Amen.
(Edward Mote, 1797–1874)*

He Will Prove the World Wrong about Judgment

*And when he comes, he will prove the world wrong about sin
and righteousness and judgment; . . . of judgment,
because the ruler of this world is condemned.*
(John 16:8, 11)

Thus this judgment proceeds from the authority and power of our Lord Jesus Christ sitting at the right hand of the Father, and the judgment is publicly preached, that the ruler of this world and all that belongs to him are already condemned and have no power against Christ. The devil must let him be Lord and must lie forever under his feet and suffer the bruising of his head.

Although the world goes on in its usual way, despising the judgment already passed on the devil and all his members, scoffing at it because they cannot see it before their eyes, Christ goes on, meekly suffering to be disdained yet manifesting to the devil and the world that he is the Lord who can break the devil's wrath and raging, cast down his enemies, and make them all into a footstool for his feet. But this no one but the Christians believe, and they hold that the Word of their Lord is true. They know his power and his kingdom and are comforted by their Lord and King. The children of the world will have no other reward than what they seek with their lord, the devil.

Sermon on John 16:5-15.   WA 21:371f.

*O Lord, help me to see myself as others see me,
and let me follow the path of Jesus. Amen.*

The New Song

O sing to the LORD a new song,
for he has done marvelous things.
His right hand and his holy arm
have gotten him victory.
(Psalm 98:1)

This is the new song about the new kingdom, new creatures, new men, born not of the law or of works but of God and the Spirit, who themselves are miracles and who work miracles in Jesus Christ our Lord.

And because the Holy Spirit commands us all to sing, it is certain that he also commands us to believe in the miracles that have been done and proclaimed for our sake. Therefore doubt and unbelief are here condemned, when they say, "How can I be sure that God, by his authority or his arm (that is, through his Son), has done such victories and miracles for my sake?" "Listen," says the Spirit, "for you, for you, for you it was done. You, you, you should sing and give thanks and be happy. That is my wish and will."

Sayings from the Old Testament.   WA 48:56

My life flows on in endless song
above earth's lamentation.
I hear the real though far-off hymn
that hails a new creation.
(Robert Lowry, 1826–1899)

The Song of the Multitude

The oracle of David, son of Jesse . . . the anointed of the God of Jacob. . . .
The spirit of the LORD speaks through me, his word is upon my tongue.
(2 Samuel 23:1-2)

Faith knows no rest or ease. It goes out, speaks and preaches, and for very joy it begins to compose sweet and lovely psalms. But it not only thinks of the sweetness and loveliness of the psalms as grammar and music, how neatly and skillfully the words are arranged, and how sweet and lovely the chanting and the music sound, but also thinks of the lovely spiritual meaning of the psalms. Yet the music helps as a wonderful creation and gift of God, especially where the congregation joins in the singing and their minds and hearts are in earnest.

David calls his psalms Israel's psalms. He does not want to ascribe them to himself alone and claim the sole glory for them. For a word or psalm needs to be accepted or rejected by the congregation or the people of God. Thus we Christians talk about *our* psalmists.

St. Ambrose wrote many lovely hymns, and they are called church hymns because the church accepted them and uses them as if the members had written them themselves and they were their hymns. That is why we do not say, "Thus St. Ambrose, Gregory, Prudentius, or Sedulius sings," but we say, "So sings the Christian church." For these are now the songs of the church, which Ambrose, Sedulius, and so forth sing with the church and the church with them. And when they die, the church remains, singing their hymns forever.

On the Last Words of David.   LW 15:274; WA 54:33f.

To you our morning song of praise, to you our evening prayer we raise;
we praise your light in ev'ry age, the glory of our pilgrimage.
(St. Ambrose, 340–397)

FRIDAY

The Psalter

Let the word of Christ dwell in you richly; teach and
admonish one another in all wisdom; and with gratitude
in your hearts sing psalms, hymns, and spiritual songs to God.
(Colossians 3:16)

In common and simple speech the psalms present to us the loftiest
thoughts of the saints in which they talk earnestly about the highest
things with God himself. This great gift their hymns pass on to us, so
that we know how their hearts felt and their mouths spoke to God and to
others.

A human heart is like a ship on a wild sea, tossed about by all
the four winds of the world. Such storms teach us to pray earnestly, to
pour forth our inmost thoughts. For when we are hemmed in by fear
and sorrow, we speak very differently about trouble than one who is
surrounded by joy. It does not come from the heart when a sad person
laughs or a glad person weeps.

Do not most of the psalms consist of such earnest prayer in the
midst of storms? Where are lovelier words of joy to be found than in the
psalms of praise and thanksgiving? There you see into the hearts of the
saints, like looking into bright, beautiful gardens, or even heaven. Again,
where are sadder and more plaintive words of sorrow to be found than
in the penitential psalms? There we can look into the hearts of the saints
as into death, or even hell. How dark and black it is there because of the
sense of the wrath of God! Thus when they speak of fear and hope, they
use such vivid words that no painter could make the pictures clear, and
no Cicero or any orator could so depict it.

Preface to the Psalter, 1531.   EA 63:29f.

Enter his gates with thanksgiving, and his courts with praise.
Give thanks to him, bless his name. (Psalm 100:4)

Music

Sing to him a new song;
*   play skillfully on the strings with loud shouts.*
(Psalm 33:3)

Music is one of the loveliest and most glorious gifts of God. Satan hates it because it has great power to dispel temptations and evil thoughts. The devil does not wait on this lady. Music is one of the finest arts. The music makes the words live. It drives away the spirit of sadness, as is seen in the story of King Saul.

Music is the best balm for a sad heart, for it restores contentment and quickens and refreshes the heart.

Music is a glorious gift of God, very much like theology. I would not part with my little gifts of music for anything in the world. We ought to teach the young this art, for it makes fine and clever people.

"O sing to the LORD a new song; sing to the LORD, all the earth" (Psalm 96:1), for God has made our hearts and minds joyful through his beloved Son, whom he gave for us and for our redemption from sin, death, and the devil. Whoever earnestly believes this cannot help speaking and singing joyfully about it so that others may hear it and discover the cause. But if we do not sing and speak about it, that is a sign that we do not believe in it, and have not entered into the new and joyful testament but are still under the old, tedious testament.

Preface to the Babst Hymnal.   LW 53:334 ; WA 35:477

For the soaring melodies of praise, for the joy of singing
and making music, I thank you, O God. Amen.

The Prayer of the Congregation

James 5

The prayer of the righteous is powerful and effective.
(James 5:16)

No one can conceive the power of prayer except one who has tried it and learned by experience. But it is a great thing that a person faced with a dire calamity may directly call on the Lord. This I know. Whenever I have prayed earnestly about a matter that has concerned me very deeply, it has been richly answered and I have received more than I have asked. Sometimes God has been slow in coming, but he has always come. See what a great thing is the fervent prayer of a true Christian! How it avails with God that a poor person should speak with his great Majesty in heaven and be not afraid of him but know that God smiles graciously for the sake of Jesus Christ, his beloved Son, our Lord and Savior! The heart and conscience need not turn back and run away. We need not be in doubt because of our unworthiness, and need not be afraid, but may believe with complete certainty that our prayers are always answered when we pray believing in Christ.

Therefore pray in your hearts, and at times with words, for, by the will of God, prayer upholds the world. Without it the world would be very different. At home I am not so brave and cheerful, though I am not content that it should be so, but in the church with the multitude, prayer comes straight from the heart and prevails.

Table Talk.   WA Tischreden 3:448

Let my prayer come before you; O Lord, hear my prayer. Amen.

Cry to God

He will surely be gracious to you and the sound of your cry;
when he hears it he will answer you.
(Isaiah 30:19)

You must learn to pray and not sit alone or lie about, hanging your head and shaking it, brooding over your thoughts, worrying about how you can escape, and looking at nothing but yourself and your sad and painful condition. Get up, you lazy villain, then fall on your knees, lift your eyes and hands toward heaven, take a psalm or the Lord's Prayer, and pour out your trouble with tears before God, lamenting and calling upon him. "I pour out my complaint before him; I tell my trouble before him" (Psalm 142:2). "Let my prayer be counted as incense before you, and the lifting up of my hands as an evening sacrifice" (Psalm 141:2). Prayer and the mentioning of trouble are sacrifices most pleasing to God. God desires it, and it is his will that you should pour out your trouble before him, and not let it lie upon yourself, dragging it about with you and being chafed and tortured by it, so that in the end you make two, or even ten or a hundred calamities out of one. God wills that you should be too weak to bear and overcome such trouble, in order that you may learn to find strength in him and that he may be praised through his strength in you. This is how Christians are made!

Exposition of Psalm 118.   WA 31:95f.

Lord, as with the psalmists of old, I bring before you my petitions.
Give me faith, enliven my hope, and give me strength to love
in my passage through life. Amen.

Prayer in the Name of Jesus

---

*Very truly, I tell you, if you ask anything of the Father
in my name, he will give it to you.
(John 16:23)*

Therefore, when you pray, remember that you may approach God
boldly and without hesitation (provided, of course, you acknowledge
your sin and earnestly desire to better your life). When you pray, say,
"Lord God, heavenly Father, I come to you with my petition, which I
urgently desire you to answer, and I pray in firm and fixed assurance.
Otherwise, I'd rather not pray. Not that I am right or worthy. In fact, I
know and confess that I have not deserved your kindness. Much more, by
a multitude of great sins, I have merited hellfire and your eternal wrath.
Yet I am a little bit obedient in this regard, that you ask me, yes, you
compel me to pray in the name of your Son, our Lord Jesus Christ. In
the assurance and firm hope of your boundless goodness, and not because
of any worthiness on my part, I bow before you and ask you for such and
such. . . ."

Moreover, as we have taught so often, we should not tempt God;
that is, we should not determine the when and where and why, or the
ways and means and manner in which God should answer our prayer.
Rather we must in all humility bring our petition before him who will
certainly do the right thing in accordance with his unsearchable and
divine wisdom. But by no means doubt that God hears our prayer, even
if it may appear that he does not do so.

Appeal for Prayer against the Turks.   LW 43:230; WA 51:605f.

---

*Lord, teach us how to pray aright, with reverence and with fear.
Though dust and ashes in your sight, we may, we must draw near.
Amen. (James Montgomery, 1771–1854)*

Amen—Your Will Be Done

So I tell you, whatever you ask for in prayer, believe that you
have received it, and it will be yours.
(Mark 11:24)

The little word "Amen" means "surely" or "truly." Think carefully about it, for it expresses the faith that we should have in all our prayers. Therefore when you are about to pray you should test and examine yourself, whether you believe or doubt that you will be heard. If you find that you doubt it, or without any conviction give it a try, your prayer is futile. For your heart is not composed. Therefore God can pour no certainty into it, just as you cannot give someone something if they do not keep their hand still. Think how you would like it if someone urgently asked you for something and in the end said, "But I don't believe you will give me it"— although you had promised for certain. You would deem such a prayer a mockery, and would withdraw all that you had promised. You might even punish the person. How then can it please God, who has promised that he will give us what we ask, when we give the lie to his promises through our doubt and, in the very act of praying, act contrary to the prayer, thus insulting the Truth to whom we pray?

Exposition of the Lord's Prayer.   LW 42:77; WA 2:126f.

Eternal Father, help me truly to say "Amen,"
for I know that your mercy is most certainly real.

Luke 24:50-53

The LORD said to my lord,
 "Sit at my right hand
until I make your enemies your footstool."
(Psalm 110:1)

Christ is seated in the heavenly places waiting for the time when his enemies will be made his footstool. That is his proper work. He does not sleep, but he watches us. He does not ask anyone to substitute for him; he does it himself. When people incline toward him, he is present to help. If we are tempted and cry to Christ, we will be helped. The last day has not yet come, and the flesh and sin and death still remain, but on the last day Christ will deliver up the kingdom to his Father. Now he rules in our hearts. He comforts us, makes us clean, and intercedes for us. On the last day all his Christians will rule in unity with him, and they will be seated at the right hand of the Father. Then the last and proper enemy will be slain. Here on earth we still have unstable faith, anxiety about food, and despair, if ever God shows his displeasure. What is now our comfort? It is Christ, our priest, who has atoned for us and looks on us and sees our enemies and reminds the Father that he is our portion. When we feel this in our conscience, we have a sure access to the Father in every need. We fail to see this only because our eyes are not sufficiently penetrating to pierce the clouds and look into heaven, and be assured that Christ is our advocate.

Sermon on Hebrews 8. WA 45:398f.

Heavenly Father, I thank you that Jesus Christ, your Son,
is my advocate and mediator. Amen.

The Grace of God Is High above Our Thinking

Likewise the Spirit helps us in our weakness;
for we do not know how to pray as we ought,
but that very Spirit intercedes with sighs too deep for words.
(Romans 8:26)

It is not a bad sign but a very good one if things seem to turn out contrary to our requests, just as it is not a good sign if everything turns out favorably for our requests. The reason is that God's excellent counsel and will are far above our counsel and will.

It sometimes happens that when we pray to God for something and he hears our prayers and begins to give us what we wish, he gives in such a way that contravenes all of our conceptions and ideas, so that he may seem to us to be more offended after our prayers and to do less after we have asked than he did before. And he does all this because it is the nature of God first to destroy and tear down whatever is in us before he gives us his good things.

When everything is hopeless for us and all things begin to go against our prayers and desires, then those unutterable groans begin. Then "the Spirit helps us in our weakness" (Romans 8:26). For unless the Spirit were helping, it would be impossible for us to bear this action of God by which he hears us and accomplishes what we pray for. Then the soul is told: "Wait for the Lord; be strong, and let your heart take courage; wait for the Lord!" (Psalm 27:14).

But those who have the Spirit are helped by him. For the work of God must be hidden and never understood, even when it happens.

Lectures on Romans.   LW 25:364–65

When I'm overcome with care and the words don't come, O Lord,
may your Spirit intercede for me. Amen.

Prayer with Christ and without Him

If you abide in me, and my words abide in you,
ask for whatever you wish, and it will be done for you.
(John 15:7)

Life apart from Christ is a wretched business. It means hard work for people and yet nothing accomplished; much praying, seeking, and knocking, yet nothing gained, found, or done, for they are not knocking at the right door. For whatever they do and pray, they do it like any other work, without faith. They have no comfort or confidence, and even no conviction that it is well pleasing to God or that he will hear them. That is why they never pray, for, as I have often said, prayer is the work of faith alone, which no one but a Christian can do. For Christians do not pray trusting in themselves, but in the name of the Son of God in which they were baptized, and they know for certain that such prayer is well pleasing to God, for he has commanded them to pray in the name of Christ and has promised to answer. Other people who begin to pray in their own name, taking a long time to prepare themselves until they are right and worthy, and so gaining merit, do not know this. If they are asked whether they are sure that they will be heard, they answer, "I have prayed, but whether I shall be answered, God alone knows." But what manner of prayer is that when you do not know what you are doing or what God will say to it?

As Christians, however, we do not so rise from prayer but, as we begin it in response to God's command and promise, we make it an offering to God in the name of Christ and know that what we have asked will not be denied us, and so we find from experience that we are helped in every time of need.

Sermon on John 15.   LW 24:241; WA 45:681

Prayer is the soul's sincere desire, unuttered or expressed;
the motion of a hidden fire that trembles in the breast.
(James Montgomery, 1818)

The Promise of the Spirit

John 15:26—16:4

I will pour out a spirit of compassion and supplication.
(Zechariah 12:10)

In all Christians the Spirit effects and produces two things: first, the Spirit convinces and assures their hearts that they have a compassionate God; second, the Spirit enables them to help others by their supplication. The result of the first is that they are reconciled to God and have all they need for themselves. Then, when they have this, they will become gods and saviors of the world by their supplication. Through the Spirit of compassion they themselves will become children of God; and then, as children of God, they will mediate between God and their neighbor and will serve others and help them attain this estate too.

Once Christians begin to know Christ as Lord and Savior, God completely permeates their hearts. Now they are eager to help everyone acquire the same benefits. For their greatest delight is in the knowledge of Christ. Therefore they step forth boldly, teaching and admonishing others, praising and confessing their treasure before everybody, praying and yearning that they too may obtain such mercy. There is a spirit of restlessness amid the greatest calm, that is, in God's grace and peace. Christians cannot be still or idle. They constantly strive and struggle with all their might, as those who have no other object in life than to disseminate God's honor and glory among the people, that others may also receive such a spirit of grace, and through this spirit also help them pray.

Sermons on John 14.   LW 24:87; WA 45:540

Gracious Spirit, dove divine! Let your light within me shine.
All my guilty fears remove; fill me with your heavenly love. Amen.
(John Stocker, 1777)

The Spirit Will Glorify Christ

I glorified you on the earth by finishing the work that you gave me to do.
(John 17:4)

If Christ had not been glorified, the Father's glory could not have come to us but would have perished with Christ. The glory of Christ and that of the Father are interlocked and interwoven. These are one indivisible glory, so that the Son receives his glory from the Father and the Father is glorified in and through the Son.

As Christ, our head, prays, so also must we who cling to him pray that he may be glorified in us. For as he fared on earth so must we fare. For his sake we—because we glorify him and praise him with our teaching and living—must submit to shame, condemnation, cursing, and death, so that in our suffering also his name and holy Word will be persecuted and reviled. But that his honor may remain and to keep his Word, he must help us out and turn the wheel so that the world must be shown to be wrong and condemned with all its shame, while we enter into the highest honor and glory. Thus his honor and praise stand out most vividly and spread through the Holy Spirit, and the mouth of Christians, into all the world. This he calls the work that the Father gave him to do, namely, drawing on himself all shame and blame, and suffering and death, for the honor of the Father—and all this for our sake that we might be redeemed and have eternal life.

Sermons on John 16–20.   WA 28:108

We give thanks, Lord God, for the ministry of your Son,
our Lord Jesus, for his preaching, teaching, and healing,
and for his obedience unto death. Amen.

Christ Is in the Father and We Are in Christ

On that day you will know that I am in my Father,
and you in me, and I in you.
(John 14:20)

The first and foremost point about Christ's being in the Father is that we do not doubt that everything this man says and does stands and must stand in heaven before all the angels, in the world before all tyrants, in hell before all devils, in the heart before every evil conscience and one's own thoughts. For if we are sure that everything he thinks, says, and wants reflects the will of the Father, I am able to defy anyone who would be spiteful and angry with me. In Christ I have the Father's will and heart. If you comprehend and see this, then you comprehend and see Christ in the Father and the Father in Christ; then you see no anger, death, or hell, but sheer grace, compassion, heaven, and life.

"Furthermore," he says, "if you know that and believe this, then you will also go on to recognize that I am in you and you are in me. Then you will realize that I am your Savior. You will show that you are in me in this way: Whatever you are, your failings and shortcomings, your sins, your damnation, your death, are all in me. That is their proper place. But whatever is in me must necessarily be perfect righteousness, life, and salvation. By faith you also come to be in me with your death, sin, and every trouble. If you are sinful in yourselves, you are justified in me; if you feel death in you, you have life in me; if you have strife in you, you have peace in me; if you stand condemned on your own account, you are blessed and saved in me."

Sermons on John 14.   LW 24:141; WA 45:589f.

I could not do without you, O Savior of the lost, whose wondrous love redeemed me at such tremendous cost. Amen. (Frances R. Havergal, 1873)

Those for Whom Christ Prays

I am not asking on behalf of the world,
but on behalf of those whom you gave me.
(John 17:9)

We have been told for whom he prays, namely, for all those who believe in his Word and love him with all their hearts and cling firmly to his Word. These may joyfully rely that they are certainly included in this prayer and will abide with Christ.

But, on the other hand, it is a terrible thing that he says, "I am not asking on behalf of the world." Let us then take care that we are not found among those for whom he will not pray. For nothing can follow but that they will certainly be lost, for Christ has cast them out from himself and will have nothing to do with them. The world should be filled with fear and petrified with horror at such judgment. But it merely mocks and laughs, and remains in its grim and stubborn blindness, feeling so secure that it casts it to the wind and lets it go in at one ear and out at the other, as if a fool had said it.

Sermons on John 16–20.   WA 28:128f.

Lord Jesus, think on me, by anxious thoughts oppressed;
let me your loving servant be, and taste your promised rest. Amen.
(Synesius of Cyrene, 375–430)

The Spirit Works in Us and through Us

I will pour out a spirit of compassion and supplication.
(Zechariah 12:10)

When Christians begin to know Christ as their Lord and Savior, through whom they are redeemed from death and brought into his kingdom and inheritance, their hearts are aglow with a flaming love of God, and they would gladly help everyone to the same experience. For they know no greater joy than that they possess this treasure, that they know Christ. Therefore they go out and teach and exhort other people, praising and testifying to it before everybody, praying and yearning that they too might attain to such grace. That is a restless spirit enjoying the highest rest in the grace and peace of God. For it cannot be silent or idle but is always striving with all its power to spread the honor and glory of God among the people, that others too may receive this Spirit of grace and may then help with the work of prayer. For where the Spirit of grace is, it quickens our hearts so that we can and may and must begin to pray.

Sermons on John 14.   LW 24:87; WA 45:540

Holy Spirit, love divine, glow within this heart of mine;
kindle every high desire; purge me with your holy fire. Amen.
(Samuel Longfellow, 1819–1892)

Comfort under the Cross

I am not asking you to take them out of the world,
but I ask you to protect them from the evil one. . . .
Sanctify them in the truth; your word is truth.
(John 17:15, 17)

All Christendom is a small group that must submit to, suffer, and—more than all other people—bear whatever grief the devil and the world can inflict on it. What persons, in view of such outward appearance, could recognize and conclude that they are genuine Christians? Reason will surely not show this. The Holy Spirit must do so. He is called "the Spirit of truth" because in spite of what they appear to be and are subjected to—according to which this message seems to amount to nothing and to be a pack of lies—he strengthens and preserves hearts in the faith. Otherwise no one would have believed for any length of time, or would still believe, that this Jesus Christ, who sits at the right hand of the Father forever, he who was so shamefully crucified as a malefactor by his own people, is true God. Or how could we conclude with certainty of our own accord that we, who believe in this crucified Christ and are condemned, cursed, and executed by the whole world as God's enemies and the devil's own, are actually God's dear children and saints? After all, we ourselves do not feel this. In fact, our heart tells us something far different, because we are still sinners full of weakness. But this is the work of the Holy Spirit; it is his power; he confirms this in our heart. Therefore we can accept it as true in accord with his Word. He enables us to live and to die by this truth.

Sermons on John 14.   *LW 24:358; WA 46:54*

Lord, strengthen and preserve my heart in faith,
whether in sorrow or joy. Amen.

Peace I Leave with You

Peace I leave with you; my peace I give to you. . . .
Do not let your hearts be troubled, and do not let them be afraid.
(John 14:27)

It is a very comforting and pleasing final word that he leaves them. It does not consist of cities and castles or of silver and gold; it is peace, the greatest treasure in heaven and on earth. He does not want his disciples to be fearful and mournful; he wants them to have true, beautiful, and longed-for peace of heart. "For so far as I am concerned," Christ says, "you shall have nothing but sheer peace and joy. All my sermons to you and all my associations with you have let you see and realize that I love you with all my heart and do for you everything that is good, and that my Father is most graciously disposed toward you. That is the best I can leave to you and give you; for peace of heart is the greatest peace." As it is said, "Joy of heart exceeds all other joy; sadness of heart surpasses all other woe."

Sermons on John 14.   LW 24:177; WA 45:623

Lord, give me a peaceful heart that I may express your peace
to those around me. Amen.

Pentecost

The Church of the Holy Spirit

Acts 2:1-13

All of them were filled with the Holy Spirit.
(Acts 2:4)

On this holy and joyful feast of Pentecost, we give thanks to our Lord God as we celebrate the great unending mercy that he manifested on earth. He revealed from heaven to us poor mortals his holy Word, which is not a plain and common word, but a special and a different Word, compared with the Law of Moses. For on this day the kingdom of Christ began through the apostles and was manifested through the gospel for all the world. Certainly, in his person, Christ possessed his kingdom from eternity, but today, on Pentecost, it was made manifest by the Holy Spirit through the apostles to all the world, and this revelation was accompanied by the great courage, daring, and joy of those wretched fishermen, the apostles, who had previously denied Christ and deserted him, because their minds were stupid and afraid and in despair.

Today, on the day of Pentecost, we celebrate the joyous, blessed, and precious kingdom of Christ, which is full of joy and confidence and courage.

Sermon for Pentecost, 1534.   WA 37:399f.

O Holy Spirit, enter in, and in our hearts your work begin,
and make our heart your dwelling. Sun of the soul, O light divine,
around and in us brightly shine. Amen. (Michael Schirmer, 1606–1673)

We Begin in Weakness

God chose what is foolish in the world to shame the wise;
God chose what is weak in the world to shame the strong.
(1 Corinthians 1:27)

Christ began his kingdom through the untaught laypersons and simple fishermen who had not studied the Scriptures. It sounds very foolish that the Christian church should have begun with those poor beggars and the scandalous preaching of the crucified Jesus of Nazareth, who was mocked, defiled, slandered, scourged, and finally as a blasphemer and rioter nailed to the cross and shamefully done to death, as his title on the cross proves: "Jesus of Nazareth, the King of the Jews." So on Pentecost the apostles preached that he suffered wrong and violence, and that those who nailed him to the cross and killed him had gravely sinned. Through this preaching, Christ's kingdom and the Christian church began. This is a daring deed of the apostles and disciples, and it is a great comfort to them that they were given power to preach such tidings openly on Pentecost.

In what does that might and strength consist? In nothing but the Word and the Spirit. See what power Peter has—indeed not Peter only but all the others as well! How sure they are of their message, how mightily do they use the Holy Scriptures! I could not master the Scriptures as well, although I am a doctor of divinity and these are fishermen who had not read the Bible.

Thus Christendom began with the word of the poor fishermen, and with the despised and disdained work of God, which is called Jesus of Nazareth, nailed to the cross.

Sermon for Pentecost, 1534.   WA 37:400

God's foolishness is wiser than human wisdom, and God's weakness
is stronger than human strength. (1 Corinthians 1:25)

The Spirit of Grace

I will ask the Father, and he will give you another
Comforter, to be with you forever.
(John 14:16, Luther's reading)

We must learn to know the Holy Spirit and believe him to be as Christ describes him and sets him before the eye of the soul, namely, that he is not a Spirit of wrath and terror but of grace and comfort, and that thus the whole Godhead shows nothing but comfort. The Father wills to comfort us, for he gives the Holy Spirit; the Son gives comfort, for he prays the Father to send him; and the Holy Spirit is himself the Comforter. There is therefore here no terror, threat, or wrath over Christians, but only gracious laughter and sweet comfort in heaven and on earth. And why is that? The reason is, he says, because you have already enough torturers and hangmen to plague and frighten you.

This is the right way of teaching about the Holy Spirit, that he is called a Comforter, and that that is his nature, character, and ministry. With regard to his Godhead, he is of indivisible divine essence with the Father and the Son. But to us he is called a Comforter, and a comforter is one who makes a sad heart glad and joyful toward God and tells you to be of good cheer for your sins are forgiven, death is slain, heaven is open, and God smiles upon you. Whoever could grasp this definition rightly would have already won the victory and would not find or see anything but sheer comfort and joy in heaven and on earth.

Sermons on John 14.   LW 24:115; WA 45:562ff.

In this world, mixed with delight and sorrow, I need your grace, O Lord
God. Be with me in times of joy and in times of grief. Amen.

Righteousness, Peace, and Joy in the Holy Spirit

*The kingdom of God is . . . righteousness and peace
and joy in the Holy Spirit.*
(Romans 14:17)

If I am to be made saintly, it is not enough to do good works outwardly, but I must do them from the bottom of my heart with love and desire, that I may be fearless, free, and joyful and stand before God with a good conscience and complete confidence. Nothing I do can give me this assurance, and no creature, but Christ alone. Such faith makes me well pleasing to God, and Christ fills my heart with the Holy Spirit, who makes me happy and glad to do anything that is good. In this way only can I be justified, and in no other; for works make you the more unhappy the longer you trust in them.

But the more you do this work and the better you know it, the more does it make your heart joyful, for where there is such knowledge the Holy Spirit cannot remain outside. And when he comes he makes the heart joyful, willing, and light, so that it freely goes and gladly and with good heart does all that is well pleasing to God, and suffers what has to be suffered, and would gladly die. The purer and greater the knowledge, the deeper grow the bliss and joy. Thus the Lord's command is fulfilled and all is done that should be done; and thus you are made just.

Sermons from the year 1523.   WA 12:547

*Holy Spirit, strong and mighty, you who render all things new,
make your work within me perfect, help me by your word so true. Amen.*
(Heinrich Held, 1664)

The Church Is His Crown

You have . . . crowned him with glory and honor.
(Psalm 8:5, Luther's reading)

David talks here about the royal adornment with which Christ, crowned as king, will be glorious in this world and in the world to come. It is the custom to adorn kings when they are to appear in splendor. Christ the king will likewise be adorned not for himself alone in his natural body but also for us in his spiritual body, which is the church. For he gathers his church through the preaching of the gospel and adorns her with his Holy Spirit. And this adornment is set over against his, of which Isaiah says (chapter 53) that the Son of Man has no form or comeliness, and few to follow him, at the time of his suffering. His own people cry, "Crucify him, crucify him!" Even his own disciples desert him and flee from him. But after his resurrection he will be gloriously adorned, and a multitude of Christians will follow him on earth. That will be the beautiful adornment with which he will be crowned in this world.

Sermons from the year 1537.   WA 45:242f.

Remember, O Lord, your church; deliver her from all evil,
perfect her in your love, and from the four winds gather her,
the sanctified, in your kingdom that you have prepared for her. Amen.
(Didache 10:5, late first century or early second century)

The Gospel Is Foolishness

Others sneered and said, "They are filled with new wine."
(Acts 2:13)

Once, on Pentecost, Christ gave the Holy Spirit visibly to the apostles
when there were seen sitting upon each of them tongues as of fire, and
they spoke in many languages, and exorcised devils and healed the sick.
Now, however, and to the end of the world, he no longer gives the Holy
Spirit and his gifts to his Christians as he did then, but invisibly and
secretly. But as little as our reason believes that Christ has overcome and
taken captive all our foes, death, and the devil, so little does it believe that
Christ pours forth gifts among us humans. For when the apostles received
the Holy Spirit on Pentecost, and began to speak with other tongues and
to preach, who believed that they were in their right mind? Indeed, they
were told by their own people that they were full of new wine, and also
that they were possessed of devils. By both Jews and Gentiles they were
done to death as blasphemers, deceivers, and rogues.

That is why the world neither sees nor understands the gifts of the
Holy Spirit but despises and scorns them. In fact, everything our Lord does
and says does not and cannot suit the world. They even deem his Word to
be heresy and the devil's teaching. On the other hand, they hold the devil's
work in high esteem, and call it the word of God. Only the Christians
recognize the Word of God and deem it to be the highest treasure on
earth; they only perceive the dignity and power of his great divine works,
although even they never sufficiently marvel at them and praise them as
they should. For as the apostles fared, we also fare in our time.

Sermon on the Fruit and Power of the Ascension, 1527. EA 18:185f.

Help me, Lord God, to recognize the activity of the Spirit in our time;
give me grace to share in your redemptive work. Amen.

The Church of Sinners

God chose what is low and despised in the world,
things that are not, to reduce to nothing things that are,
so that no one might boast in the presence of God.
(1 Corinthians 1:28-29)

May a merciful God preserve me from a Christian church in which everyone is a saint! I want to be and remain in the little flock and that church where there are the fainthearted, the feeble, and the ailing, who feel and recognize the wretchedness of their sins, who sigh and cry to God incessantly for comfort and help, who believe in the forgiveness of sin, and who suffer persecution for the sake of the Word, which they confess and teach purely and without adulteration. Satan is a cunning rogue. Through his fanatical activity he wants to trick the simpleminded into the belief that the preaching of the gospel is useless. "Greater effort" is necessary, they say. "We must lead a holy life, bear the cross, and endure persecution." By such a semblance of self-styled holiness, which runs counter to the Word of God, many a person is misled. But Christ is our righteousness and our holiness. In him, not in ourselves, we have perfection (Colossians 2:10). I find comfort in and cling to the words of St. Paul in 1 Corinthians 1:30, that Christ "became for us wisdom from God, and righteousness and sanctification and redemption."

Sermons on John 1.   LW 22:55; WA 46:583

Heavenly Father, in a confusing world and in a time of ambiguity,
become for me wisdom and righteousness and sanctification. Amen.

The Holy Trinity

Romans 11:33-36

From him and through him and to him are all things.
To him be the glory forever. Amen.
(Romans 11:36)

Festivals in the year other than Trinity Sunday center on the works and wonders that the Lord has done. At Christ's nativity we celebrate that God was made a human being, at Easter that he rose from the dead, at Pentecost that he poured out the Holy Spirit and instituted the church, and all the other festivals of the year speak of our Lord God as he is seen clothed in some work. But this festival shows us how God is in himself, in his divine nature without any wrappings and works. Here you must soar high above all reason, leaving all creatures far below, and must swing yourself up and listen only to what God says of himself and of his innermost being. In no other way can we know this. There God's folly and the world's wisdom clash.

Therefore we should not dispute about how it can be that God the Father, the Son, and the Holy Spirit are one God, for it is by its very nature beyond all reason, but it should be enough for us that God speaks in this way about himself and reveals himself thus in his Word.

This message should make our hearts joyful toward God. For we see that all three persons, the whole Godhead, turn to us in order that we poor, wretched people should be helped against sin, death, and the devil, that we may be brought to justification, the kingdom of God, and eternal life.

Sermons on John 3.   WA 52:346

Holy, holy, holy! Lord God Almighty!
All your works shall praise your name in earth and sky and sea.
Holy, holy, holy, merciful and mighty!
God in three persons, blessed Trinity! Amen.
(Reginald Huber, 1783–1826, alt.)

The Unsearchable Majesty of God

*It is he alone who has immortality and dwells
in unapproachable light, whom no one has ever seen
or can see; to him be honor and eternal dominion. Amen.
(1 Timothy 6:16)*

The secret will of the divine majesty is not a matter for debate. Human temerity, which is always neglecting necessary things in its eagerness to probe this one, must be called off and restrained from busying itself with the investigation of these secrets of God's majesty. This is impossible to penetrate, because he dwells in light inaccessible, as Paul testifies (1 Timothy 6:16). Let us occupy ourselves instead with God incarnate, or as Paul puts it, with Jesus crucified, in whom are all the treasures of wisdom and knowledge, though in a hidden manner (Colossians 2:3). Through him it is furnished abundantly with what we ought to know and ought not to know. It is God incarnate, moreover, who is speaking here: "I would . . . you would not"—God incarnate, I say, who has been sent into the world for the very purpose of willing, speaking, doing, suffering, and offering to all persons everything necessary for salvation. Yet he offends very many who, being either abandoned or hardened by that secret will of the divine majesty, do not receive him as he wills, speaks, acts, suffers, and offers. It is likewise the part of this incarnate God to weep, wail, and groan over the perdition of the ungodly, when the will of the divine majesty purposely abandons some to perish. It is not for us to ask why he does so but to stand in awe of God who both can do and wills to do such things.

The Bondage of the Will.   LW 33:145

*As the heavens are higher than the earth, so are my ways higher than
your ways and my thoughts than your thoughts. (Isaiah 55:9)*

TUESDAY

God Is Unsearchable

How unsearchable are his judgments and how inscrutable his ways!
(Romans 11:33)

Why, then, do we poor, wretched humans rack our brains over the nature of God, while we yet fail to grasp by faith the rays of the divine promises or comprehend a spark of God's commands and works, both of which he has confirmed with words and mighty works?

Truly, we ought to teach God's unsearchable and unfathomable will; but to take it on ourselves to understand it is a very dangerous thing, through which we may stumble and break our neck. It is my habit to restrain and direct myself by the word that the Lord Christ spoke to Peter, "What is that to you? Follow me" (John 21:22). For Peter also disputed and brooded over the works of God, asking in what manner he would deal with another, that is, what might befall John. Again, when Philip said, "Show us the Father" (John 14:8), what did he reply? "Do you not believe that I am in the Father and the Father is in me? . . . Whoever has seen me has seen the Father" (John 14:9-10). For Philip, too, was anxious to behold the majesty and presence of the Father. Again, even if we knew all these hidden judgments of God, of what use and benefit could it be to us over and above the command and promise of God?

Yet over and above all things, practice faith in God's promises and in the works of his commandments.

Table Talk.   WA Tischreden 6:39f.

Who has directed the spirit of the LORD, or as his counselor
has instructed him? (Isaiah 40:13)

The Holy Spirit Brings Christ into Our Hearts

. . .that Christ may dwell in your hearts through faith.
(Ephesians 3:17)

The Holy Spirit teaches us the knowledge of Christ. The Spirit pours Christ into the heart, setting it all on fire with love and making it steadfast through faith in him. Where he dwells, there is fullness of life, whether the soul be weak or strong.

That Christ dwells in our hearts means nothing else than to know who he is and what we may hope of him. This means to know that he is our Savior through whom we have been brought into that state where we can call God our Father and receive through him the Spirit who gives us courage in the face of all calamities. Thus he has made our hearts his abode, and we cannot lay hold on him in any other way, because he is not a dead thing but the living God. But how can he be contained in the heart? Not by thoughts but by living faith alone. He cannot be possessed through works, nor can looking draw him. Only the heart can hold him. If, then, your faith is right and sound, you both have and feel Christ in your heart, and know everything that he thinks and does in heaven and on earth, and how he rules through his Word and Spirit, and what is the mind of both those who possess him and those who do not possess him.

Sermons from the year 1525. WA 17/1:436

Take my life and let it be consecrated, Lord, to thee. Amen.

The Spirit of Adoption

For you did not receive a spirit of slavery to fall back into fear,
but you have received a spirit of adoption. When we cry,
"Abba! Father!" it is that very Spirit bearing witness. . . .
(Romans 8:15)

Here is described the power of Christ's kingdom and the true work and
lofty ministry that is accomplished by the Holy Spirit in the faithful. That
is the comfort through which the heart, freed from the fear and terror of
sin, is set at rest and the heartfelt prayer that awaits the answering help of
God in faith. Neither of these can be brought about through the law or
one's own sanctity. For in this way we can never receive certain comfort
of God's mercy and love toward us; rather we always remain in fear and
anxiety about wrath and condemnation, and because we are in such
doubt, we flee from God and cannot call on him.

Where there is faith in Christ, on the other hand, there the Holy
Spirit pours both comfort and childlike confidence into the heart. The
heart no longer doubts God's gracious will and help, because he has
promised both grace and help, fulfilment and comfort, not because of
our own worthiness but because of the merit and the name of Christ, his
Son. Of these two works of the Holy Spirit, comfort and supplication,
the prophet also says that God will begin a new message and work in
the kingdom of Christ when he will pour forth the Spirit of grace and of
prayer. It is the same Spirit who assures us that we are children of God,
and moves our hearts that we cry to him with heartfelt supplication.

Sermon on Romans 8:12-17.   WA 22:137f.

When the trials of life overwhelm me, Lord God, let me rely on your grace
shown in the work of your Son, Jesus Christ, our Lord. Amen.

If, in Fact, We Suffer with Him

And if children, then heirs, heirs of God and joint heirs with Christ—
if, in fact, we suffer with him so that we may also be glorified with him.
(Romans 8:17)

There you hear the high praise, honor, and glory of Christians. Who can adequately praise and express it? No words can express it, nor can reason grasp it.

But here is found that deep human weakness within us, for if we could believe this and not doubt it, what is there to fear, and who is there to harm us? For whoever can say to God from the bottom of the heart, "You are my beloved Father and I am your child," will obviously defy all the devils from hell, and with a joyful heart despise all the world's threatening and boasting. For in this Father we have a Lord before whom all creatures must tremble, and without his will they can do nothing. Thus they possess such an inheritance and dominion that no creature can harm or hurt them. But he adds this little word, "if, in fact, we suffer with him," that we may know that we must live in such a way on earth that we give proof that we are devout and obedient children who do not follow the lust of the flesh but suffer for the kingdom's sake whatever may befall us, and what hurts the flesh. If we do that, we should and shall find glorious comfort in the words and shall rejoice in the truth of them, "For all who are led by the Spirit of God [that they follow not the flesh] are children of God" (Romans 8:14).

Sermon on Romans 8:17.   WA 22:139

When peace, like a river, attends all my way;
when sorrows, like sea billows, roll;
whatever my lot, you have taught me to say,
It is well, it is well with my soul. Amen.
(Horatio G. Spafford, 1828–1888, alt.)

The Children of God

*It is that very Spirit bearing witness with our spirit
that we are children of God.
(Romans 8:16)*

The knowledge that we are children of God—and that we may be fully assured of it—is not derived from ourselves or from the law. It is the witness of the Holy Spirit who bears witness to it, against the law and the feeling of our own unworthiness, and in spite of our weakness he makes us fully assured of it. Such witness is accomplished in such a way that we are made aware of it and feel the power of the Holy Spirit at work within us through the Word, and our experience agrees with the Word or the message. For you can feel it, if you are in sorrow and affliction and you receive comfort from the gospel, and are enabled to overcome fear and doubt, so that your heart can firmly believe that you have a gracious God. Then you no longer need flee from him. but through such faith you can joyfully call on him and expect help from him. Where there is such faith, the experience follows that we receive help, as St. Paul says, "Suffering produces endurance, and endurance produces character, and character produces hope, and hope does not disappoint us" (Romans 4:4-5).

This is the true inward witness by which you perceive that the Holy Spirit is working within you.

Sermon on Romans 8:16.   WA 22:138f.

*Beloved, we are God's children now; what we will be
has not yet been revealed. (1 John 3:2)*

What True Faith Consists In

Acts 4:32-35

Faith is the assurance of things hoped for,
the conviction of things not seen.
(Hebrews 11:1)

The noblest and dearest virtue of faith is that it closes its eyes and simply and joyfully leaves everything in the hands of God. It does not desire to know why God acts as he does, and it still holds him to be the highest good and the purest justice, although to reason, the senses, and experience, nothing appears but wrath and injustice. That is why faith is called the conviction of things not seen, and even the very opposite to what is seen. Therefore this is the highest honor and love toward God and the highest degree of such honor and love, that in these contrary things you can regard and praise him as good and just. Here the natural eye must be completely plucked out, and there must be nothing but sheer faith. Otherwise there will be a grim and fearful vexation of spirit.

Letter to Hans von Rechenberg, 1522.   LW 43:52; WA 10/2:323

I trust in you, O LORD; I say, "You are my God."
My times are in your hand. Amen. (Psalm 31:14-15)

Increase Our Faith

The apostles said to the Lord, "Increase our faith!"
(Luke 17:5)

In the Christian community no one possesses more than another. St. Peter and St. Paul have no more than Mary Magdalene or you or I. In sum, they are brothers and sisters, and there is no difference between the persons. Mary, the mother of the Lord, and John the Baptist and the thief on the cross all possess the very same blessing possessed by you and me and by all who are baptized and do the Father's will. What is this precious possession? They have the knowledge that their sins are forgiven. They have comfort and help promised them through Christ in every kind of need, against sin, death, and the devil. I have the same, and you, and all believers have it also.

But it also is true that you and I do not believe it as firmly as did John the Baptist and St. Paul; and yet it is the one and only treasure. It is the same as when two persons hold a glass of wine, one with a trembling, the other with a steady hand. Or when two persons hold a bag of money, one in a weak, the other in a strong hand. Whether the hand be strong or weak, as God wills, it neither adds to the contents of the bag nor takes away. In the same way there is no other difference here between the apostles and me than that they hold the treasure more firmly. Nevertheless I should and must know that I possess the same treasure as all holy prophets, apostles, and all saints have possessed.

Sermons from the year 1530.   WA 32:85f.

Do not remember the sins of my youth or my transgressions; according to your steadfast love remember me, for your goodness' sake, O LORD! Amen.
(Psalm 25:7)

God's Will Is Unsearchable

His understanding is unsearchable.
(Isaiah 40:28)

There can be no faith unless all that I believe is hidden and invisible, for what I see I do not need to believe. But nothing can be more deeply hidden than when it seems absurd, and I see and perceive and understand it as the opposite to what faith shows it to be. Thus God acts in all his works. When he wills to bring us to life, he puts us to death. When he wills to make us saintly, he smites our conscience and makes us first sinners. When he wills to raise us up into heaven, he casts us first into hell, as the Scriptures say, "The Lord kills and brings to life; he brings down to Sheol and raises up" (1 Samuel 2:6).

Thus God hides his eternal and unspeakable goodness and mercy under eternal wrath, his justice under injustice. Here is the highest degree of faith, to believe that the God who makes so few souls blessed is nevertheless the most merciful God; to believe that the God whose will it is that some should be condemned is nonetheless the most just God.

But if by reason we could understand how God is good, merciful, and just when he shows such cruel wrath and injustice, how could faith be necessary? But as reason cannot understand, faith is there, and you can practice faith when such things are preached to you.

The Bondage of the Will.   LW 33:62

Truly, you are a God who hides himself, O God of Israel, the Savior.
(Isaiah 45:15)

The Lord Dwells in Thick Darkness

The LORD has said that he would dwell in thick darkness.
(1 Kings 8:12)

Faith is such a knowledge that, although it is completely and utterly dark and nothing is visible, it is yet sure and, in such utter darkness, sees that it really holds Christ, just as in former times our Lord God was seated in the midst of darkness on Mount Sinai and in the temple. Therefore our righteousness, which makes us appear just before God and well pleasing to him, is not the love that gives this appearance to faith, but it is faith itself, and the hidden mystery and the secret knowledge in the heart, that is a trust in what is invisible, which means in Christ invisible and yet really present. But the reason why faith makes us just is that it seizes Christ, the noble and precious treasure, and keeps him present. But human thought cannot express how he is present, for as I have said, it is pure darkness, which means that it is a hidden, high secret, and unsearchable knowledge. Therefore, where there is such a full trust and genuine confidence of the heart, there, certainly, is Christ within the dark mist and in the faith. That is the right justification, which causes the person to be regarded as righteous and acceptable before God.

Lectures on Galatians.   LW 26:130; WA 40/2:288f.

He made darkness his covering around him,
his canopy thick clouds dark with water. (Psalm 18:11)

Felt and Unfelt Forgiveness

And forgive us our debts, as we also have forgiven our debtors.
(Matthew 6:12)

God is well disposed toward many people, forgiving with all his heart all their trespasses, yet without telling them of this. Instead, this inner and external treatment of them leads them to believe that they have a very ungracious God who is determined to condemn them here in time and also in eternity. Outwardly he torments them; inwardly he terrifies them. One of these was David, when he exclaimed in Psalm 6:1, "O LORD, do not rebuke me in your anger." On the other hand, God secretly retains the sins of others and is really angry with them but keeps them ignorant of this. God treats them in such a way that they believe that they are his dear children. Outwardly they are well off; inwardly they are happy and sure of heaven. These are described in Psalm 10:6, "We shall not be moved; throughout all generations we shall not meet adversity." Thus God occasionally allows comfort to come to the conscience and fills us with cheerful confidence in his mercy to strengthen and inspire us with hope in God even in times when our conscience is fearful. On the other hand, God at times saddens and terrifies a conscience so that even in happy days we will not forget the fear of God.

The first mode of forgiveness is bitter and hard for us, but it is the one most sublime and precious. The second is easier for us, but not as good.

Exposition of the Lord's Prayer.   LW 42:63; WA 2:116f.

Have mercy on me, O God,
according to your steadfast love;
according to your abundant mercy
blot out my transgressions. Amen. (Psalm 51:1)

Nothing Will Harm Us

*We know that all things work together for good for those
who love God, who are called according to his purpose.
(Romans 8:28)*

God is a master who knows how to convert whatever would hinder and
harm us into that which furthers and helps us. Whatever is intended to
take our life must serve to preserve it. Whatever would cause us to sin
and damn us must help to strengthen our faith and hope, must make our
prayer more fervent and cause it to be heard more richly.

Here is the master who always works the opposite of what the
world has in mind and who puts its worst schemes to good use. He is
the God who "calls into existence the things that do not exist" (Romans
4:17), who reverses and renews all things. To be sure, when Christians
are trampled on and beheaded, this does not look like honor and glory,
joy and bliss; it seems to be the very opposite. He says, however, "I can
call into existence the things that do not exist and change sadness and all
heartache into sheer happiness. I can say, 'Death and grave, be life! Hell,
become heaven and bliss! Poison, be precious medicine and refreshment!
Devil and world, be of even greater service to my beloved Christians
than the blessed angels and the pious saints!' For I can and will cultivate
my vineyard in this way. All kinds of suffering and adversity will only
improve it."

Sermon on John 15.   LW 24:197; WA 45:640f.

*Lord God, you bring hope where there is despair; you turn sorrow into
gladness; you create faith where there is doubt. Restore my soul. Amen.*

Faith Means Watching

I lie awake;
I am like a lonely bird on the housetop.
(Psalm 102:7)

The world sleeps, as the apostle says, "Let us not fall asleep as others do, but let us keep awake and be sober" (1 Thessalonians 5:6). For temporal desires are opposed to the eternal good as the pictures in a dream are the opposite of the real thing. Thus Isaiah says that sinners have the same experience as when a thirsty person dreams he is drinking, and when he awakes his soul is unsatisfied (Isaiah 29:8). Hence this sleep is nothing but the love and desire for creatures. But to wake is to hold fast and to look to and long for the eternal good. But in this we are alone, and no one is with us; for all the others are sleeping. He says "on the housetop" as if he meant: The world is a house in which all persons are enclosed and are sleeping. I alone am outside the house, on the roof, not yet in heaven and still not in the world. The world is below me, and heaven is above me. I hover between the life of the world and eternal life, lonely in the faith.

The Seven Penitential Psalms.   *LW 14:180; WA 1:198f.*

I wait for the LORD, my soul waits, and in his word I hope. (Psalm 130:5)

God's Love and Our Response

1 John 3:13-18

God's love has been poured into our hearts
through the Holy Spirit that has been given to us.
(Romans 5:5)

Mark here that it says "God's love." For through it alone do we love God. Here there is nothing to be seen or felt, either inwardly or outwardly, that you might love or fear, or on which you might ground your confidence. No, love is caught up high above all things, into the invisible God who surpasses all feeling and all understanding, and is carried right into the innermost darkness.

This high virtue that is in us is not born of ourselves, as the apostle says, but we must pray to God for it. Thus it follows that it "is poured" into us, not born in us or originated in us. This takes place "through the Holy Spirit"; it is not acquired by moral effort and practice, as our moral virtues are. "Into our hearts," that is, into the depths and the midst and center of our hearts, not on the surface of the heart, as foam lies on water. This is the kind of love that the hypocrites have, who imagine and pretend that they have love. But a period of testing only proves the pride and impatience that lie deep within them. "That has been given to us," that is, whom we do not deserve; rather we deserve the direct opposite.

That this is actually so is confirmed by what follows, namely, that it is really given and not merited. So Christ was slain for the sake of the weak, and by no means for the strong and deserving.

Lectures on Romans. LW 25:294

We love because he first loved us. (1 John 4:19)

Continue in My Love

As the Father has loved me, so I have loved you; abide in my love.
(John 15:9)

It is the devil's joy and delight to strive for nothing else than to destroy love among Christians and to create utter hatred and envy. For he knows very well that Christendom is built and preserved by love.

Therefore Christ admonishes us so solemnly and earnestly to hold firmly to love above all else after we have come to faith in him and are now his branches. He places both himself and his Father before our eyes as the noblest and most perfect examples. It is as if he would say, "My Father loves me so much that he transmits all his power and might to me. To be sure, he lets me suffer now, but he takes to heart all that I do and suffer as though this were happening to him, and he will raise me from the dead, make me Lord over all things, and completely glorify his divine majesty in me. So do I love you. I shall not leave you in your sins and in death, but I will stake life and limb to rescue you. I shall communicate to you my purity, holiness, death, resurrection, and all that I can do. Therefore you should let my love for you be reflected in your love for one another. Though you are sorely tempted and tried for my sake and hard pressed to forsake me, stand firm and be patient. Let my love be stronger, greater, and mightier than the suffering you feel."

Therefore we should follow this example of Christ and learn to practice this command among one another, each one according to one's ability.

Sermons on John 15.   LW 24:246; WA 45:686f.

And now faith, hope, and love abide, these three;
and the greatest of these is love. (1 Corinthians 13:13)

Love for Love

We love because he first loved us.
(1 John 4:19)

As there is no fire without heat and smoke, so is there no faith without love. For when through faith we know how dearly God loves us, we must gain a sweet and loving heart toward God, and this heart cannot stay by itself alone. It must flow forth and freely show its gratitude and love.

But as God does not need our work and has not commanded us to do anything for him but to praise and thank him, Christians make haste to give themselves wholeheartedly to their neighbors, serving and helping them freely with their counsel, for they know that God showed them his grace freely out of sheer mercy, without any merit, even while they were still in sin, while they were God's foes and never gave a thought to God. But now when they see their neighbors in error or sin, they cannot help but show them the right way. They lead them to the place where they themselves have found comfort and help; they preach the gospel to them and lead them to the forgiveness of sins. After that, if they see them naked, they clothe them; hungry, they feed them; thirsty, they give them to drink, and so forth. To sum up, "Do to others as you would have them do to you" (Matthew 7:12). And so, whatever way you can serve your neighbors, do it gladly and willingly, before they ask you.

Sermons from the year 1527.   WA 17/2:275f.

Lord, when I am tempted to respond in pettiness, when I want to speak my resentment, let me think on your steadfast love to me. Amen.

God Is Love

God is love.
(1 John 4:16)

See what "God is love" means. It is so clear that anyone must see and grasp it if they will but open their eyes. For the gracious gifts of God stand every day before your eyes whichever way you look: the sun, the moon, and the heavens filled with light; the earth full of leaves, grass, and corn, and many kinds of plants, prepared and given to us for good. Moreover, God's love is experienced through father and mother, house and homestead, peace, safety, and security through worldly government, and so forth. And over and above all this he gave his beloved Son for you and through his gospel brought him home to you, to help you in every grief and affliction. What more could he have done for you or what more or better could you wish? His love is such a burning fire, I hold, that no human thought could fathom it. The one who does not see or heed it must be as blind as a bat—or as hard as a stone, or dead.

Now since you (says St. John) who desire to be Christian and to know God, see and know that God is nothing but pure love, most richly poured forth and shed abroad upon us, take this to your heart, that you should do the same toward your neighbors. For it is impossible that anyone who feels such fire of God's love should not be at least a little warmed and kindled by it.

Sermons from the year 1532.   WA 36:429

Lord God, even as I worship you as the creator of all that is
and as the Lord of the nations, I thank you for your tender mercies
and your heart of steadfast love. Amen.

Not to Receive Thanks but to Give Thanks

And sustain in me a willing spirit.
(Psalm 51:12)

That is, sustain me with the Holy Spirit. The Spirit makes us free and willing, persons who do not serve God out of painful fear or improper love. For all who serve out of fear are not firmly established as long as the fear lasts. In fact, they are forced; they serve with resentment. If there were no hell and punishment, they would not serve at all. Even those who serve God out of love of reward or some good thing are not firmly established. For if they know of no reward or if the good thing does not materialize, they stop. All these have no joy in God's salvation. Nor do they have a clean heart or a right spirit. They are lovers of themselves more than of God. Those, however, who serve God with a good and honest will are firm in their service of God, whether things go this way or that way, are sweet or sour. They are established and made firm by God with a noble, free, princely, and unconstrained will. In Hebrew the little word for "willing spirit" means "free," "willing," or "unconstrained." What is done because of force does not last, but what is done willingly remains firm.

The Seven Penitential Psalms.   LW 14:172; WA 18:191f.

[God] desires everyone to be saved and to come
to the knowledge of the truth. (1 Timothy 2:4)

In Suffering Preserve Your Love for Him

Those who love me will keep my words.
(John 14:23)

The church on earth must exist and fight in weakness, poverty, and affliction, fear, death, shame, and blame. Calamity will force you to step out of yourself and not to rely on the counsel, help, and strength of others, but you must have Christ in your heart, so that you hold his name, Word, and kingdom higher, dearer, and more precious than all things on earth. To him who does not do this but loves his own honor and power, the world's praise, lust, joy, and friendship more, this word is preached in vain. As Christ himself soon after says, "Whoever does not love me does not keep my words" (John 14:24).

But he does not say to love with words alone. There must be living works and the evidence of love, as the words "keep my words" mean. That refers to a love that fights and overcomes. For it is the nature of true love to do all things for the sake of the beloved, and there is nothing too hard for her to suffer and to bear that she would not do with joy.

If his unspeakable goodness were to go right to our hearts, nothing would be too vexing or too hard for us to suffer or to bear for his sake, that we only remain in his love. This means, then, not only hearing the Word with joy, but holding on to it firmly and winning the victory.

Sermon on John 14:23-31. WA 21:453f.

In times of suffering, Lord God, let me find comfort in the love of others
and in your steadfast love for me. Amen.

Brotherly Love

Love one another with mutual affection.
(Romans 12:10)

No feeble love is demanded here but a love that comes from the heart, so that our heart bears us witness that the sorrow of others hurts us as much as if it were our own and their prosperity cheers us as much as if it were our own, just as parents are delighted when their children do well and are very troubled when they fall or fail.

Here we learn how far we still are from fulfilling the command "You shall love your neighbor as yourself" (Leviticus 19:18), which means that we should love them so deeply that we should be entirely theirs, with body and soul, with possessions and honor. It is a great thing to love. It is far greater to love like a brother, but the greatest of all is to love as a father loves his child—an ardent and untiring love that flows from the heart.

Sermons from the year 1527.   WA 17/2:277f.

Behold, how good and pleasant it is when brothers dwell in unity!
(Psalm 133:1 RSV)

Justification

Luke 15:1-10

Take heart, son; your sins are forgiven.
(Matthew 9:2)

These words indicate that in this spiritual kingdom there is—and should be—sheer forgiveness of sins.

We must study with diligence what forgiveness of sins means. "Forgiveness of sins"—it is easily said. If only it could be won and done with words! But when it comes to the serious encounter, nothing is known of it. For it is a great thing, which I must believe and grasp with my heart, namely, that all my sins are forgiven and that through this faith I am justified before God. That is a wonderful justice and very different from the justice of the judges and of the wise and prudent people in the world. For they all say that justice is to be found within our hearts and souls as a quality brought into them. But the gospel teaches us that Christian righteousness is not a quality within our hearts or souls; instead, we should learn that we are redeemed and made just through the forgiveness of sins.

Sermon on St. Matthew's Day. EA 6:171ff.

In you alone, O God, we hope, and not in our own merit.
We rest our fears in your good Word and trust your Holy Spirit.
Your promise keeps us strong and sure; we trust the cross,
your signature, inscribed upon our temples. Amen.
(Martin Luther, 1483–1546)

We Are Justified Not in Ourselves but in Christ

He will prove the world wrong . . . about righteousness,
because I am going to the Father.
(John 16:8, 10)

This righteousness is completely concealed not only from the world but
also from the saints. It is not a thought, a word, or a work in ourselves.
No, it is entirely outside and above us; it is Christ's going to the Father,
that is, his suffering, resurrection, and ascension. Christ placed this
outside the sphere of our senses; we cannot see and feel it. The only way
it can be grasped is by faith in the Word preached about him, which
tells us that he himself is our righteousness. Thus St. Paul says, Christ
"became for us wisdom from God, and righteousness and sanctification
and redemption" (1 Corinthians 1:30), in order that before God we may
boast not of ourselves but solely of this Lord.

This is a peculiar righteousness. It is strange indeed that we are to
be called righteous or to possess a righteousness that is really nothing
whatever in us but is entirely outside us in Christ. Yet it becomes truly
ours by reason of his grace and gift, as though we ourselves had achieved
and earned it. Reason, of course, cannot comprehend this way of
speaking, that our righteousness is something that involves nothing active
or passive on our part. Yes, it is something in which I do not participate
with my thoughts, perception, and senses, in which nothing at all in me
makes me pleasing to God and saves me, but in which I leave myself and
all human thoughts and ability out of account and cling to Christ, who
sits at the right hand of God and whom I do not even see. Faith must lay
hold of this, must be founded on it, and must take comfort from it in
times of temptation.

Sermons on John 16.   LW 24:346; WA 46:44f.

No merit of my own I claim, but wholly lean on Jesus' name.
(Edward Mote, 1797–1874)

We Are Justified through Faith Alone

They are now justified by his grace as a gift,
through the redemption that is in Christ Jesus.
(Romans 3:24)

The ground must be kept firm and unshaken, that faith alone, without works, without any merit, reconciles us to God and sanctifies us, as St. Paul says, "But now, apart from the law, the righteousness of God has been disclosed" (Romans 3:21). This and other similar sayings we must firmly rely on and not be moved, for they say that forgiveness of sins and justification are granted to faith alone without works.

Consider the parable Christ gives in Matthew, "Every good tree bears good fruit, but the bad tree bears bad fruit" (Matthew 7:17). There you see that it is not the fruit that makes the tree good, but the tree must be good, or be made good, before it bears good fruit.

Thus it is undoubtedly true that we must be justified without any good works and before we can do any good works. Therefore it is certain that there must be something greater and more precious than all good works, which makes us saintly and good, before we can do what is good, just as we must be sound in body before we can do sound work. The same great and precious thing is the noble Word of God, proclaimed in the gospel, that offers us the grace of God in Christ. Whoever hears and believes it is made saintly and just. Therefore it is called a Word of life, of grace, and a Word of forgiveness. But whoever does not hear and believe it cannot be sanctified in any other way.

Sermon on Unrighteous Mammon.   WA 10/3:283f.

By grace I am an heir of heaven;
*   why doubt this, O my trembling heart?*
If what the Scriptures promise clearly
*   is true and firm in every part,*
this also must be truth divine: by grace a crown of life is mine.
(Christian L. Ludwig Scheit, 1742)

Here Begins the Joyous Exchange

The righteousness of God through faith in Jesus Christ
for all who believe . . .
(Romans 3:22)

Faith not only leads to the soul being made like the divine Word, full of grace, free, and blessed, but it unites the soul with Christ as a bride with her bridegroom. From this marriage it follows, as the apostle teaches (Ephesians 5:30), that Christ and the soul become one body. In this they have all things common, be they good or ill, so that what belongs to Christ now belongs to the believing soul, and what belongs to the soul now belongs to Christ. Since Christ possesses every good and blessedness, these now belong to the soul. Since the soul is burdened with sin and wretchedness, these now become Christ's.

Here now begins the joyful exchange. Because Christ is God and man, and because he has done no sin, and his pity is invincible, eternal, and almighty, when he, through the wedding ring, which is faith, takes upon himself the sins of the believing soul as though he had committed them, they must be swallowed up and drowned in him. For his invincible righteousness is stronger than all sin. Thus the soul is cleansed from all sin through her dowry; that is, because of her faith she is free and unhampered and endowed with the eternal righteousness of Christ, her bridegroom.

On the Freedom of a Christian.   LW 31:351; WA 7:25f.

Heavenly Father, I claim the gift of righteousness through your unbounded grace. Make me an instrument of your peace. Amen.

We Are Justified without Merit

All have sinned and fall short of the glory of God; they are now justified by his grace as a gift, through the redemption that is in Christ Jesus.
(Romans 3:23-24)

However great and heavy sin may be, God's grace is still greater. My sin and my saintliness must remain here on earth, for they concern this life and my doings here; but there, with God, I have a different treasure, where Christ is seated, covering me with his wings, and overshadowing me with his mercy.

You say, "How can that be, since I feel my sin daily, and my conscience condemns me, and holds the wrath of God before me?" Answer: You should learn that Christian justification, whatever you may think or imagine, is nothing but the forgiveness of sins, which means that it is such a kingdom or sovereignty as deals only with sins and with such overflowing grace as takes away all wrath.

It is called forgiveness of sins because we are outright sinners before God and there is nothing in us but sin, although we may possess all human righteousness. Therefore when you look at this article you have two things: first, that sin takes away all your sanctity, however devout you may be, on earth; and, second, forgiveness brings to naught all sin and wrath, so that your sin cannot cast you into hell nor can your sanctity lift you into heaven.

Therefore, before the world I will be devout and do as much as I can, but before God I will gladly be a sinner and not be called by any other name. Otherwise there would be no forgiveness or grace, but it would have to be called a crown of righteousness and of my own deserving. Apart from forgiveness there is and remains nothing but sin that condemns us.

Sermons from the year 1529.   WA 29:573f.

Not the labor of my hands can fulfill your law's demands;
could my zeal no respite know, could my tears forever flow,
all for sin could not atone; you must save and you alone.
(Augustus M. Toplady, 1776, alt.)

The Kingdom of Grace

For great is his steadfast love toward us,
and the faithfulness of the LORD endures forever.
Praise the LORD!
(Psalm 117:2)

There is a kingdom of grace that is mightier in us and over us than all wrath, sin, and evil.

You must picture this kingdom in childlike fashion, as though through the gospel God has built over us who believe in him a great new heaven, which is called the heaven of grace. It is far greater and more beautiful than the heaven [sky] you can see, and in addition it is certain, imperishable, and eternal.

Whoever lives underneath this heaven can neither sin nor abide in sin; for it is a heaven of grace, everlasting and eternal. If we stumble or sin, we do not fall out of this heaven, unless we do not wish to remain and would rather go to hell with the devil, as the unbelievers do. And though sin makes itself felt or death shows its teeth and the devil frightens you, far more grace is here to rule over our sin, and far more life is here to rule over death, and far more of God is here to rule over all the devils, so that sin, death, and the devil are nothing more in this kingdom than black clouds under the lovely sky, which hide it for a while, but are not able to cover and conceal it forever but must remain beneath it and suffer it to be above and to remain supreme. In the end they must all pass away.

All this cannot be accomplished through works but through faith alone.

Exposition of Psalm 117.   LW 14:27; WA 31/1:245

I am mortal, changeable and unsteady. Your faithfulness, O God,
is steadfast and your grace unchangeable. I thank you. Amen.

Joyful Faith

Christ redeemed us from the curse of the law by becoming a curse for us.
(Galatians 3:13)

What more could God do? How could a heart restrain itself from being happy, glad, and obedient in God and Christ? What work or suffering could there be to which it would not gladly submit, singing with love and joyful praise to God? If it fails to do so, faith has certainly broken down. The more faith there is, the more joy and freedom there is; the less faith, the less joy. This is indeed true Christian salvation and freedom from the law and from the judgment of the law, that is, from sin and death. Not that there is no law or death, but that both death and law become as if they were not. The law does not lead to sin, nor death to doom, but faith walks through them into everlasting life.

Exposition of Galatians 4:1-7.   WA 10/1(i):367f.

God's gift to his sorrowing creatures is to give them joy worthy
of their destiny. (Johann Sebastian Bach, 1685–1750)

Forgive One Another

Luke 6:36-43

Be merciful, just as your Father is merciful.
(Luke 6:36)

How does God, our heavenly Father, show his mercy? He gives us freely out of sheer goodness all that is good for body and soul, for time and eternity. If God should give us according to our merit, he could give us nothing but hellfire and eternal condemnation. Therefore, whatever good and honor he gives us, it is out of sheer mercy. God sees that we are stuck in death, and he has mercy on us and gives us life. God sees that we are children of hell, and he has mercy upon us and gives us heaven. God sees that we are poor, naked, hungry, and thirsty, and he has mercy upon us and clothes us, feeds us, gives us drink, and satisfies us with all that is good. Thus all that we have in body and spirit he gives us, out of sheer mercy, and pours out all his goodness on us. That is why Christ says here, "Be merciful, just as your Father is merciful."

The mercy of Christians must not seek its own, but must be complete and comprehensive, regarding friend and foe alike, as our Father in heaven does. For where this mercy is absent, faith also is absent.

Sermons from the year 1522.   WA 10/3:224f.

Forgive my sins, O Lord, and enable me to forgive those
who sin against me. Amen.

Sinners and Irony

The Pharisee, standing by himself, was praying thus,
"God, I thank you that I am not like other people: thieves,
rogues, adulterers, or even like this tax collector."
(Luke 18:11)

All commandments are here broken and nullified, for the Pharisee denies God and does no good to his neighbor. Thereby he has gone to ruin, for he has not fulfilled one letter of the law. For if he had said, "O God, we are all sinners; this poor sinner is also, and so am I, like all other people," he would then have fulfilled God's first commandment, namely, that he had given honor and praise to God. And if he had afterwards said, "O God, I see that this man is a sinner, and is in the jaws of the devil; help him, dear Lord," and had thus taken him on his back and carried him before God and prayed to God for him, he would also have fulfilled the other commandment, namely, that of Christian love, as St. Paul says and teaches, "Bear one another's burdens, and in this way you will fulfill the law of Christ" (Galatians 6:2).

But now he comes along praising himself that he is just, boasting most gloriously of his supposed good works, of how he fasts and gives a tenth of all that he has. After that he is so full of hatred toward his neighbor that, if God would let him be judge, he would thrust the poor tax collector into the deepest depth of hell. Is not that an evil heart and dreadful to hear about, that I should wish all people to be doomed while I alone should be praised?

This has been set before us that we should be on our guard against it.

Sermons from the year 1522.   WA 10/3:301f.

Save me, Lord God, from a self-righteous attitude toward others.
Give me a heart of compassion. Amen.

Let All Things Be a Cloak to Cover Sinners

Love covers a multitude of sins.
(1 Peter 4:8)

Learn here to seek your neighbors as lost sheep, to cover their shame with your honor, and to let your sanctity be a cover for their sins. But now when people come together, they hack one another to pieces to prove how fiercely they fight against sin. Therefore you men, whenever you come together, do not hack the people to pieces. And likewise you women, when you come together, cover the shame of others and do not make wounds that you cannot heal. If you come across two people in a chamber, throw your cloak over both and close the door. Why? Because you would that it should so be done to you.

That is what Christ does. He too keeps silent and covers our sin. He too could bring shame upon us, and tread us under his feet, but he does not do so. You must do the same. A virgin must place her crown on a harlot; a saintly wife must give her veil to an adulteress, and all that we have we must make into a cloak to cover sinners. For each person will have his lost sheep to recover, and each woman her piece of silver; and all that is ours must also belong to another.

Sermons from the year 1522.   WA 10/3:220f.

O divine Master, grant that I may not so much seek to be consoled, as to console; to be understood, as to understand; to be loved, as to love. Amen.
(Francis of Assisi, 1181–1226)

How to Forgive Each Other's Sins

For if you forgive others their trespasses,
your heavenly Father will also forgive you.
(Matthew 6:14)

How would you like to have God deal with you as you deal with your neighbor, as this petition says? How would you like it if God would retain your sins and spread them abroad into all the world? Or how would you take it if another person were to broadcast all your evils? You would certainly want everyone to keep quiet about them, forgive them, cover them up, and pray for you. As it is, you are flying in the face of nature and its law that says, "In everything do to others as you would have them do to you" (Matthew 7:12). Do not ever suppose that either the slightest or the gravest sins of a backbiter, slanderer, or malicious judge are forgiven until he performs the one good work of bridling and changing his evil tongue.

If you really want to do something about your neighbor's sin, however, then observe the noble and precious golden rule of Christ. He says, "If another member of the church sins against you, go and point out the fault when the two of you are alone" (Matthew 18:15). You are not to tell other people about it but to keep it between the two of you.

Oh, if we would only busy ourselves with this noble work, how easily we could atone for our sins, even in the absence of much else! Even if we sin again, God will say, "This one has covered up and forgiven his neighbor's guilt. Gather around, all you creatures, and in turn cover up his sin. This one's sin shall not be remembered forever."

Exposition of the Lord's Prayer.   LW 42:68; WA 2:120

Help me, Lord God, to act toward others
as you have dealt with me. Amen.

Forgive without Limit

*Then Peter came and said to him, "Lord, if another member
of the church sins against me, how often should I forgive him?
As many as seven times?"*
(Matthew 18:21)

God's kingdom, the forgiveness of sins, has no limit, as the text of the
Gospel so beautifully shows when Peter asked his question of the Lord.
Jesus answered with the parable in which he earnestly exhorts us, in fear
of the loss of God's grace, to forgive our neighbor's trespasses, without
any reluctance, because God forgives us such endless sin and guilt. The
debt that we owe God is a million dollars, which means that it is infinite.
It is so great we could not pay it with all our possessions and with all our
powers, for we cannot blot out even the smallest sin. And since God in
his kingdom forgives us so much out of sheer grace, we ought also to
forgive our neighbor a little.

Christ speaks as follows: "In my heavenly kingdom, where there
really is nothing but forgiveness of sins, that is, the Christian church, I
will forgive all those who pardon another's sin." And again, "To the one
who will not show mercy to a neighbor, I will also show no mercy. I am
like a lord and king with regard to you all, but you are like fellow servants
among one another."

Sermons from the year 1524.   WA 15:730f.

*I know, O Lord, that love covers a multitude of sins. Give me grace
to treat others with kindness and understanding. Amen.*

Love without Reward

For if you love those who love you, what reward do you have?
Do not even the tax collectors do the same?
(Matthew 5:46)

Christians should have good and helpful hearts and prove their goodness even to an evildoer. To be helpful to the good and to your friends is easy, for even murderers can render service to their friends, and the nonbelievers can be good, kind, and helpful as long as they feel sure that the help will be returned. But when they receive no help in return, their goodness and love dry up. And then it is plain to be seen that there is no well nor living fountain of love, but only water poured into the sand, which is a pagan kind of helpfulness. But if I do a good deed to someone and that person repays me with evil and I say, "Go on; my heart will not grow weary of doing good. I will not wish you evil or encourage you to do evil. I shall rebuke you, but if you do not heed, go on. If the mayor and judge do not punish you, you will find one in heaven who will punish you. He has still so many devils, so many rogues on earth, so much water, fire, logs, stones, plagues, and pestilence, that he can fully punish you. And since I know that your sin will not remain unpunished, I will keep a generous and charitable heart, which is ready at all times to give counsel." That is called a Christian heart and Christian love, which the nonbelievers do not have.

Christians should have wells that cannot dry up or be exhausted, even if their generosity is poured out like water into sand.

Sermon on the Fourth Sunday after Trinity, 1533.   WA 37:101

Give me strength, Lord God, not to become weary with well-doing.
Amen.

Be Christlike in All Your Doings

*As God's chosen ones, holy and beloved, clothe yourselves with compassion,
kindness, humility, meekness, and patience.
(Colossians 3:12)*

It is not enough to be charitable and forgiving toward your neighbor
with countenance, gestures, mouth, or tongue. It must be from the heart,
or God will not forgive you, and you will be cast out of his kingdom of
grace. Again, if we feel God's mercy toward us, we should gladly forgive
our brothers and sisters who have offended us. Our merciful Father
forgives us our sin in order that we also should forgive others and show
mercy to them, as he is merciful to us and forgives sin, death, guilt, and
pain. If we do thus, we are in the kingdom of God. For the goodness of
God lives in our hearts, making us loving and good. Christ is seated at
the right hand of the Father, but he rules nonetheless in the hearts and
consciences of all the faithful, so that they both love him and fear him,
live in awe of him and obediently follow him as a loyal people follows
its king. And in all their character and conduct they become like him, as
he says, "Be perfect, even as your heavenly Father is perfect" (Matthew
5:48). God is perfect in that he suffers our evil, wretchedness, sin, and
imperfection, and forgives us, so that we should likewise forgive our
brothers and sisters.

Sermons from the year 1524.   WA 15:733

*Heavenly Father, help me to see each person
as the brother or sister for whom Christ died. Amen.*

Sanctification Is the Work of God

1 Peter 3:8-15

As he who has called you is holy, be holy yourselves in all your conduct;
for it is written, "You shall be holy, for I am holy."
(1 Peter 1:15-16)

"Because I am your Lord and God and you are my people, you must be like me." For a true lord brings it about that his people are like him, walk in obedience, and are guided by his will. Now just as God our Lord is holy, so God's people are also holy. Therefore we are all holy if we walk in faith. Scripture does not say much about the deceased saints; it speaks about those who are living on earth. Thus the prophet David describes himself in Psalm 86:2, "Preserve my life, for I am holy" [Luther's reading].

For the one who is a Christian enters with the Lord Christ into a sharing of all his goods. Now since Christ is holy, he too must be holy, or he must deny that Christ is holy. If you have been baptized, you have put on the holy garment, which is Christ, as Paul says (Galatians 3:27). The little word "holy" designates that which is God's own and that you belong to him, which means you are "consecrated." Thus Peter says, "You have now consecrated yourselves to God as his own. Therefore see to it that you do not let yourselves be led again into the worldly lusts. But let God alone reign, live, and work in you. Then you are holy, just as he is holy."

Sermons on 1 Peter, 1523.   LW 30:32; WA 12:287

As God's chosen ones, holy and beloved, clothe yourselves with compassion,
kindness, humility, meekness, and patience. (Colossians 3:12)

Sanctified in Christ

But you were washed, you were sanctified, you were justified
in the name of the Lord Jesus and in the Spirit of our God.
(1 Corinthians 6:11)

We honor Christ and not ourselves when we praise this working of sanctification, which we receive because we enter into his suffering and holiness.

That I recognize myself as a sinner is right, with respect to my own person, but since through faith in Christ I am no longer a child of Adam but a child of God, I am truly holy. There is a fine distinction: inasmuch as I am a human being and a child of Adam, I belong to hell. If I had on my side all kinds of self-appointed piety, austerity, fervent devotion, and good works, and wished to rely on them, I should be damned and lost.

But if you believe that through Christ, who died for your sin and is risen for your salvation, you have become a joint heir with Christ and a child of God, and have been baptized in that faith, you can say, "Now I am no longer Adam's child, no longer a sinner, so long as I belong to this brotherhood." If you can be bold and audacious about it, do so. I am still studying the matter, for it is no easy thing that a sinner should say, "I have a chair in heaven next to St. Peter." And yet we must praise this sanctity and glory in it. Thus alone is the golden brotherhood.

Sermons from the year 1530.   WA 32:92f.

Lord God, let your Word be a light to my path in this world,
that I might show the fruits of your grace in all that I do. Amen.

Sanctified by God

*We must always give thanks to God for you, brothers and sisters beloved
of the Lord, because God chose you as the first fruits for salvation through
sanctification by the Spirit and through belief in the truth.*
(2 Thessalonians 2:13)

Therefore we ought to regard as holy, along with Christ, those who keep his Word and earnestly witness to it, especially when they are suffering persecution or temptation, even if they are poor and feeble, having no appearance of special sanctity. For we can never perceive it written on a person's forehead whether he or she is holy and just. But this we can see: where the Word brings forth fruit, so that people have to suffer for it, these, we know, must be living saints.

Then the false humility of our hypocrites speaks: God forbid that anyone should be so presumptuous as to allow oneself to be called a saint! Are we not all sinners? Answer: All such thoughts spring from the old illusion that when sanctity is mentioned, people think of mighty deeds and look to the saints in heaven, as if they themselves had won and merited their position. But we say that the true saints of Christ must be good strong sinners and remain such saints as are not ashamed to pray the Lord's Prayer, "Hallowed be your name; your kingdom come; forgive us our debts," and so forth, for we confess that the name of God is not sanctified in us as it should be, nor has his kingdom come, nor is his will being done. They are called holy not because they are without sin or sanctified through works. On the contrary, they are sinners in themselves and are condemned with all their works, but are made saints with a sanctity that is not their own, but Christ the Lord's, which is given to them through faith and becomes their own.

Sermons on John 16–20.   WA 28:175ff.

*"By their fruits you will know them," you have said, O Lord.
Nourish me in the life of faith. Amen.*

Sanctified through Faith

. . . that they may receive forgiveness of sins and a place
among those who are sanctified by faith in me.
(Acts 26:18)

God has made provision that we should become holy in a spiritual way. It is a spiritual word, that in our innermost spirit we are made holy before God. He spoke this word in order to make it evident that there is no holiness except that which God works in us. Hence the gospel calls us holy even while we are still here on earth, if we have faith.

You must be holy, and yet you must not bear yourself as though you thought you were holy of yourself or by your own merit, but because you have God's word that heaven is yours, that you are devout, and that through Christ you have become holy. This you must confess if you wish to be a Christian. For we could show no greater disdain and blasphemy toward the name of Christ than by denying his blood the honor that it washes us clean of sin and makes us holy. Therefore you must believe and confess that you are holy through this blood and not through your own devotion. Thus you leave your life and possessions above with Christ and await and accept whatever may happen to you.

Sermons on 1 Peter, 1523.   LW 30:7; WA 12:262f.

Oh, for a closer walk with God, a calm and heavenly frame;
a light to shine upon the road that leads me to the lamb!
(William Cowper, 1778)

Curved In on Ourselves

*Not that I have already obtained this or have already
reached the goal; but I press on to make it my own,
because Christ Jesus has made me his own.
(Philippians 3:12)*

In *particular cases* human nature knows and wills what is good but in *general* neither knows nor wills it. The reason is that it knows nothing but its own good, or what is good and honorable and useful for itself, but not what is good for God and other people. Therefore it knows and wills more what is particular, yes, only what is an individual good. And this is in agreement with Scripture, which describes us as so turned in on ourselves that we use not only physical but even spiritual goods for our own purposes and in all things seek only ourselves.

This "curvedness" is now natural for us, a natural wickedness and a natural sinfulness. Thus we have no help from our natural powers but need the aid of some power outside of ourselves. This is love, without which we always sin against the law "You shall not covet," that is, turn nothing in on yourself and seek nothing for yourself, but live, do, and think all things for God alone. For then we will know the good in every way along with all particular good things, and we will judge all things. Thus the law is impossible for us.

Lectures on Romans.   LW 25:345

*Each day, O God, I present myself to you as a frail human;
forgive my errors through your steadfast grace. Amen.*

In God's Workshop

Every branch that bears fruit he prunes.
(John 15:2)

It is always the case that we understand our own work before it is done, but we do not understand the work of God until it has been done. "In the latter days you will understand it clearly" (Jeremiah 23:20), which is to say that in the beginning or at first we understand our own counsel, but in the end we understand God's. "So that when it does occur, you may believe" (John 14:29). Just as in the case of an artist who comes upon some material that is suitable and apt for making into a work of art, the suitableness of the material is in a certain sense an unfelt prayer for the form that the artist understands and heeds as he gets ready to make what this material calls for through its suitability, so God comes upon our feeling and thinking, seeing what it is praying for, what it is suitable for, and what it desires. Then, heeding the request, he begins to mold the form that suits his art and counsel. Then of necessity the form and the model of our thinking are destroyed.

Lectures on Romans. LW 25:367

Mold me, O God, into the person you intend me to be. Amen.

Faith in Sanctification

*It is that very Spirit bearing witness
with our spirit that we are children of God.*
(Romans 8:16)

Those who with firm faith and hope are confident that they are children of God *are* children of God, for no one can have such a confidence except through the Holy Spirit.

If you believe that your sin can only be canceled by God, that is good. But now believe this as well, that through Christ your sins have really been forgiven. That is the witness that the Holy Spirit gives to your heart: your sins are forgiven. Thus we are justified through faith. That is the apostle's meaning (you must firmly believe for yourself, and not only with regard to the elect, that Christ died for your sins also and has atoned for them).

It is the same in regard to merits. If you believe that you cannot have them except through him, it is not yet enough until the Spirit of truth has produced the testimony that you have these merits through him. This happens when you believe that the works that you do are acceptable and pleasing to God, whatever they may finally turn out to be. But you can have the confidence that they are pleasing to him when you realize that through these works you are nothing in his sight, even though they are good and are done out of obedience and even though you do no evil works. It is this humility and restraint regarding good works that makes them pleasing to God.

Thus also concerning eternal life it is not enough to believe that he gives it to you freely, but it is also necessary to have the testimony of the Spirit that you will come to eternal life by God's favor.

Lectures on Romans.   LW 25:359

*Come down, O love divine, seek out this soul of mine
and visit it with your own ardor glowing.
O Comforter, draw near, within my heart appear,
and kindle it, your holy flame bestowing.*
(Bianco de Siena, d. 1434)

The Meaning of Baptism

Romans 6:3-11

For if we have been united with him in a death like his, we will certainly be united with him in a resurrection like his. We know that our old self was crucified with him so that the body of sin might be destroyed, and we might no longer be enslaved to sin.
(Romans 6:5-6)

This is a true apostolic saying. What he had referred to as being baptized into Christ's death and buried with him in baptism (Romans 6:3-4), he here describes as being "united with him in a resurrection like his." Thus he binds and knits together Christ's death and resurrection and our baptism, in order that baptism should not be thought of as a mere sign, but that the power of both Christ's death and resurrection is contained in it. For our sin is slain through his death—taken away, in order that it may no longer live in us but die and be dead forever.

Being immersed in the water in baptism indicates that we too die in Christ, but emerging again from the water means and imparts to us new life in him, just as he did not remain in death but rose again. But such a life should not and cannot be a life in sin, because sin has already been slain in us and we have died to sin; it must be a new life of righteousness and holiness. Thus we are now said to be "united with him" and, as it were, baked into one loaf, and we receive into ourselves the power of both his death and his resurrection, and also the fruit or consequence of it is found in us, since we have been baptized in him.

Sermon on the Sixth Sunday after Trinity, 1535.   WA 22:96f.

Lord God, I bless your name for giving me new life by union with Christ in baptism. Amen.

Baptized into Christ's Death

*Do you not know that all of us who have been baptized
into Jesus Christ were baptized into his death?
(Romans 6:3)*

The significance of baptism is a blessed dying unto sin and a resurrection in the grace of God, so that the old self, conceived and born in sin, is there drowned, and a new self, born in grace, comes forth and rises. Therefore sins are drowned in baptism and, in place of sin, righteousness comes forth.

The meaning of such dying and drowning of sin is not perfectly evident in this life, not until the body dies and crumbles to death. The sacrament or sign of baptism is soon performed, as we see. But the meaning of it, the spiritual baptism and drowning of sin, is continued all through our earthly life and cannot be fully achieved while we are alive on earth. Only at the hour of our death is it completed. Then the person is truly sunk into baptism, and the meaning of it is fulfilled. Therefore this whole life is nothing but an increasing baptism unto death—and whoever is baptized is condemned to death.

Therefore the life of Christians, from baptism up to the grave, is nothing but the commencement of a blessed dying, for at the last day God will make them new and different.

The Holy and Blessed Sacrament of Baptism, 1519.   LW 35:30; WA 2:727f.

*All who believe and are baptized shall see the Lord's salvation;
baptized into the death of Christ, they are a new creation.
(Thomas H. Kingo, 1634–1703)*

The Nature of the Children of God

. . . baptizing them in the name of the Father
and of the Son and of the Holy Spirit.
(Matthew 28:19)

We call a child devout who is born of upright parents, who obeys
and is like them in every respect. Such a child rightfully possesses and
inherits property and the full name of the parents. Thus we Christians,
through our rebirth in baptism, became children of God. If we pattern
ourselves after our Father and all his ways, all his goods and names
are likewise our inheritance forever. Now our Father is and is called
merciful and good, as Christ says, "Be merciful, just as your Father is
merciful" (Luke 6:35). He also says, "Learn from me; for I am gentle
and humble in heart" (Matthew 11:29). God is, furthermore, just, pure,
truthful, strong, guileless, wise, and so on. All these are names of God
and are comprehended in the words "your name" in the Lord's Prayer,
for the names of all virtues are also names given to God. And since
we are baptized into these names and are consecrated and hallowed
by them, and since they have thus become our names, it follows that
God's children should be called and also be gentle, merciful, chaste, just,
truthful, guileless, friendly, peaceful, and kindly disposed toward all, even
toward our enemies. For the name of God, in which we were baptized,
works all this in us.

Exposition of the Lord's Prayer, 1519.   LW 42:28; WA 2:87f.

Save me, O God, by your name, and vindicate me by your might.
Hear my prayer, O God; give ear to the words of my mouth. Amen.
(Psalm 54:1-2)

The Meaning of the Sacrament of Baptism

*So you also must consider yourselves dead to sin
and alive to God in Jesus Christ.
(Romans 6:11)*

Baptized persons are sacramentally altogether pure and guiltless. This means nothing else than that they have the sign of God. That is to say, they have the baptism by which it is shown that their sins are all to be dead, and that they too are to die in grace and at the last day to rise again to everlasting life, pure, sinless, and guiltless. With respect to the sacrament, then, it is true that they are without sin and guilt. Yet because all is not yet completed and they still live in sinful flesh, they are not without sin, even though they have begun to grow into purity and innocence.

You ask, "How does baptism help me, if it does not altogether blot out and remove sin?" First, you give yourself up to the sacrament of baptism and to what it signifies. That is, you desire to die, together with your sins, and to be made new at the last day. God accepts this desire at your hands and grants you baptism. From that hour God begins to make you a new person. God pours into you his grace and the Holy Spirit, who begins to overcome nature and sin and to prepare you for death and resurrection.

Second, you pledge yourself to continue in this desire and to destroy your sin more and more as long as you live, even until your dying day. This too God accepts. God trains and tests you all your life, with many good works and with all kinds of sufferings. Thereby God accomplishes in baptism what you have desired, namely, that you may become free from sin, die, and rise again at the last day, and so fulfill your baptism.

The Holy and Blessed Sacrament of Baptism, 1519.   LW 35:34; WA 2:730

*Remind me each day, Lord God,
that I am baptized and that I am yours. Amen.*

Our Baptism Is Our Comfort in Sin

He saved us . . . according to his mercy,
through the water of rebirth and renewal by the Holy Spirit.
(Titus 3:5)

If any fall into sin, they should all the more remember their baptism, how God has here made a covenant with them to forgive all their sins, if only they will fight against them even until death. On this truth, on this alliance with God, we must joyfully dare to rely. Then baptism again goes into force and operation. Then our hearts again become peaceful and glad, not in our own works or "satisfaction," but in the mercy of God promised to us in baptism, a mercy that God will keep forever. This faith we must hold so firmly that we would cling to it even though all creatures and all sins attacked us. For any who let themselves be forced away from this faith make God a liar in the promise in the sacrament of baptism.

The Holy and Blessed Sacrament of Baptism, 1519.   LW 35:37; WA 2:733

With one accord, O God, we pray, grant us your Holy Spirit.
Consider our infirmity through Jesus' blood and merit.
Grant us to grow in grace each day by holy baptism
*   that we may eternal life inherit. Amen.*
(Thomas H. Kingo, 1634–1703)

The Water and the Blood

This is the one who came by water and blood, Jesus Christ,
not with the water only but with the water and the blood.
(1 John 5:6)

Thus the apostle always mingles blood with baptism in order that the red and innocent blood of Christ may be seen in it. To human eyes there appears to be nothing but pure, colorless water. That is true, but St. John wishes to open for us the inward and spiritual eyes of faith, that we may perceive not water only but also the blood of our Lord Jesus Christ.

Why? Because Holy Baptism was won for us through that blood he shed for us when he paid for our sin. This blood and the merit and power of it he has attached to baptism, that we should receive it in this way. For if we receive baptism in faith, that is like being openly washed with the blood of Christ and being made clean from sin. For we do not attain to forgiveness of sin through our own works, but through the dying of the Son of God and through the shedding of his blood. Such forgiveness is contained in the holy sacrament of baptism.

Sermons from the year 1540.   WA 49:13

May the death of Jesus, O God, I pray, point to the end of bloodshed on the face of the earth. Make me also an instrument of your peace. Amen.

Saints

As he who called you is holy, be holy yourselves in all your conduct.
(1 Peter 1:15)

I will not call myself holy for what I have done nor be called holy by anyone else or praised for my sanctity. Nor will I boast of holiness. I am holy because I can declare with unswerving faith and with an undaunted conscience, "Even though I am a poor sinner, still Christ is holy with his baptism, Word, sacrament, and Holy Spirit." This is the only genuine holiness given to us by God.

You ask, "But how do I attain this? And what does the Holy Spirit have to do with me?" Answer: "He baptized me; he proclaimed the gospel of Christ to me; and he awakened my heart to believe. Baptism is not of my making; nor is the gospel; nor is faith. He gave these to me. For the fingers that baptized me are not those of a human being; they are the fingers of the Holy Spirit. And the preacher's mouth and the words that I heard are not his; they are the words and message of the Holy Spirit. By these outward means he works faith within me and thus he makes me holy." Therefore just as we should not deny that we are baptized and are Christians, so we should not deny or doubt that we are holy.

Sermons on John 14–15.   LW 24:170; WA 45:616f.

I know, Lord God, that I have no claim on your justice and no holiness of my own. Grant me grace each day of my life. Amen.

Sanctification: The Response of the Justified Sinner

Romans 6:19-23

*But now that you have been freed from sin and enslaved to God,
the advantage you get is sanctification. The end is eternal life.
(Romans 6:22)*

St. Paul says, "Do you not know that if you present yourselves to anyone as obedient slaves, you are slaves of the one whom you obey, either of sin, which leads to death, or of obedience, which leads to righteousness?" (Romans 6:16). This means that as you now through grace have received the forgiveness of sins and are now just, you are bound to obey God and live according to his will. For you must be in the service of one master, either of sin, which brings you into death and the wrath of God, if you remain in it, or of God in grace, to serve him in newness of life. Therefore you must no longer be obedient to sin, for you are now released from its power and dominion.

Sin will not be able to rule over you, for you are no longer under the law but under grace. That is, you can now resist sin because you are now in Christ and have received the power of his resurrection.

Sermon on the Seventh Sunday after Trinity, 1534.   WA 22:106f.

*In my finitude and weakness, O God,
allow me a glimpse of what I can be. Amen.*

Sanctify the Lord in Your Hearts

Sanctify the Lord God in your hearts.
(1 Peter 3:15, Luther's reading)

What does St. Peter mean when he says that we should sanctify God? How can we sanctify him? Must he not sanctify us? Answer: In the Lord's Prayer we also say, "Hallowed be your name," that we should hallow his name, even though God himself hallows his name. Therefore this is the procedure: You must sanctify him in your hearts, says St. Peter. That is, when our Lord God sends us something—whether good or bad, whether it benefits or hurts, whether it is shame, honor, good fortune, or misfortune—I should consider this not only good but also holy, and I should say, "This is pure, precious holiness, and I am not worthy of being touched by it." Thus the prophet says in Psalm 145:17, "The LORD is just in all his ways, and kind in all his doings." When in such matters I give praise to God and regard such works as good, holy, and precious, I sanctify God in my heart.

Sermons on 1 Peter, 1523.   LW 30:103; WA 12:358

Bless the LORD, O my soul,
and all that is within me,
bless his holy name. Amen.
(Psalm 103:1)

TUESDAY

Before God We Are Sinners

In my vain life I have seen everything; there are righteous people
who perish in their righteousness.
(Ecclesiastes 7:15)

It is not enough to confess with the mouth that we are sinners. What
is easier than that, especially when you are at peace and live without
temptation? But when you have confessed with your mouth that you
are such a person, then you must also earnestly feel the same way about
yourself in your heart, and you must conduct yourself in this manner in
every act and in your entire life. For there are only a few who confess and
believe that they are sinners. How can we confess that we are sinners if we
are unwilling to endure even a word of criticism against ourselves or our
actions or ideas but immediately rush into the controversy and do not
even confess with the mouth that we are liars but rather contend that we
are truthful and well intentioned and that we have been wickedly resisted
and falsely accused? But if we are compelled to endure something, we
become furious and wear everyone out by complaining of the injury that
we alone of all people have suffered. Look at the hypocrite who confesses
that he is a sinner but is willing to do and to suffer nothing that befits a
sinner but only that which is proper for a righteous person and a saint.

But in which way must we spiritually become sinners? It is not
possible in a natural way, for in that way we cannot *become* sinners,
because we are such already. All the force necessary to bring about this
change lies hidden in our mind, our self-estimation and our opinion of
ourselves. Every statement in Scripture and every action of God has the
purpose of bringing about this change.

Lectures on Romans. LW 25:216–17

If you, O LORD, should mark iniquities, Lord, who could stand?
But there is forgiveness with you, so that you may be revered. Amen.
(Psalm 130:3-4)

Our Works Are the Seal of Our Faith

We are what he has made us, created in Christ Jesus for good works,
which God prepared beforehand to be our way of life.
(Ephesians 2:10)

We must receive before we can give out. Before we can do works of mercy, we must first receive mercy from God. We do not lay the first stone, nor does the sheep seek the shepherd, but the shepherd the sheep. Therefore with regard to works, remember that they merit nothing before God, but without merit, we receive everything that we have from God.

After that, we may regard works as a sure sign, like a seal on a letter, assuring me that my faith is right. The reason is that if I feel in my heart that the work flows from love, I am sure that my faith is right. If I forgive my brother or sister, such forgiving makes me certain that my faith is right and confirms me, and gives me proof of my belief that God has forgiven me and continues to forgive me day after day; but if I do not forgive, I must certainly conclude that I lack faith.

Sermon on the Fourth Sunday after Trinity, 1526.   WA 10/1(ii):317f.

As you, O God, have dealt with me in mercy and steadfast love,
so give me strength to deal in grace and mercy with others. Amen.

How to Fast

Make no provision for the flesh, to gratify its desires.
(Romans 13:14)
(Luther's reading: Make provision for the flesh,
yet so as not to fulfill its desires.)

There is nothing in us more dangerous than our reason and will. It is the first and highest work of God in us and the best discipline to lay aside our works and to let go of our reason and will, committing ourselves to God in all things, especially when they are running spiritually and smoothly.

The discipline of the flesh follows, to mortify its coarse and evil desires and win peace and rest. Such desires we must overcome with fasting and watching and work. Thus we learn why and how much we should fast, watch, and work. There are unfortunately many blind people who esteem their discipline, such as fasting, watching, or working, in themselves as good works and practice them in order to win great merit. Such fasting is not fasting at all, but a mockery of fasting and of God.

Therefore I leave it to everyone to choose the days, the food, and the amount of fasting, but we must not stop there, but keep watch over our flesh. Inasmuch as we find it lascivious and wanton, we should discipline it with fasting, watching, and working—but no more.

Sermon on Good Works, 1520.   WA 9:270f.

O Lord God, in our world of conspicuous consumption and vulgarity,
let me learn self-discipline, giving thanks for my great blessings. Amen.

Joy and the Cross

The joy of the LORD is your strength.
(Nehemiah 8:10)

See how daring and bold the prophet is! Who gave him such a stout and defiant courage? From where did he receive it? From the Savior alone. The more people would drive us away from him, the firmer we cling to him. The more sorrow, misery, and harm people do us, the more we rejoice, for our joy is eternal. And the more people want to drag us away from it, the greater it becomes.

But someone may ask, Can ever a soul lose such joy? Yes, and as soon as we lose it we are surrounded by everlasting pain, from which, though it is in itself eternal, God saves his people. Hence the joy also is eternal, though we may lose it while we are here on earth. This should be understood as follows: Christ is my Savior. If I know and believe it, it is an eternal joy to me, so long as I build on it. When, however, the heart and conscience are devoid of Christ, the joy has ceased. Grace continues, but the conscience can stumble and fall. This I say that you may not be offended if many of your number fall away from the gospel and deny Christ. For where Christ is with his comfort and joy, the cross and persecution are not far away.

But I fear that we have neither the cross nor the joy because we receive so little of the gospel. We remain forever in our old nature and despise the dear and precious treasure of the gospel.

Sermon on the First Sunday in Advent, 1524.   EA 17:113

When suffering comes into my life, merciful God,
let me be assured of your steadfast love. Amen.

Put to Death the Deeds of the Body

If by the Spirit you put to death the deeds of the body, you will live.
(Romans 8:13)

Putting sin to death through the Spirit happens when we recognize our weakness and sin, feel that sinful desires are stirring in us, remember the Word of God and the forgiveness of sins through faith, strengthen ourselves, and resist our lusts and do not submit to them so that they cannot proceed to actions.

This makes the difference between those who are Christians and are holy, and the others who are without faith and the Spirit, or have ceased to care and have lost them. For although the faithful still suffer from sinful desires of the flesh as the others do, yet they continue in repentance and in the fear of God and keep their faith, so that their sins are forgiven for Christ's sake, because they resist and do not give way to sin. Therefore they continue in forgiveness, and their weakness is not unto death and condemnation as with the others, who without repentance and faith continue willfully in their lusts, contrary to their conscience, and thus thrust away both faith and the Holy Spirit.

Sermon on the Eighth Sunday after Trinity, 1535.   WA 22:134f.

When my shortcomings overwhelm me, Lord God, show me the way once again to joy and gladness. Amen.

The Christian Hope

Romans 8:12-17

We wait for the blessed hope and the manifestation
of the glory of our great God and Savior, Jesus Christ.
(Titus 2:13)

Through the gospel we have been given a treasure that is not goods and gold, power and honor, joy and happiness of this world, and not even life on this earth, but it is hope—a living and blessed hope that will awaken us to life and blessedness in body and soul, perfectly and eternally. To this treasure the gospel calls us, and in this treasure we are baptized. Therefore let us live this earthly life bearing in mind that we shall leave it behind, and let us stretch out after that blessed hope as "toward the goal for the prize of the heavenly call of God in Jesus Christ" (Philippians 3:14) and seek it and await it at all times.

But how long shall we wait for that blessed hope? Will it remain but a hope forever, and will it never be fulfilled? No, he says, our blessed hope will not always remain a hope, but it will eventually be made manifest so that we shall no longer only hope and wait for it. Instead, what we now believe and hope for will then be made manifest in us and we shall possess with full certainty what we now await. But meanwhile we must wait for that blessed hope until it is revealed.

Sermons from the year 1531.   WA 34/2:117

And now, O LORD, what do I wait for? My hope is in you. Amen.
(Psalm 39:7)

The Living Hope

He has give us new birth . . . into an inheritance that is imperishable,
undefiled, and unfading, kept in heaven for you.
(1 Peter 1:3-4)

While we live on earth we must live in hope. For although we know that through faith we possess all the riches of God (for faith certainly brings with it the new birth and inheritance), we do not yet see them. Therefore they still stand in hope, and are laid aside a little while, so that we cannot see them with our eyes. This he calls the hope of life.

St. Peter declares that we await the precious inheritance in the hope into which we have entered through faith. For this is the sequence: out of the Word comes faith, out of faith the new birth, and out of the new birth we enter into hope, so that we are sure of the heavenly good and await it with certainty.

If you are a Christian waiting for your inheritance or salvation, you must keep to this alone and must despise everything that is on earth and must confess that all earthly reason, wisdom, and holiness are nothing. The world will not be able to bear this. Therefore you must consider that you will be condemned and persecuted. And therefore St. Peter gathers faith, hope, and the holy cross into one unity; for the one follows from the other.

Sermons on 1 Peter, 1523.   LW 30:16; WA 12:267ff.

In this world, Lord God, I walk by faith and not by sight.
Give me a solid hope for the life to come. Amen.

The Nature of Hope

In hope we were saved. Now hope that is seen is not hope.
For who hopes for what is seen?
(Romans 8:24)

Although grammatically this statement may be figurative, yet theologically it is most direct and affirmative because of the expression of a very intense emotion. Hope that comes from a desire for something we love always increases the love by delay. Thus it happens that the thing hoped for and the person hoping become one through the tenseness of the hoping. Thus love transforms the lover into the beloved. Hope changes the one who hopes into what is hoped for, but what is hoped for does not appear. Therefore hope transfers us into the unknown, the hidden, and the dark shadows, so that we do not even know what we hope for, and yet we know what we do not hope for. Thus the soul has become hope and at the same time the thing hoped for, because it resides in that which it does not see, that is, in hope. If this hope were seen, that is, if the one who hopes and the thing hoped for mutually recognized each other, then we would no longer be transferred into the thing hoped for, that is, into hope and the unknown, but we would be carried away to things seen, and we would enjoy the known.

Lectures on Romans.   LW 25:364

O God, our help in ages past, our hope for years to come,
still be our guard while troubles last, and our eternal home. Amen.
(Isaac Watts, 1674–1748)

A Christian Is in the Process of Becoming

Who forgives all your iniquity,
who heals all your diseases.
(Psalm 103:3)

You must understand that Christians are divided into two parts: the inner being, which is faith, and the outer being, which is the flesh. Now when one looks at Christians according to faith, they are pure and completely clean; for the Word of God finds no uncleanness in them. When it enters the heart so that the heart clings to it, it must also make the heart completely clean. Therefore all things are perfect in faith. Accordingly, we are kings and priests and God's people. But since faith is now operative while we are in the flesh and still dwelling on earth, we sometimes feel evil inclinations, such as impatience, fear of death, and so on. All these are still weaknesses of the old self, for faith has not yet completely permeated him and still does not have full power over the flesh.

You can understand this from a parable in Luke 10:34ff. concerning the man who went down from Jerusalem to Jericho and fell among the murderers, who beat him and left him half dead. Later the Samaritan attended to him, bound up his wounds, looked after him, and had him cared for. Here you see that since this man is now being cared for, he is no longer mortally ill but is now sure to live. Only one thing is lacking: he is not completely well. Life is there, but he does not yet have perfect health but is still in the care of the physicians. He must continue to be cared for. Thus we also have the Lord Christ completely and are certain of eternal life. Nevertheless, we do not yet enjoy perfect health. Something of the old self still remains in the flesh.

Sermons on 1 Peter, 1523.   LW 30:68; WA 12:322f.

Merciful God, you are the source of all life and all goodness and all healing. Create in me health of body and of mind. Amen.

Growth

Grow in the knowledge of God . . . be made strong
with all the strength that comes from his glorious power.
(Colossians 1:10, 11)

We must earnestly and diligently study the Word of God and pray not simply that we may learn to know the will of God but that we may be filled with it and always walk in his way and continue in it, and so seek strength and comfort.

For it is the nature of the riches of this knowledge that whoever has it has never enough and never tires of it; rather the more and the longer we drink of it, the more are our hearts filled with joy and the more we thirst for it, as the Scriptures say, "Those who drink of me will thirst for more" (Sirach 24:21). As St. Peter says, the dear angels in heaven also never tire of it but have everlasting joy in it and desire to look into what is revealed and preached to us (1 Peter 1:12).

Therefore, unless we too hunger and thirst (as we ought to do much more than the angels) to know and to understand God's will more perfectly until we also attain to an everlasting vision in the life hereafter, there is nothing more of it in us than a mere froth that can neither quench our thirst nor satisfy us and can neither comfort us nor make us better.

Sermon on the Twenty-fourth Sunday after Trinity, 1536.   WA 22:378f.

As Jesus grew in wisdom and in favor with all, so, Lord God,
let me grow and become mature. Amen.

We Wait for New Heavens and a New Earth

In accordance with his promise,
we wait for new heavens and a new earth.
(2 Peter 3:13)

Because we are to be new persons, God wills that we shall have new and different thoughts, minds, and understanding, not judging things as they appear to reason and to the world, but as they are before his eyes. God desires further that we should rule ourselves according to the invisible and new nature that is to be, for which we hope and which is to follow our earthly sufferings and this wretched nature. Therefore we should not covet this life and mourn and lament that we must leave it, nor that this whole world and all that is in it and so many great and famous people must perish. Instead, we should have mercy on the poor dear Christians, both the living who now suffer oppression, and the dead who are lying in their graves longing to rise and be transformed, like the grain that is turned in the ground in the winter, or the sap in the trees that cannot rise because of the cold and waits for the summer to come, that they may come forth and produce green leaves and blossoms.

Sermons from the year 1531.   WA 34/2:481

I wait for the LORD, my soul waits, and in his word I hope;
my soul waits for the Lord more than those who watch for the morning.
(Psalm 130:5-6)

The New Glory

Father, I desire that those also, whom you have given me,
be with me where I am, to see my glory, which you have given me.
(John 17:24)

"My dear Christians should not only be with me, but should receive
a bright and clear view of my glory," as he said shortly before in other
words: "The glory that you have given me I have given them" (John
17:22). For now, on earth, we know and hold this glory in faith, but we
do not see it except through a mirror and in a veiled Word. That is, we
hear the preaching and understand it with our hearts, that Christ is raised
from the dead and ascended into heaven where he is seated in the glory
and majesty of the Father as the only mighty Lord over all creation. But
it is still a veiled knowledge, like a thick cloud over the bright sun. For no
one's heart can hold it and no one's understanding can comprehend that
the glory is so great, especially as Christ now, in his Christians, appears
so different. But there, in the world to come, another light will shine,
so that we shall no longer hold it only in faith and in the preaching and
teaching of the Word, but we shall see it all radiant before our eyes and
shall look upon it with unspeakable and eternal joy.

Sermons on John 16–20, 1528.   WA 28:194f.

Almighty God, I look for the glory that is to be revealed;
keep my eyes focused on that goal. Amen.

The Christian's Life in the World

Luke 16:1-12

His master commended the dishonest manager because he had acted shrewdly; for the children of this age are more shrewd in dealing with their own generation than are the children of light.
(Luke 16:8)

Luke says that the Lord commended the dishonest manager. This must not be taken to mean that it pleases him if we are unjust toward others. He praises only the manager's swiftness and prudence, and desires that we should be as earnest and diligent in a good cause as this manager was in a bad cause, for his own benefit and for his master's harm.

In contrast, we see how the children of light—the true Christians—are lazy, weary, careless, and slow with regard to the things of God. Therefore Christ judges rightly when he says that the children of the world are more diligent and wise than are his children, for the devil has a hundred servants at work where Christ has hardly one. What shall we do about it? We cannot alter it, for the world will not listen to our words. We must preach and continue to rebuke, threaten, and admonish people, the lazy, weary Christians as well, and we must all remind ourselves to take as an example the industry with which the world serves the devil, so that we should exercise ourselves in good works as the children of Adam do in evil works. We might attain a little of their industry, especially as we are children of light.

Sermon on the Ninth Sunday after Trinity, 1544.   WA 52:430ff.

O Lord, let your grace work in me willingness to volunteer my talents and the energy to do good in my community. Amen.

Our Vocation Is Divinely Ordained

Render service with enthusiasm, as to the Lord,
and not to men and women.
(Ephesians 6:7)

God has need of many and various offices and stations, and therefore he bestows many different kinds of gifts, so arranging things that one always needs the other and none can do without the other. What would princes, nobles, and regents be if there were not others, such as pastors, preachers, teachers, farmers, craftsmen, and so on? They would not and could not learn or do everything alone and by themselves.

Therefore none should look to oneself alone, but rather each should look up to heaven and say: God has created all stations, and before him none is the lowest, except those who are arrogant and proud, and none is better, except those who cast themselves down to the lowest place.

Therefore even though another station may be humbler than yours, you must nevertheless know that it too has been created and ordained by God. Conversely, you must know that you too have been put in your station in order that you may humble yourself and serve others, as, for example, servants or maidservants serve their master and mistress; and you should do this for God's sake.

God does not ask whether you are a lord or a servant, a husband or a wife. Remain in the state to which you have been called, and learn to serve God in it by serving your neighbor.

Sermons from the year 1544.   LW 51:352–53; WA 49:611f.

There are varieties of gifts, but the same Spirit; and there are varieties
of services, but the same Lord; and there are varieties of activities,
but it is the same God who activates all of them in everyone.
(1 Corinthians 12:4-6)

Unless the Lord Builds the House . . .

Unless the LORD builds the house,
those who build it labor in vain.
(Psalm 127:1)

Let the Lord build the house and keep it, and do not interfere with his work. The concern for these matters is his, not yours. For whoever is the head of the house and maintains it should be allowed to bear the burden of care. Does it take a lot to make a house? So what! God is greater than any house. He who fills heaven and earth will surely also be able to supply a house, especially since he takes the responsibility on himself and causes it to be sung to his praise.

But this does not mean that God forbids you to work. Work you should and must, but do not ascribe the fact that you have food to eat and that your house is furnished to your work, but to God's grace and blessing alone. For where it is ascribed to our own work, covetousness and worry immediately raise their heads, and they hope by much labor to acquire many possessions. Hence the strange contradiction occurs that some who work extremely hard have scarcely enough to eat, while others who work leisurely are blessed with all good things. This means that God will have the honor, for he alone makes things grow. For even if you were to till the earth for a hundred years and do all the work in the world, you could not make it bring forth one blade of grass; but while you are asleep, and without your work, God will bring the blade out of the little kernel, and he adds many kernels according to his will.

Exposition of Psalm 127. LW 45:324; WA 15:365f.

Bless the labors of my hands, Lord God,
to do your work in my time and place. Amen.

Our Works Shall Be God's Tabernacle

Indeed, all that we have done, you have done for us.
(Isaiah 26:12)

What to God is our work in field and garden, in town and house, in struggling and in ruling but the work of children, through which God bestows his gifts on the land, in the house, and everywhere? Our works are God's masks, behind which he remains hidden, although he does all things. If Gideon had not obeyed and gone to battle with Midian, the Midianites would never have been conquered, although God could, of course, have conquered them without Gideon. God could also give you grain and fruit without your plowing and planting, but that is not his will. Neither is it his will that your plowing and planting should produce grain and fruit, but you must plow and plant and say a blessing on your work and pray, "Now help, O God; give us now grain and fruit, dear Lord; for our plowing and planting will not yield us anything. It is your gift."

God is the giver of all good gifts; but you must get involved and take the bull by the horns, which means you must work to give God an occasion and a mask.

Exposition of Psalm 147.   WA 31/1:435f.

I know, Lord God, that you build the house, but let me do my part
also for my family and in service of others. Amen.

Ministry and State

We have gifts that differ . . . ministry, in ministering.
(Romans 12:6-7)

There must be difference of ministries and states, for there is not *one* state but many. But the many varied states can be gathered up in one unity of the Spirit. So the body has many members. Not all can be eyes, and each member is itself and has its own office. Yet there is but *one* life and drink and food to sustain all the members and the one body, although there are many various members. See, then, how in the same way, under the great diversity of the various states and persons called for in this life and ordained by him, God has created one being and one unity with this intent, that each of us in fulfilling our ministry should do the work allotted to us as our state demands. We should perform it with the humility that regards all states and persons as equal before God and having the one as much favor with God as the other. Then we cannot pride ourselves before God and our neighbor, thinking highly of ourselves because our state is lofty. But we can know that unless we preserve in our higher state the spirit of true humility, we sin much more shamefully and will be condemned much more severely than anyone of lower degree.

Therefore let all fight the good fight in their own callings. If you are a husband or wife, you have your calling from God, and so have the servant, the maid, and the mayor.

Sermons from the year 1531.   WA 34/1:578

Straighten my priorities, Lord God.
Let me do my duty to family, community, and country. Amen.

FRIDAY

The Strain and Stress of Life

*By the sweat of your face you shall eat bread until you return
to the ground, for out of it you were taken.
(Genesis 3:19)*

The man is not burdened with childbearing; that is the woman's affliction. He has a different calling, namely, that he should look after his wife and child and keep them. This demands so much care and labor that every man shuns it and none is willing to bear the burden; yet it must be borne. For if you do not take a wife and do not eat your bread in the sweat of your brow, God takes the punishment he has laid on your body and lays it on your soul. That is a poor exchange. He desires to be gracious and helpful to your soul, but he chastens your body.

If man and woman are truly joined in marriage, they do not have an easy time, for married life means labor and sorrow, or else it is not right before God. Wherefore, if in your married life you have to endure much sorrow and labor, be of good cheer and remember that it is so ordained that it is God's holy will that people should marry. Therefore in the name of God, I burden myself with trouble and give myself to marriage willingly and cheerfully. If you refuse to do this, and wish to do better, your soul will be lost, however well it may go with your body.

Therefore God curses the soil so that of all that it bears, not half should be grain but most should be thorns and thistles, which otherwise would not grow. Because God wills that humans should labor, he ordains that by far the greater part shall be thorns and thistles. Therefore the sum and substance is that God in this way wills to keep us in check.

Exposition of Genesis, 1527.   WA 24:103f.

*See me through the thorns and thistles of life, O Lord,
and turn my toil into joy. Amen.*

Holy Matrimony

Let marriage be held in honor by all.
(Hebrews 13:4)

Regarding marriage, as with any other estate that God has called into being, the cardinal point is that everyone should know for certain that matrimony is ordained and appointed by God. Almost the chief thing to know in married life is that we should learn to look on marriage in the light of its highest honor, which is that it is ordained by God and is supported by God's Word.

If we consider it in a godly and Christian way, the greatest thing is that on wife and on husband the Word of God is written. If you can look upon your wife as though she were the only woman in the world and there were none besides; if you can look upon your husband as though he were the only man in the world and there were none besides, then no king, and not even the sun, will shine brighter and clearer in your eyes than your wife and your husband. For here you have the Word of God that gives you your husband and your wife and says, "The man shall be yours; the woman shall be yours. That pleases me well. All angels and all creatures find pleasure and rejoice therein." For no adornment is above the Word of God, through which you look upon your wife as a gift from God.

Would to God that every man might go through life with such a mind, that he could say from the bottom of his heart, "I am certain beyond a doubt that God is well pleased that I remain here and live with this woman to whom I am joined in holy matrimony, for God himself has ordained it thus, and his Word tells me so. This Word comforts those who are joined together in married life and gives them a good conscience.

A marriage sermon on Hebrews 13:4, 1531.   WA 34/1:50ff.

Bless my home, Lord God, and let me treat all those
who come and go in it with respect and love. Amen.

People and State

Luke 19:41-48

If you, even you, had only recognized on this day the things
that make for peace! But now they are hidden from your eyes.
(Luke 19:42)

Thus it shall be with all who have no fear of God and look more to their own selves than to God. In this manner God avenged the death of all the holy prophets. I am distressed at heart for my country. For now she has the day of her gracious and merciful visitation. If she makes light of it and does not receive it but scoffs and sneers at it, then Germany will lose the splendor of this glorious day and—God have mercy on her—she is ruined. The wind blows ill; for even now, at the time of the grace of her Lord, she remains unmindful of the eternal good. As the Lord says, "If you comprehended it, you would weep, and you would receive forgiveness of your iniquities." Again, "Now I have not come as a hangman, judge, and persecutor, to destroy you; I have come as a Father, preacher, and Savior, to give you counsel and to help you. But if you let the sun go down, you will be lost."

The Lord spent three days preaching in the temple, because he had never before been so deeply moved, for he sensed the peril of the hour pressing on him. The dear Lord Jesus would gladly have seen a different response.

Sermons from the year 1531.   WA 34/2:84ff.

Lord God of all nations, may justice and compassion spread
throughout our land, and may our leaders strive
for peace in deed as well as in word. Amen.

The Powers Are Ordained by God

Be strong, and let us be courageous for the sake of our people, and
for the cities of our God; and may the LORD do what seems good to him.
(2 Samuel 10:12)

We Christians must understand that all worldly rule and power, until its
time is run, is based on an ordinance or command of God and on the
prayer of Christians. Those are the two pillars that carry the whole world.
If they give way, all must tumble to the ground, as will be seen on the
day of judgment. Even now, in our time, it is apparent that all kingdoms
and powers are weakened and beginning to crumble because those two
pillars are very close to sinking and breaking. The world does not want
it otherwise, for it will not receive the Word of God (although the Word
honors and sustains it), but persecutes and kills innocent Christian folk
and does not cease to rage against the pillars that support it, like an
insane husband tearing his own house to pieces. Well, we shall support
things as long as we can, although we receive no thanks for it. But if her
fall and destruction come to pass, and the Word of God and Christian
prayer are silenced, then may the devil, the god of this world, have mercy
on her.

Sermons on John 14–16.   LW 24:81; WA 45:535

Let the prayers of the faithful rise to you, O Lord,
and let your truth prevail in our land. Amen.

The Peace of the City

Seek the welfare of the city.
(Jeremiah 29:7)

It is the duty of the city council and the magistrates to devote great care and attention to the young. All the town's goods, honor, life, and limbs are entrusted to their faithful hands, and they would not act honestly before God and the people if they failed to seek the town's welfare and improvement day and night. But the welfare of a town does not consist only in gathering treasures, building firm walls and fine houses, and making many firearms and armor. But this is the town's greatest and highest good, that it has many fine, scholarly, dignified, sensible, and honorable citizens, for they would be able to gather and treasure goods and keep them and use them properly.

Since a town must have such people, and since there are complaints on every hand because of the lack of them, we must not wait until they grow of themselves. We cannot build them of stones or carve them from wood, and God will not perform a miracle as long as we are able to meet the need by our own hands. Therefore we must undertake the work, whatever the cost and labor involved, and train them ourselves. For who is to blame that capable people are now so few in every town, except the councils and magistrates, who have left the young folk to grow like trees in the forest and have not seen to it that they are trained and trimmed? Now the tree has grown so irregular that it is of no use for building but has become crooked lumber that is good only for firewood.

Now it has become a dire necessity, not only for the sake of the young, but for the maintaining of both spiritual and secular estates, that we devote ourselves seriously and earnestly to this matter while there is still time.

To the Councilors of All German Cities.   LW 45:356–7; WA 15:34f.

I pray, O Lord, that the young people of my community will grow to healthy maturity, eager to work for the common good. Amen.

Secular Authority

[The authority] is God's servant for your good.
(Romans 13:4)

Secular authority is an image, symbol, and likeness of the authority of Christ. The ministry of the Word brings eternal justification, eternal peace, and eternal life, and the secular authority maintains temporal peace, justice, and life. Yet secular authority is a glorious divine ordinance and a wonderful gift of God, who has instituted and appointed it and wills that it shall remain as a necessity for all time. For if it were lacking, no one could save himself from the neighbor, but they would all devour each other like unreasoning beasts. Secular authority protects your body that no one may kill you, protects your wife that no one may take her and abuse her, and protects your children that no one may abduct them and take possession of them. It protects your house and home that no one may break into it and plunder it, and your fields, cattle, and all your possessions that no one may seize and steal and run away with them or damage them.

Do you not think that if the birds and animals could speak, when they see worldly government among men, they would say, "O great and noble humans, compared with us you are not human beings but gods. You enjoy secure possession of life and land, while we are not safe from each other in respect of life or home or good, not even for an hour. Woe to your ingratitude, that you do not see what glorious life our God has given you compared with us beasts."

A Sermon on Keeping Children in School.   WA 32/2:554f.

I give thanks, heavenly Father, for all good government.
Raise up, I pray, faithful servants in our land. Amen.

A Paternal Government

One must be subject, not only because
of wrath but also because of conscience
(Romans 13:5)

If you are a burgomaster, or anyone who bears the name of father, see to it that you carry out your paternal office. Parents, take care to raise up good people who in turn will raise up their children in piety. A prince and the cities need good people. The prince needs councilors; the cities need pastors and learned men. If you note that your children can become able leaders, send them to school. If you do not do this, you will have to give account, and you are a rogue who is against the prince and the city and disobedient to your God.

Our civil authorities are appointed not only to punish the wicked but that the good may be defended, and peace and security maintained, and these are without doubt Christian works of great mercy, love, and goodness.

Worldly authority is not ordained in order that the rulers may exploit and abuse their subjects but that they get the best and greatest profit for them. The Romans used to call their princes *patres patriae* (fathers of the country). We should blush that we never call or regard our princes as fathers of the land. Our prince is our father, and so is our mayor, for through him, as through a father, God gives us food and protects our home. Therefore we must honor, obey, and love them, so that a subject should regard the prince as the greatest treasure and should beware of rebellion.

Sermon on the Fourth Commandment, 1528.   LW 51:148, 150; WA 30/1:70

I urge that supplications, prayers, intercessions, and thanksgivings be
made for everyone, for kings and all who are in high positions.
(1 Timothy 2:1–2)

Civil Offices

Those authorities that exist have been instituted by God.
(Romans 13:1)

We must distinguish between an occupation and the person who holds it, between a work and the person who does it. An occupation or a work can be good and right in itself and yet be bad and wrong if the one who does the work is evil or wrong or does not do the work properly. The occupation of a judge is a valuable divine office. This is true of the office of both the trial judge who declares the verdict and the executioner who carries out the sentence. But when the office is assumed by one who uses it to gain riches or popularity, then it is no longer right or good. The married state is also precious and godly, but there are many rascals and scoundrels in it. It is the same with the profession or work of the soldier; in itself it is right and godly, but we must see to it that the persons who are in this profession and who do the work are the right kind of persons, that is, godly and upright.

I am speaking here about external righteousness, which is to be sought in offices and works. I am dealing here with such questions as whether the Christian faith, by which we are accounted righteous before God, is compatible with being a soldier, going to war, stabbing and killing, as military law requires us to do to our enemies in wartime. Is this work sinful or unjust? Should it give us a bad conscience before God? Must a Christian only do good and love, and kill no one, nor do anyone any harm? I say that this office or work, even though it is godly and right, can nevertheless become evil and unjust if the person engaged in it is evil and unjust.

Whether Soldiers, Too, Can Be Saved, 1526. LW 46:94; WA 19:626

I pray, Lord God, for those who struggle against evil
in defense of justice and freedom. Amen.

God and Caesar

He said to them, "Then give to the emperor the things
that are the emperor's, and to God the things that are God's."
(Luke 20:25)

It has been ordained that the Holy Spirit—not the world, prince, or emperor—is to be the judge through the Word. The world must stand ready to submit to reproof and judgment. Wherever the world presumes to judge and to condemn in spite of God's Word, we must know that such judgment is condemned and is of the devil. We must resist it as condemned by God and say, "Dear prince, emperor, and world, I know that I as well as my life and my property am under your authority, and insofar as your power over life and property is concerned, I must and will be glad to obey you. But when you presume to exceed your jurisdiction and trespass into God's power—where you should not and cannot be the judge but should let yourself, together with me and all creatures, be judged through God's Word—there I must and will not be obedient to you. No, I must and will do the very opposite, in order that I may be obedient to God and cling to his Word."

Beloved, we are not baptized in the name of kings, princes, and the multitude but in the name of Christ and God himself; neither are we called kings or princes or the multitude; but we are called Christians. No one must attempt to guide souls unless they know how to show them the way to heaven. But no one can do that except God alone. Therefore, in the things that concern the soul's salvation, nothing must be taught and received but the Word of God alone.

Sermons on John 16. LW 24:351; WA 46:48

Straighten my priorities, O God. In this world
of many false gods—power, money, lust, and violence—
help me to have no other gods before you. Amen.

Our Neighbors

Luke 18:9-14

*Two men went up to the temple to pray,
one a Pharisee and the other a tax collector.
(Luke 18:10)*

Let us consider this fool, the Pharisee. He does the most glorious works! First, he thanks God. He fasts twice a week for the glory of God. He gives a tenth of all his worldly goods. He has not committed adultery, has never done violence to anyone or stolen anything. He has led such a saintly life. Would you not call that an honorable life? Indeed, the world would have to praise him. In fact, he praises himself. But there, at that moment, God's judgment falls on him, saying that all his works are blasphemy. Lord God, have mercy! How terrible is this judgment! We are shocked to the limit, for not one of us is half as saintly as the Pharisee!

Mark, then, how deeply the sword of God cuts and how it pierces to the innermost soul! Here everything must be laid in ruins or dashed to the ground and humbled, or the soul cannot exist before God. It is as though a godly woman must fall down and kiss the feet of the worst harlot, indeed, even her footsteps.

The tax collector stands there and humbles himself. He makes no mention of fasts or works or anything. Yet the Lord says that his sin is not so great as that of the hypocrite. Let us take care that we do not exalt ourselves above the most insignificant sinner. If I lift myself up above my neighbor, even by the breadth of a finger, yes, above the worst sinner, I shall be thrown down.

Sermons from the year 1522.   WA 10/3:300f.

*My God, accept my heart this day, and make it always thine,
that I from thee no more may stray, no more from thee decline.
(Matthew Bridges, 1848)*

Despising the Neighbor

The Pharisee, standing by himself, was praying thus,
"God, I thank you that I am not like other people:
thieves, rogues, adulterers, or even like this tax collector."
(Luke 18:11)

Notices how he also tramples on the second table of the law and rages against his fellow humans. There is no Christian love in him at all, nothing to show any love and concern about his neighbor's honor and salvation. He treats him in a scandalous way and tramples him under his feet and does not regard him as a human being. Where he ought to save him and help him so that he should suffer no evil or injustice, he himself inflicts on him the greatest wrong. For where he knows and perceives his brother sinning against God, he does not consider for a moment how to convert him or save him from the wrath of God and from condemnation, so that he may change. There is in his heart no mercy or compassion for a poor sinner's misery and distress. To his mind it is but fit and proper that the tax collector should be left in his misery and condemnation. He withholds from him all the proper ministry of love and service.

What service can such a person render to the kingdom of God—one who can rejoice and find great pleasure in the sin and disobedience of all the world toward God and who would be grieved if anyone's heart were inclined toward God, intending to keep his commands, one who would not stoop to help him in the slightest way, even where he might, and unwilling to ward off from his brother evil and destruction? What could one hope for or look for in someone whose heart is so bad that he cannot desire his neighbor's salvation?

Sermon on the Eleventh Sunday after Trinity, 1544.   WA 22:200f.

Nothing in my hands I bring, O Lord; simply to your grace I cling. Amen.

Let Each Be Like Christ to the Other

Let each of you look not to your own interests,
but to the interests of others.
(Philippians 2:4)

Christians are filled and made rich by faith and should increase their faith until it is made perfect. For this faith is their life, their righteousness, and their salvation. It saves them, makes them acceptable, and bestows on them all things that are Christ's. Although Christians are thus free from all works, they ought in this liberty to empty themselves and to serve, help, and in every way deal with their neighbors as they see that God through Christ has dealt and still deals with them. This they should do freely, having regard for nothing but divine approval. All our work should be directed toward the good of our neighbor, because for each of us our faith suffices and all our works and all our life are left to him to use in a free service of love to our neighbor.

Well, then, my God has given me—unworthy and condemned as I am, without any merit on my part—freely and out of pure mercy, through and in Christ, the unsearchable riches of salvation and piety, so that henceforth I need nothing more than to believe that this is true. Should I not in return gladly and freely serve such a Father, who has thus poured his superabundant blessings on me, and do whatever pleases him? Shall I not also become a Christian to my neighbors, as Christ has become to me, and do for them everything that is helpful toward their salvation, because through my faith all my wants are satisfied in Christ?

Thus springs from faith, love, and desire for God, and out of love a free, willing, and cheerful life spent in free service to our neighbor.

The Freedom of a Christian. LW 31:365–6; WA 7:35f.

Make me sensitive, Lord God, to the sorrows and joys of those around me.
Let me be to them a conduit of your grace. Amen.

The Christian's Faith and Vocation

We have gifts that differ. . . . If ministry is given to us,
let us wait on our ministering.
(Romans 12:7, Luther's reading)

Christians, among themselves and by and for themselves, need no law
or sword, since it is neither necessary nor useful for them. Since true
Christians live and labor on earth not for themselves alone but for their
neighbors, they do by the very nature of their spirit even what they
themselves have no need of, but is needful and useful to the neighbor.
Because the sword is most beneficial and necessary for the whole world
in order to preserve peace, punish sin, and restrain the wicked, Christians
submit most willingly to the rule of the sword, pay taxes, honor those
in authority, serve, help, and do all they can to assist the governing
authority, that it may continue to function and be held in honor and fear.

In this way the two propositions are brought into harmony with
each another: at the same time you satisfy God's kingdom inwardly and
the kingdom of the world outwardly. You suffer evil and injustice, and
yet at the same time you punish evil and injustice; you do not resist evil,
and yet at the same time you do resist it. In the one case, you consider
yourself and what is yours; in the other, you consider what is your
neighbor's. In what concerns you and yours, you govern yourself by the
gospel and suffer injustice toward yourself as a true Christian; in what
concerns the person or property of others, you govern yourself according
to love and tolerate no injustice toward your neighbor. The gospel does
not forbid this; in fact, in other places it actually commands it.

Temporal Authority.   LW 45:95, 96; WA 11:253 f.

I know, Lord God, that my citizenship is in heaven. But help me
to foster justice and mercy in my course through this life. Amen.

Blessed Are the Meek

The Lord's servant must not be quarrelsome but kindly to everyone,
an apt teacher, patient, correcting opponents with gentleness.
(2 Timothy 2:24-25)

If you are truly meek, your heart grieves over any evil that befalls your enemy. Those who do that are the true children and heirs of God and brothers and sisters of Christ, who did the same for us all on the holy cross. Thus we see that a godly judge is pained when he has to pronounce judgment on the evildoer, and that he grieves over the death that the law inflicts on such a one. But the deed is not what it seems, for it appears to be full of wrath and severity. But so fundamentally good is meekness that it remains even under such angry deeds, and the heart suffers most grief when duty calls to anger and severity.

Yet we must take care that our meekness does not run counter to the honor and the command of God. For example, it is not right that magistrates should look aside, leaving sin to rule, and that we should remain silent about it. Our possessions and honor and loss we should not regard, and should not be angry because of anything that may happen to them. But God's honor and command we must defend, and the loss and injustice that our neighbor suffers we must redress, the magistrates with the sword, other people with words and penalties, yet always grieving over those who have deserved such punishments.

Sermon on Good Works, 1520.   WA 9:292f.

Heavenly Father, help me to move beyond anger and thoughts
of revenge at those who injure me. Purify my heart. Amen.

That We May Bring a Sinner into Heaven

Rule in the midst of your foes.
(Psalm 110:2)

"Not among your friends, not in the midst of roses and lilies, but in the midst of thorns and foes I have appointed your rod." And it follows that all who want to serve God and follow Christ must suffer much disappointment and nuisances, as Christ himself says, "In me you . . . have peace. In the world you face persecution" (John 16:33). Thus it is ordained by God, and it will not be otherwise: your reign will be in the midst of your enemies. Whoever will not suffer thus will not be found in the kingdom of Christ. He wants to be in the midst of friends, to sit among lilies and roses and not live with wicked people but with saints.

O you blasphemers and betrayers of Christ! If Christ had done as you are doing, who would ever have been saved? He emptied himself of his Godhead, his piety, and his wisdom, and he desired to be with sinners that he might make them full. Yes, and he took them to himself and did not wish to have to do with the spiritually minded, the pious, and the just. And what are you doing? The very opposite. You are unwilling to bear your brother's sin, and load yourselves with your own justification and wisdom, but Christ emptied himself of his own justice and wisdom and burdened himself with the sin and iniquities of others. See how faithfully you follow Christ!

The children of God do not flee the company of evil persons; instead they seek it that they may help them. They do not want to go to heaven alone; they want to bring with them the greatest sinner, if they can.

Sermon on Psalm 110, 1518.   WA 1:696

O God, let me be a light to the path of the lost and hopeless,
that your grace may bring deliverance in the midst of despair. Amen.

The Strong and the Weak

Welcome those who are weak in faith, but not
for the purpose of quarreling over opinions.
(Romans 14:1)

The apostle desires above all that those who are weak be tolerated and helped by those who are stronger, and second, that the weak should not make hasty judgment. Thus he is encouraging them to preserve peace and unity. For even though a weak faith is not sufficient for salvation, yet such people are to be welcomed in the meantime so that they may be strengthened and not allowed to remain in their weakness, as those do who are disdainful of them and are concerned only about their own salvation.

What God does not forbid but leaves free, that must remain free to everyone; and no one is to be obeyed who forbids what God has left free. Rather it is the duty of everyone to fight against such prohibitions with words and deeds, and to do the thing in a spirit of defiance.

Lectures on Romans. LW 25:492

Merciful Father, save me from pettiness and from judging
those whose lives differ from mine in inconsequential ways.
Make me open to others beyond my own circle. Amen.

Sickness and Suffering

Mark 7:31-37

There is no wealth better than health of body.
(Sirach 30:16)

O dear Lord God, what a precious thing is a healthy body! How little do we give him thanks for it! God has burdened our poor flesh with many kinds of sickness and disease, and still we fail to understand. We ought every day to perceive how sinful we are by nature. Oh, blindness upon blindness!

When our heart is grieved and sad, the weakness of the body follows. Sickness of the heart is true sickness, such as sadness, temptation, and the like. I am a true Lazarus, and well tried in sickness.

It is true that our sufferings are great, but what are they compared with the sufferings of Christ, the Son of God, the Crucified? There we may well be put to silence.

Table Talk.   WA Tischreden 4:202

Remain with me, O God, through sickness and health.
Give me comfort and hope in time of distress. Amen.

The Discipline of God's Law

The law was our disciplinarian until Christ came,
so that we might be justified by faith.
(Galatians 3:24)

It is proper that the law and God's commandments provide me with the correct directives for life; they supply me with abundant information about righteousness and eternal life. The law is a sermon that points me to life, and it is essential to remember this instruction; but it must be borne in mind that the law does not *give* me life. It resembles a hand that directs me to the right road; such a hand is a useful member of the body. However, if I do not have feet, a wagon to travel in, or horses to ride on, I shall never go by that road. The hand gives me the proper direction, but it will not conduct my steps along the way. Thus the law serves to indicate the will of God, and it leads us to a realization that we cannot keep it. It also acquaints us with human nature, with our capabilities, and with our limitations. The law was given to us for the revelation of sin; but it does not have the power to save us from sin and rid us of it. It holds a mirror before us; we peer into it and perceive that we are devoid of righteousness and life. And this image impels us to cry, "Oh, come, Lord Jesus Christ, help us and give us grace to enable us to fulfill the law's demands!"

Sermon on John 1, 1537.   LW 22:143; WA 46:661

I long for your salvation, O LORD, and your law is my delight. Amen.
(Psalm 119:174)

The Fearful Heart

My heart is in anguish within me;
the terrors of death have fallen upon me.
(Psalm 55:4)

All suffering that afflicts the flesh can be endured. The heart can even despise all physical suffering and rejoice in it, but when the heart is tormented and broken, that is the greatest anguish and suffering of all. In bodily afflictions you suffer but half, for joy and happiness may still fill the soul and heart, but when the heart alone must bear the burden, it takes great and lofty spirits, and special grace and strength to endure it.

Why then does God let such suffering and affliction befall those whom he loves most?

First, because he wants to save his people from pride, so that the great saints who have received such special grace from him should not venture to put their trust in themselves. Therefore it must be thus mingled and salted for them that they do not always possess the power of the Spirit, but that, at times, their faith grows restless and their hearts faint, so that they perceive what they are and confess that they can achieve nothing unless the pure grace of God sustains them.

Again, God lets such affliction befall them as an example to others, to shake the self-confident souls, and to comfort those who are afraid.

In the third place comes the right and true cause why God acts thus, namely, in order to teach his saints where they should seek true comfort, and to be content to find Christ and to abide with him.

Sermon on the First Sunday after Epiphany, 1525.   WA 17/2:22f.

Eternal God, Lord of life, bring comfort to those to whom death draws near. In my weakness give me strength, and in my despair give me hope. Amen.

On Being Alone

I am not alone, because the Father is with me.
(John 16:32)

Those who want to be true Christians should seek such help and strength as to be so disposed and equipped that they need no one else's help but are strong in themselves, so that if they fall on evil they do not need to stand around seeking help from other people. Christ must be our example, that we may learn and know that our strength comes alone through his grace. David had experienced this; therefore he says, "Look on my right hand and see—there is no one who takes notice of me; no refuge remains to me; no one cares for me" (Psalm 142:4).

Such is the lot of Christians at all times. They are forsaken and left to themselves. Those who would like to stand by them and help them have little faith and therefore cannot help; and those who could and should help turn away and become their worst enemies. Therefore we must have our strength in ourselves, and not in others.

This example of our Lord Christ we must learn and mark well, because the suffering of a Christian begins in loneliness, for the time is sure to come when you are left alone, and if it does not occur in this life, it occurs at the hour of death. Therefore every Christian should be armed with the strength that is Christ and be united to him who is our only help and comfort, according to his promise.

Sermons on John 16–20, 1528.   WA 28:214f.

Where can I go from your spirit? Or where can I flee from your presence?
. . . If I take the wings of the morning and settle at the farthest limits
of the seas, even there your hand shall hold me fast. Amen.
(Psalm 139:7, 9–10)

Wait for the Lord Your God

I wait for the LORD.
(Psalm 130:5)

There are some people who want to show God the goal and to determine the time and the manner and at the same time suggest how they wish to be helped. And if things do not turn out as they wish, they become faint-hearted or, if they can, they seek help elsewhere. They do not wait upon God; instead God should wait for them and be ready at once to help them in the way they have planned. But those who truly wait upon God ask for grace, and they leave it free to God's good pleasure how, where, and by what means he shall help them. They do not despair of help, yet they do not give it a name. They rather leave it to God to baptize and name it, however long it may be delayed. But whoever names the help does not receive it, for he does not await and suffer the counsel, will, and tarrying of God.

Exposition of Four Comforting Psalms, 1526.   EA 37:423f.

Wait for the LORD; be strong, and let your heart take courage;
wait for the LORD! (Psalm 27:14)

To Be Nothing before God

Do not forsake me, O LORD;
O my God, do not be far from me.
(Psalm 38:21)

"I am lonely, forsaken by all and despised. Receive me, and do not forsake me." It is God's nature to make something out of nothing; therefore God cannot make anything out of the one who is not yet nothing. Humans, however, can change one thing into another, which is a futile occupation. Therefore God accepts only the forsaken, cures only the sick, gives sight only to the blind, restores life only to the dead, sanctifies only the sinners, gives wisdom only to the unwise. In short, he has mercy only on those who are wretched, and gives grace only to those who are not in grace.

Therefore no arrogant saint or just or wise person can be material for God; neither can such a one do the work of God. That person remains confined within his or her own work and becomes a fictitious, pretended, false, and deceitful saint, that is, a hypocrite.

The Seven Penitential Psalms, 1517.   LW 14:163; WA 18:183f.

Take my love; my Lord, I pour at thy feet its treasure store;
take myself and I will be ever, only, all for thee. Amen.
(Frances R. Havergal, 1874)

Saturday

God Works Wonders in the Saints

But know that the Lord has set apart the faithful for himself.
(Psalm 4:3)

God works wonders in his saints and leads them wonderfully, against all human reason and wisdom, so that those who fear God and are Christians learn to cling to things invisible and are brought back to life through being given over to death. For the Word of God is a light that shines in a dark place, as every example of faith shows.

God deals with the saints and Christians as with the godless and the enemies of Christ—at times, even worse. God treats them as the master of the house treats his son and servants. His son he strikes and flogs more often than the servants, and yet for him he saves a treasure for an inheritance. Otherwise I should be at a loss to say why God allows his dear children to have such hard times in this world.

Table Talk.   WA Tischreden 1:519f.

O Lord, in the rough patches of my life, give me confidence in your steadfast love, and let your shining face be my strength. Amen.

Good Works

Luke 10:25-37

You shall love the Lord your God with all your heart . . .
and your neighbor as yourself.
(Luke 10:27)

There you have good works described in total. These we should practice toward one another, as our heavenly Father has done toward us and is still doing unceasingly. You have often heard that we need no works to please God, but we need them for our neighbor. We cannot make God any more powerful or richer through our works, but we can make our neighbor stronger and richer by them. Our neighbor needs them, and they should be directed there and not to God. You have often heard this, and it is still ringing in your ears. Would to God that it would go into your hands and be expressed in works!

Faith is due to God alone; faith receives divine works that God alone can do, and these works of God we can receive alone through faith. Then we should be busy for our neighbors' sake and direct our works toward them, that these works may serve them.

My faith I must bring inwardly and upward to God, but my works I must do outwardly and downward to my neighbor.

Sermon on the Fourth Sunday after Trinity, 1526.   WA 10/1(ii):314f.

You have shown me, Lord God, who is my neighbor. Renew my heart
to deal justly and with understanding toward all. Amen.

Works and Faith

"No human being will be justified in his sight"
by deeds prescribed by the law.
(Romans 3:20)

I have often warned you that you should keep works and faith separate, for although this has been so often said and preached to you that you know it well, yet whenever it comes to the point that you should judge according to it and do right, everybody does wrong. Faith, I say, you must have toward God in your conscience, and no law must strike against it, be it the law of humans or the law of God. Therefore, if you hear someone saying, "You must do this," wanting to force such work or deed upon your conscience and setting it in opposition to God, remember that that is surely the devil's teaching. And you should keep the two as far apart as heaven and earth, or day and night, so that your faith remains within your heart and conscience alone, but your works are drawn away from the conscience to the body. Faith belongs to heaven above; works must be related to earth. Faith is directed to God, works to the neighbor. Faith is above the law and is outside of the law. Works are placed under the law and are the slaves of the law.

Sermons from the year 1525.   WA 17/1:105f.

Teach us the lesson you have taught, to feel for those your blood has bought,
that every word and deed and thought may work a work for you. Amen.
(Godfrey Thring, 1877)

God Meets Us in Our Neighbor

*Just as you did it to one of the least of these who are members
of my family, you did it to me.*
(Matthew 25:40)

Dear Lord God, we are so blind that we do not take such love to heart. Who could ever have discerned that God lets himself so low that he receives all these works that we do to the poor and needy as if they had been done to him? Thus the world is full of God. In every yard, in every lane you may find Christ. Do not gaze up into the sky and say, "If I could but once see our Lord God, how readily I should render him any service in my power!" You are a liar, says St. John. Listen, wretched person, do you wish to serve God? You have him in your home, with your servants and children; teach them to fear God and put their trust in him alone, and love him. "Go and comfort your sad and sick neighbors; help them with all your possessions, wisdom, and skill. Bring up your children that they may know me; give them a good and saintly schoolmaster; spare no cost with them; I shall reward you richly.

"See that you do not fail to see me. I shall be close to you in every poor and wretched person who is in need of your help and teaching; I am there, right in the midst. Whether you do little for him or much, you do it to me. You will not give the cup of cold water in vain. You will receive fruit a thousandfold, not because of your work, but because of my promise."

Sermons from the year 1526.   WA 20:514f.

*Help me, Lord God, to see in everyone I meet the brother or sister
for whom Christ died. Amen.*

Almsgiving

But when you give alms, do not let your left hand know what your right hand is doing, so that your alms may be done in secret.
(Matthew 6:3-4)

Paul says the same thing in Romans 12:8, "He who contributes, let him do it with singleness" [Luther's reading]. "Contributing with singleness" means that one does not seek one's own glory or popularity, gratitude, or reward, and is not concerned about whether any human being is grateful or not. Such a person contributes freely, just as God grants gifts every day and causes his sun to shine regardless of the thankful or the unthankful. A heart is truly single in its motivation if it neither seeks nor desires nor looks at anything except the will of God and the glory of God.

It is really disgraceful the way the world carries on. It may be pious or it may be wicked, but either way it is worthless. Either it tries openly to be a devil with its wicked works, or it tries to be God himself with its good works. Both of these are intolerable. Therefore no persons can do a truly good work unless they are Christians. If they do it as humans, then they are not doing it for the glory of God, but for their own glory and advantage. On the other hand, if they claim that it is for the glory of God, that is a lie that smells to high heaven.

Giving alms in secret means that the heart is not ostentatious or desirous of gaining honor and reputation from it but is moved to contribute freely, regardless of whether it makes an impression and gains the praise of the people. For it is concealed by the singleness of a heart that does not ask or worry, but leaves it for God to decide whether its reward will be gratitude or ingratitude, good or evil.

Sermons on Matthew 5–8, 1532.   LW 21:134; WA 32:410f.

Incline my heart, O God, to those who suffer poverty. May our society provide the means for all to have the necessities of life. Amen.

Without Reward

You received without payment; give without payment.
(Matthew 10:8)

If (the saints) did good works for the sake of obtaining the kingdom, they would never obtain it but would rather belong among the ungodly who with an evil and mercenary eye "seek their own" even in God. But the children of God do good with a will that is disinterested, not seeking any reward but only the glory and will of God, and being ready to do good even if there were neither a kingdom nor a hell. These things are, I think, sufficiently established by that one saying of Christ's from Matthew 25:34, "Come, you that are blessed by my Father, inherit the kingdom prepared for you from the foundation of the world." How can they merit that which is already theirs and is prepared for them before they are born? We could instead more truly say that the kingdom of God merits *us* as its possessors and thus place merit where they place reward, and reward where they place merit. For the kingdom is not *being* prepared; it *has been* prepared, while the children of the kingdom are being prepared, not preparing the kingdom. That is to say, the kingdom merits its children, not the children the kingdom.

The Bondage of the Will.   *LW 33:153*

As you, heavenly Father, have given me grace,
so let me act with compassion toward others. Amen.

Love Your Enemies

Love your enemies.
(Matthew 5:44)

What sort of a good deed is it if we are kind only to our friends? Does not even a wicked person behave that way to friends? Even dumb beasts are good and gentle to their kind. Therefore a Christian must seek for something higher and serve with meekness even undeserving and ungrateful people, and wicked persons and enemies. So our heavenly Father makes his sun to rise on the evil and on the good and sends rain on the ungrateful as on the grateful.

Yet here we shall find how hard it is to do good works according to the will of God, how our nature writhes and winces at it, although we are quite ready and willing to do the good works of our own choice. So turn to your enemies, to the ungrateful, and do them good, and you will find out how near you are to this commandment or how far you are away from it, and how all through life you will be occupied in practicing this work. For if your enemy is in need of you and you do not give help when you can, it is like stealing what belongs to that person, for it was your duty to help.

Sermon on Good Works, 1520.   WA 9:297f.

O Lord, when I am tempted to respond with anger and peevishness,
show me the better way. Amen.

To Please Our Neighbor

Each of us must please our neighbor for the good purpose
of building up the neighbor.
(Romans 15:2)

Christians live for one purpose only, namely, to do good to others, and not to destroy the persons but their vices, and this they cannot do unless they are willing to deal with the weak. It would be a foolish work of charity if you feed the hungry, give drink to the thirsty, clothe the naked, visit the sick, but would not allow the hungry, naked, sick, and thirsty to visit you and be in your company. If you would not allow the wicked and the frail to be with you, that would be the same as saying that you did not wish to help one soul to sanctity.

Therefore let us learn from this epistle that the Christian way of living does not consist in *finding* saintly, righteous, and holy people, but in *making* them. Let it be the Christian's work and practice on earth to make such people, whether by punishment or prayer or by suffering for them or in whatever way they can. Likewise, a Christian lives not to find rich, strong, and healthy people, but to make the poor rich, the weak strong, and the sick healthy.

Sermon on the Second Sunday in Advent, 1522. WA 10/1(ii):69

O divine Master, grant that I may not so much seek to be consoled, as to console; to be understood, as to understand; to be loved, as to love. Amen.
(Francis of Assisi, 1181–1226)

Fruit

Galatians 5:16-24

Abide in me as I abide in you. Just as the branch cannot bear fruit by itself unless it abides in the vine, neither can you unless you abide in me.
(John 15:4)

It will always be true that the one who is a Christian must have emerged and grown naturally from Christ the vine.

When I am baptized or converted by the gospel, the Holy Spirit is present. The Spirit takes me as a piece of clay and makes of me a new creature, which is endowed with a different mind, heart, and thoughts, that is, with a true knowledge of God and a sincere trust in his grace. The very essence of my heart is renewed and changed. This makes me a new plant, one that is grafted on Christ the vine and grows from him. My holiness, righteousness, and purity do not stem from me, nor do they depend on me. They come solely from Christ and are based only in him, in whom I am rooted by faith, just as the sap flows from the stalk into the branches. Now I am like him and of his kind. Both he and I are of one nature and essence, and I bear fruit in him and through him. This fruit is not mine; it is the vine's.

Thus Christ and the Christians become one loaf and one body, so that the Christian can bear good fruit—not Adam's or his own, but Christ's.

Sermons on John 14–15.   LW 24:226; WA 45:667

O Master, let me walk with thee in lowly paths of service free;
tell me thy secret, help me bear the strain of toil, the fret of care. Amen.
(Washington Gladden, 1836–1918)

Bearing Fruit

You did not choose me but I chose you. And I appointed you
to go and bear fruit, fruit that will last.
(John 15:16)

I chose you and spent all this on you that you might bear much fruit and
live in such a way that you can be recognized as my true disciples. You do
not need this to wipe out your sins. No, that lies beyond your power and
falls solely into the domain of my calling and friendship. But you must
do this, in the first place, for the honor and glory of God and as evidence
of your obedience. In the second place, you must do this for the welfare
and improvement of your neighbor, in order that it may be seen that your
faith is true and that you belong to Christ. This happens when the fruits
appear, so that people see that you are kind and generous and patient,
and that you cause no grief or harm to others.

Sermons on John 14–15.   LW 24:262; WA 45:700f.

Let your Spirit work in me the fruits of righteousness, O Lord. Amen.

Fruit Is in Christ Alone

Apart from me you can do nothing.
(John 15:5)

It is a tremendous comfort and inspiration for us to know that our lives and works are not in vain but are pleasing to God and are called true fruit, and for us to be able to say with our whole heart, "I was baptized in the name of Christ. I did not invent this baptism or institute it through my monastic order or rule, nor did it come into being by human choice. No, Christ my Lord himself is the author; this I know for certain. In the second place, I know and profess before all the world that by the grace of God I believe in that man, and I am resolved to remain with him and to surrender life, limb, and everything rather than deny him. In this faith I stand and live. Then I go forth, eat and drink, sleep and wake, rule, serve, labor, act, and suffer all in the faith in which I am baptized; and I know that this is good fruit and is pleasing to God."

The life of such a person, whether great or small and no matter what it is called, is nothing but fruit and cannot be without fruit; for in Christ that person has been born into a new existence, in order to be constantly full of good fruit. Everything such a person does becomes easy, not troublesome or vexatious. Nothing then is too arduous or too difficult to suffer and bear.

Sermons on John 14–15.   LW 24:230; WA 45:671

Lord God, grant me to grow in grace each day by Holy Baptism
that I may eternal life inherit. Amen.

The Good and the Corrupt Trees

In the same way, every good tree bears good fruit,
but the bad tree bears bad fruit.
(Matthew 7:17)

No good work helps a person toward saintliness or salvation who has no faith. The opposite is also true. No evil work can make that person evil and condemned, but only unbelief, which makes both the person and the tree evil, and then the person does the evil works. Therefore, if we grow saintly or wicked, it does not begin with works but with faith, as the sage says, "The beginning of human pride is to forsake the Lord; the heart has withdrawn from its Maker" (Sirach 10:12). So also Christ teaches that we must not begin with works, and says, "Either make the tree good, and its fruit good; or make the tree bad, and its fruit bad" (Matthew 12:33), as though he would say, "Whoever would have good fruit must begin with the tree and make it good." Therefore whoever would do good works must begin not with the works, but with the *person* who is to do the works. But the person cannot be made good except through faith; neither can that one be made evil except through unbelief. It is true that works make a person saintly or evil in the sight of humans; that is to say, they indicate outwardly who is saintly and who is wicked, as Christ says, "You will know them by their fruits" (Matthew 7:20). But all this is in outward appearance only.

The Freedom of a Christian, 1520.   LW 31:362; WA 7:32f.

Create in me a clean heart, O God,
and put a new and right spirit within me. Amen.
(Psalm 51:10)

Love Is the Fulfilling of the Law

You see that faith was active along with his works,
and faith was brought to completion by the works.
(James 2:22)

Love is the fulfilling of the law.
(Romans 13:10)

Faith and love should be distinguished in this way: faith is concerned with the person and love with the works.

I say this so that the nature and meaning of faith, love, and the law may be rightly grasped, and that to each is ascribed what properly belongs to it. Faith justifies but it does not fulfill the law; love does not justify but it fulfills the law; the law demands love and works but does not mention the person; the person feels the law, but love does not feel it at all.

Faith, then, although it cannot fulfill the law, yet possesses that by which the law can be fulfilled, for it gains the Spirit and the love by which it can be fulfilled. Again, though love does not justify, yet it gives proof of what makes a person just, namely, faith. To sum up, as St. Paul himself here says, "Love is the fulfilling of the law," as if he said that it is one thing to fulfill the law and another to make possible the fulfilling of the law. Love fulfills the law in the sense that it is itself the fulfilling of the law, but faith fulfills it in the sense that it provides the doer and love remains the deed.

Sermon on the Fourth Sunday after Epiphany, 1525.   WA 17/2:97f.

May my faith become active in love, O Lord. Amen.

Perfect in Love

Be perfect, therefore, as your heavenly Father is perfect.
(Matthew 5:48)

We cannot be or become perfect in the sense that we do not have any sin, as some dream about perfection. Here and everywhere in Scripture "to be perfect" means that the teaching be completely correct and perfect, and then, that life move and be regulated according to it. Here, for example, the teaching is that we should love not only those who do us good but our enemies too. Whoever teaches this and lives accordingly teaches and lives perfectly.

But some people love only their friends. Such a love is chopped up and divided; it is only half a love. What Jesus wants is an entire, whole, and undivided love, where one loves and helps his enemy as well as his friend. So I am called a truly perfect person, one who has and holds the teaching in its entirety.

Now if my life does not measure up to this in every detail—as indeed it cannot, since flesh and blood incessantly hold it back—that does not detract from the perfection. Only we must keep striving for it, and moving and progressing toward it every day. This happens when the spirit is master over the flesh, holding it in cheek, subduing and restraining it, in order not to give it room to act contrary to this teaching. It happens when I let love move along on the true middle course, treating everyone alike and excluding no one. Then I have true Christian perfection, which is not restricted to special offices or stations, but is common to all Christians—as it should be.

Commentary on the Sermon on the Mount, 1532.   LW 21:129; WA 32:406

O Lord, I have not yet attained the goal,
but I press on with your grace. Amen.

God's Will for You

The mighty one has done great things for me; and holy is his name.
(Luke 1:49)

It may be that someone will be frightened by such great deeds of God, unless the person believes not only that God has the power and the knowledge to do such mighty deeds but also that he has the will and the love to act thus. Yet it is not enough to believe that God wills to do great deeds with others but not with you, thus excluding yourself from such divine action, as those do who do not fear God in the height of their power but give in faintheartedly when they are in trouble. For such a faith is futile and dead, like a delusion from a fairy tale. You must rather, without any wavering or doubt, realize his will toward you and firmly believe that he will do great things also to you and is willing to do so. Such a faith has life and being; it pervades and changes the whole person. It constrains you to live in fear if you are prosperous and to be comforted if you are in need. The more prosperous you, are the more you should live in fear; and the deeper you are cast down, the more you should be comforted. With this faith all things are possible, as Christ says (Mark 9:23); it alone abides. Such a faith also comes to experience the works of God and thus attains to the love of God and leads to songs and praise of God, so that the believer esteems God highly and truly magnifies him.

Commentary on the Magnificat, 1521.   LW 21:306; WA 7:553f.

Bless the Lord, O my soul, and all that is within me.
Bless his holy name. Amen.

On Anxiety and Trust in God

Matthew 6:24-34

---

*Look at the birds of the air; they neither sow nor reap nor gather
into barns, and yet your heavenly Father feeds them.
Are you not of more value than they?
(Matthew 6:26)*

God sets before us the example of the creatures that we may learn from
them to trust in God and not be anxious. For the little birds fly before
our eyes to shame us; we should take off our hats to them and say, "My
dear doctor, I must confess, I cannot do what you do. You sleep the
whole night through in your little nest without any anxiety. At dawn you
rise and are happy and gay. You perch on a little flower and sing your
praise and thanks to God. Then you seek your food and find it. Shame on
me! What a fool I am that I fail to do the same, although I have so much
reason to do it!"

If the little bird can live without anxiety and bear itself in that
respect like a living saint, though it has neither field nor barn, neither
chest nor cellar, and sings and praises God and is happy and gay because
it knows that there is one who cares for it, whose name is "our Father in
heaven," why do we not do the same—we who have the advantage that
we can work, till the soil, gather the fruit, and store it and lay it up till we
need it? Yet we cannot leave off living in such shameful anxiety.

Sermon on the Fifteenth Sunday after Trinity, 1544.   WA 52:473f.

---

*Cast your burden on the LORD, and he will sustain you; he will never
permit the righteous to be moved. (Psalm 55:22)*

Without Anxiety

I want you to be free from anxieties.
(1 Corinthians 7:32)

Despairing unbelief is still so deep in us that we always live in anxiety about food and drink. The reason is that we want to know how God will sustain us. We want to have our barn well full of grain and our chest full of gold and to bind God to our barn and chest, but his will is to be free and master over all, over time and place and person and everything. Leave it to him to determine how he will feed us, give grain and gold as and when we need them. Our course is to say, "I will do my work today and I will see how he will give me food, and the same again tomorrow," and thus we should understand that he will feed us and we shall have no need to be anxious.

Therefore we should leave all care to him. The work we do and the pains we take are not contrary to faith but are useful for the training of the flesh; but anxiety is contrary to God. The woman should mind the children, run the house, and wait for God to show what is his will for her. Similarly, the man should work and commit himself to God. God will not desert him. He has promised that very clearly. All that we achieve with our anxiety is that we stand in God's way and hinder his work in us.

Sermons on Genesis, 1527.   WA 24:115f.

Be still, my soul, the Lord is on your side! Bear patiently the cross of grief or pain. Leave to your God to order and provide; in every change he faithful will remain. (Katherina von Schlegel, 1697–c. 1768)

God Lays It Down, We Pick It Up

The eyes of all look to you,
*   and you give them their food in due season.*
(Psalm 145:15)

No animal works for its living, but each has its own task to perform, after which it seeks and finds its food. The little birds fly about and warble, make nests, and hatch their young. That is their task. But they do not gain their living from it. Oxen plow; horses carry their riders and have a share in battle; sheep furnish wool, milk, cheese, and so on. That is their task. But they do not gain their living from it. It is the earth that produces grass and nourishes them through God's blessing.

Similarly, we must necessarily work and busy ourselves at something. At the same time, however, we must know that it is something other than our labor that furnishes us sustenance; it is the divine blessing. Because God gives us nothing unless we work, it may seem as if it is our labor that sustains us—just as the little birds neither sow nor reap but would certainly die of hunger if they did not fly about to seek their food. The fact that they find food, however, is due not to their own labor but to God's goodness. For who placed their food where they can find it? For where God has not laid up a supply, no one will find anything, even though they all work themselves to death searching. We can see this with our eyes and grasp it with our hands, yet we will not believe. Again, where God does not uphold and preserve, nothing can last, even though a hundred thousand fortresses were thrown up to defend it; it will be shattered and ground to dust till no one knows what has become of it.

Exposition of Psalm 127, 1524.   LW 45:327; WA 15:367f.

These all look to you
*   to give them their food in due season;*
. . . when you open your hand,
*   they are filled with good things. Amen.*
(Psalm 104:27-28)

Cast Your Burden on the Lord

Cast your burden on the LORD,
and he will sustain you;
he will never permit
the righteous to be moved.
(Psalm 55:22)

Whoever desires to be a Christian must learn to believe this and to exercise this faith in all affairs, in physical and in spiritual things, in doing and in suffering, in living and dying, and to cast aside all anxious thoughts and cares and throw them cheerfully off. Yet we must not throw them into a corner, as some have vainly tried to do, for they will not let themselves be stripped of their power so long as they are allowed to dwell in the heart. But you must cast both your heart and your care upon God's back, for God has a strong neck and shoulders, and can well carry them. Moreover, God bids us cast them on him, and the more we cast on him, the more God is pleased, for he promises to bear your burden for you, and everything that concerns you.

"Cast all your anxieties on him, because he cares for you" (1 Peter 5:7).

If we could learn this casting off of care, we would know by experience that it is true. But the one who does not learn such casting off of care must remain a downcast, dejected, defeated, rejected, and hopelessly confused person.

Sermon on the Third Sunday after Trinity, 1544. WA 22:34f.

When my way grows drear, precious Lord, linger near. When my life is almost gone, hear my cry, hear my call, hold my hand lest I fall. Take my hand, precious Lord, lead me home. Amen.
(Thomas A. Dorsey, 1899–1993)

God Comes Often in Disguise

Why, O LORD, do you stand far off?
Why do you hide yourself in times of trouble?
(Psalm 10:1)

When we suffer with respect to our body or possessions or honor or friends or whatever we have, let us ask whether we believe that we are not well pleasing to God and if, whether our sufferings and afflictions are small or great, God has graciously ordained them for us.

Faith sees through what seems to our feelings and understanding to be the expression of his anger and holds a sure confidence in his good purpose. God is hidden here, as the bride sings, "Look, there he stands behind our wall, gazing in at the windows, looking through the lattice" (Song of Solomon 2:9). This means that he is hidden beneath the sufferings that seek to separate us from him like a wall, and he sees us and does not leave us. For there he stands ever ready with his gracious help, and is seen through the windows of a struggling faith.

Sermon on Good Works, 1520. WA 9:233

In the dark night of despair, O Lord, let me have a glimpse
of your luminous presence. Amen.

The Ways of God Are Hidden from Us

I will instruct you and teach you the way you should go;
I will counsel you with my eye upon you.
(Psalm 32:8)

"You ask that I deliver you. Then do not be uneasy about it; do not teach me, and do not teach yourself; surrender yourself to me. I am competent to be your master. I will lead you in a way that is pleasing to me. You think all is lost if things do not go as you feel they should. But your thinking harms you and hinders me. Things must go not according to your understanding but beyond your understanding. Submerge yourself in a lack of understanding, and I will give you my understanding. Lack of understanding is real understanding; not knowing where you are going is really knowing where you are going. My understanding makes you without understanding. Thus Abraham went out from his homeland and did not know where he was going (Genesis 12:1ff.). He yielded to my knowledge and abandoned his own knowledge; and by the right way he reached the right goal.

"That is the way of the cross. You cannot find it, but I must lead you like a blind person. Therefore not you, not a human being, not a creature, but I through my Spirit and the Word will teach you the way you must go. You must not follow the work that you choose, not the suffering you devise, but that which comes to you against your choice, thoughts, and desires. It is there that I call you; there you must be a pupil. There your Master has come to you."

The Seven Penitential Psalms, 1517.   LW 14:152; WA 18/1:171f.

Your word is a lamp to my feet
and a light to my path. Amen.
(Psalm 119:105)

God Does Not Abandon Those Who Trust Him

*. . . knowing that suffering produces endurance, and endurance
produces character, and character produces hope.*
(Romans 5:3-4)

When God wants to strengthen our faith, he first weakens it by feigning to break faith with us. God thrusts us into many tribulations and makes us so weary that we are driven to despair, and yet God gives us strength to be still and persevere. Such quietness is endurance, and endurance produces character, so that when God returns to us and lets his sun rise and shine again, and when the storm is over, we open our eyes in amazement and say, "The Lord be praised that I have been delivered from evil. God dwells here. I did not think that all would end so well."

Within a day or two, within a week or a year, or even within the next hour, sin brings another cross to us: the loss of honor or possessions, bodily injury, or some mishap that brings such trouble. Then it all begins again and the storm breaks out once more. But now we glory in our afflictions because we remember that on the former occasion God was gracious to us, and we know that it is God's good will to chastise us that we may have reason to run to him and to cry, "He who has helped me so often will help me now." That very longing in your heart (which makes you cry, "Oh, that I were free! Oh, that God would come! Oh, that I might receive help!") is hope, which does not put to shame, for God must help such a person.

In this way God hides life under death, heaven under hell, wisdom under folly, and grace under sin.

Sermons from the year 1527.   WA 17/2:274f.

Even when my way seems dark and hope flees, I know, O Lord, that the darkness is not dark to you. You are there. Amen. (See Psalm 139:12.)

Being Strengthened in the Inner Being

Ephesians 3:13-21

I pray that, according to the riches of his glory, he may grant that you may be strengthened in your inner being with power through Spirit.
(Ephesians 3:16)

Worldly people are full of courage and of high spirits, and so are Christians. Christians are much stronger through the Holy Spirit, for they fear neither the world nor the devil, neither death nor misfortune. This is called spiritual strength. For the little word "spirit" rightly means courage, which is bold and daring. For spiritual strength is not the flesh and bones but the heart and courage itself, and, by contrast, weakness means timidity and cowardice and lack of courage.

Therefore St. Paul says, "This is what I desire and pray for you from God, that he may give you a strong and daring mind, such a powerful and joyful spirit that fears no shame, poverty, sin, devil, and death, that you will be certain that nothing can harm you and that you will not want." Worldly courage endures no longer than there is some earthly good on which to rely. But true courage trusts in God alone and has no other good or gold than God alone. In him it withstands all evil and wins an altogether different heart and courage from that of the world.

Sermons from the year 1525. WA 17/1:435

Even though I walk through the darkest valley, I fear no evil; for you are with me. Amen. (Psalm 23:4)

Our Affirmation of Faith

Our message of the gospel came to you not in word only,
but also in power and in the Holy Spirit and in full conviction.
(1 Thessalonians 1:5)

How often the apostle Paul demands *plērophoria* (the Greek word he uses)—that most sure and unyielding *affirmation* of conscience! In Romans 10:10 he calls it "confession," saying, "One confesses with the mouth and so is saved." And Christ says, "Everyone therefore who confesses me before others, I also will confess before my Father" [Matthew 10:32, Luther's reading].

Nothing is better known or more common among Christians than affirmation. Take away affirmations and you take away Christianity. The Holy Spirit is given to Christians from heaven that he may glorify Christ [in them] and make them firm and sure in their witness to Christ, so that they will live and die for it.

The Holy Spirit is no skeptic, and it is not doubts or mere opinions that he has written on our hearts but assertions more sure and certain than life itself and all experience.

The Bondage of the Will. LW 33:20, 24

I believe; Lord, help my unbelief. Amen.

The Lord Will Be Your Confidence

The LORD will be your confidence.
(Proverbs 3:26)

Christ, your righteousness, is greater than your sins and those of the whole world. His life and his consolation are stronger and mightier than your death and hell.

This conviction leads to a confident and staunch heart that can scorn the devil with all his terror and torment, defy all his might, and say, "Sin, if you want to condemn me, you will first have to condemn Christ, my dear Savior, priest, and intercessor with the Father. Death, if you want to devour me, you must begin on top, with Christ, my head. Devil and world, if you want to torment and frighten me, you must first pull him down from his throne. In brief, I will fear nothing, even if lightning were to strike this moment and throw everything into confusion. For Christ is mine with his suffering, death, and life; the Holy Spirit, with his comfort; and the Father himself, with all his grace. He sends the Holy Spirit to preach Christ into my heart and to fill it with his consolation.

Sermons on John 14–17.   LW 24:292; WA 45:727

Care for me, O God of grace; help me that I never, anxious,
look to future days but may trust you ever. Amen.
(Laudamille Elisabeth, 1640–1672)

Christ Leads Us On

I am confident of this, that the one who began a good work among you
will bring it to completion by the day of Jesus Christ.
(Philippians 1:6)

"Hold firmly to me! Through my Word I have made the beginning
and have brought you to me. And now if you prove this, if you fight to
remain in me, you will be greatly troubled at first, and it will be difficult
for you. It will seem that you are all alone and that I have forsaken you
and am abandoning you to fear and all wretchedness. But just hold fast,
and I will prove that I love you. Then you will feel in your hearts how
pleasing your faith, your confession, and your suffering are to God. And
from this you will recognize and experience ever better who I am, how
powerful I am, and what I am working in you. Thus I will manifest
myself from day to day, until you have been so tried that you can place all
your trust in heaven and repel the devil."

Such confidence follows when, in days of trial, we test and experience
the doctrine we have already believed. Thus we become aware that we
are in Christ and that Christ is in us. If before this there was wrath and
displeasure anywhere, these have now vanished. For Christ is our dear
bishop and mediator before God, and he shall remain our only Master and
Lord. And no one shall accuse or terrify us, carp at us or teach us.

Sermons on John 14–15.   LW 24:153; WA 45:600f.

To you, O Lord, the Rock that is higher than I,
my soul in its conflicts and sorrows would fly. Amen.

Holding Forth the Word of Life

Give attention to the public reading of scripture, to exhorting, to teaching.
(1 Timothy 4:13)

I am often aware of temptation, and even today I cannot guard and cross myself against it too carefully. I confess this freely as an example to anyone; for here am I, an old doctor of theology and a preacher, and certainly as competent in Scripture as such smart alecks. At least I ought to be. Yet even I must become a child; and early each day I recite aloud to myself the Lord's Prayer, the Ten Commandments, the Creed, and whatever lovely psalms and verses I may choose, just as we teach and train children to do. Besides, I must deal with Scripture and fight with the devil every day. I dare not say in my heart, "The Lord's Prayer is worn out; you know the Ten Commandments; you can recite the Creed." I study them daily and remain a pupil of the Catechism. I feel, too, that this helps me a lot, and I am convinced by experience that God's Word can never be entirely mastered, but that Psalm 147 speaks truly, "His understanding is beyond measure" (verse 5).

Sermon on of Psalm 117.   LW 14:8; WA 31/1:227

In this life I know the temptations to power, property, and fame.
Keep me steadfast, O God, in your Word. Amen.

A Wonderful and Precious God

I thank you that you have chastened me and have become my salvation.
(Psalm 118:21, Luther's reading)

This is a joyful verse. It sings and dances along in sheer delight. Are you not a wonderful and precious God, who rules over us so wonderfully and so graciously? You exalt us when you humble us. You justify us when you show us to be sinners. You lead us into heaven when you cast us into hell. You give us victory when you allow us to be defeated. You bestow life on us when you give us over to death. You comfort us when you allow us to grieve. You make us joyful when you allow us to weep and lament. You make us sing when you allow us to weep. You make us strong when we suffer. You make us wise when you make us fools. You make us rich when you make us poor. You make us masters when you allow us to serve—and innumerable similar wonders are all contained in this one verse and for all of which Christians give thanks in these few words: "I give thanks to you, for you have chastened me and have become my salvation."

Sermons from the year 1532.   WA 36:171

With the psalmists of old, Lord God, I long to sense your shining face
in the midst of sorrow and tears. Amen.

The Testimony of the Spirit within Us

Likewise the Spirit helps us in our weakness.
(Romans 8:26)

Let no one think that he or she will be freed from all sin, lust, and evil thoughts; yet each must continue to yearn for such freedom and cry to God, "Ah, if only I could be set free from sin." So the voice of the Holy Spirit will cry out in us until the last day. Therefore sin always abides in us poor Christians. We fall into sin, not wilfully or out of wickedness but from weakness, which God can well forgive. Therefore it is the best comfort that we have within us the testimony of the Holy Spirit, which means that when we are in need and cry to God, he will be gracious to us and will help us. For our position is now so different from what it was before, when we were in need. Now we can trust in God and know that he will not forsake us, and thus we show that we are truly Christians.

On Many Important Matters, 1537. WA 45:405

O Holy Spirit, enter in, and in my heart your work begin,
and make my heart your dwelling. In your radiance life from heaven
now is given, overflowing, gift of gifts beyond all knowing.
(Michael Schirmer, 1606–1673)

One Holy Catholic Church

Ephesians 4:1-6

. . . that they may be one.
(John 17:21)

To all who believe, the promise is given for Christ's sake and by the power of this prayer, that they shall be one body and one loaf with all Christians. They are promised that what happens to them for good or ill shall happen to the whole body for good or ill. Not only one or two saints, but all the prophets, martyrs, apostles, all Christians, both on earth and with God in heaven, shall suffer and conquer with them, shall fight for them, help, protect, and save them, and shall undertake for them such a gracious exchange that they will all bear their sufferings, want, and afflictions, and they will partake of all their blessings, comfort, and joy.

How could anyone wish for anything more blessed than to come into this fellowship and be made a member of the body that is called Christendom? For who can harm or injure a person who has this confidence, who knows that heaven and earth, and all the angels and the saints, will cry to God when the smallest suffering comes? If a sin attacks them to frighten, bite, and oppress their conscience, threatening them with the devil, death, and hell, God speaks with the great company of heaven, "Sin, leave them to me unmolested! Hell, leave them undevoured. Death, leave them untouched." But this cannot be done without faith, because to the eyes of the world and of reason, the opposite appears to happen.

Sermons on John 16–20, 1528.   WA 28:182

I love your church, O God! Its walls before you stand, dear
as the apple of your eye and graven on your hand. Amen.
(Timothy Dwight, 1752–1817)

The True Church

Your life is hidden with Christ in God.
(Colossians 3:3)

The church is ruled by the Spirit of God and the saints are led by the Spirit of God (Romans 8:14). And Christ remains with his church even to the end of the world (Matthew 28:20).

But here is the task, to determine whether those whom you call the church are the church, or rather, whether after being in error all their lives they were at last brought back before they died. In the time of Elijah, everybody and everything in the public life of this people had so far fallen into idolatry that Elijah thought he alone was left; and yet, although kings and priests and everything that could be called the people or church of God was going to perdition, God had kept for himself seven thousand (1 Kings 19:18). But who saw them or knew them to be the people of God?

What happened in Christ's own time, when all the apostles fell away and he himself was denied and condemned by the whole people, and scarcely more than a Nicodemus, a Joseph, and the thief on the cross were saved? Were these then called the people of God? They were the remnant of the people, but they were not so called, and what was so called was not the people of God.

Who knows but that the state of the church of God throughout the whole course of the world from the beginning has always been such that some have been called the people and the saints of God who were not so, while others, a remnant in their midst, really were the people or the saints, but were never called so?

On the Bondage of the Will.   LW 33:85–86

Remember, O Lord, your church. Deliver her from all evil, perfect her in
your love, and from the four winds gather her, the sanctified,
in your kingdom. Amen. (Didache 10:5)

The Church Is Founded on the Word of God

The words that you gave to me I have given to them.
(John 17:8)

This constrains us and makes us sure, namely, that a real Christian knows that the church never ordains or institutes anything apart from the Word of God. Any church that does so is no church except in name only, as Christ says in John 10, verses 27 and 5: "My sheep hear my voice. . . . They will not follow a stranger, but they will run from him because they do not know the voice of strangers." It is not God's Word just because the church speaks it; instead the church comes into being because God's Word is spoken. The church does not constitute the Word but is constituted by the Word. The Word of God is a sure sign by which we may know where the church is.

How can we know where the church is if we do not hear her preaching and the testimony of the Spirit?

On the Misuse of the Mass, 1521. LW 36:145; WA 8:491f.

Heavenly Father, open my ears that I may hear your Word. Amen.

The People Whose Sins Are Forgiven

The people who live there will be forgiven their iniquity.
(Isaiah 33:24)

"The kingdom of Christ is not one of condemnation. I am not here to condemn you but to remit the sins of those who, like you, are where death, the devil, evil consciences, accusers, and judges have come to plague them. The principle in my kingdom is: I forgive you your sin, for in my kingdom no one is without forgiveness of sins. Therefore you too must have forgiveness. My kingdom must not be in disorder. All who enter it and dwell in it must be sinners. But as sinners they cannot live without the forgiveness of sins."

Thus only those sinners belong in the kingdom of Christ who recognize their sin, feel it, and then catch hold of the Word of Christ, "I do not condemn you." These people constitute the membership of Christ's kingdom. He admits no saint; he sweeps them all out; he expels from the church all who lay claim to holiness. If sinners enter, they do not remain sinners. He spreads his cloak over their sins and says, "If you have sinned, I remit your sins and cover them." To be sure, sin is there. But the Lord in this kingdom closes his eyes to it, covers it, forgives it, and does not impute it to the sinner. Thus you are made a living saint and a true member of Christ.

Sermons on John 6–8.   LW 23:318; WA 33:509

If you, O Lord, should mark iniquities,
Lord, who could stand?
But there is forgiveness with you,
so that you may be revered. Amen.
(Psalm 130:3-4)

The Keys of the Kingdom

*Truly I tell you, whatever you bind on earth will be bound in heaven,
and whatever you loose on earth will be loosed in heaven.
(Matthew 18:18)*

Whatever is bound on earth is bound in heaven. God here binds himself
to the judgments of the holy Christian church on earth, when she uses
her judgment aright, so that the judgment of the church becomes God's
judgment. Holy Scripture teaches here that the Lord Christ has ordained
in the church a great spiritual order, that he and the church shall have
power with regard to public sins and vices to bind and banish those
responsible through the Word. He does not say that he reserves some
power to himself, but what the church binds shall be bound in his
sight—that, and nothing else.

Therefore, wherever you see that sin is punished or forgiven, publicly
or otherwise, you may know that the people of God are there. Where
there are not the people of God, there are not the keys either. For Christ
has left them behind so that there shall be a public symbol and sanctuary
where the Holy Spirit can sanctify sinners and where Christians can bear
witness that they are one holy people under Christ in this world. And
those who will not turn away from their sins and be sanctified must be
expelled from this holy people—that is, bound and locked out by the
keys.

On the Councils and Church, 1539. LW 41:153; WA 50:632

Nothing in my hands I bring; simply to your cross I cling. Amen.

The Sanctuary of the Cross

*Blessed are you when people revile you and persecute you
and utter all kinds of evil against you falsely.
(Matthew 5:11)*

The holy Christian people are externally recognized by the holy possession of the sacred cross. They must endure every misfortune and persecution, all kinds of trials and evil from the devil, the world, and the flesh (as the Lord's Prayer indicates) by inward sadness, timidity, fear, outward poverty, contempt, illness, and weakness, in order to become like their head, Christ. The only reason they must suffer is that they steadfastly adhere to Christ and God's Word, enduring this for the sake of Christ. They must be pious, quiet, obedient, and prepared to serve the government and everybody with life and goods, doing no one any harm. No people on earth have to endure such bitter hate; they must be called heretics, knaves, and devils, the most pernicious people on earth, to the point where those who hang, drown, murder, torture, banish, and plague them to death are rendering God a service. No one has compassion on them; they are given myrrh and gall to drink when they thirst. All of this is done not because they are adulterers, murderers, thieves, or rogues but because they want to have none but Christ, and no other God. Wherever you see or hear this, you may know that the holy Christian church is there, as Christ says in Matthew 5:11-12, "Blessed are you when people revile you . . . and utter all kinds of evil against you falsely on my account. Rejoice and be glad, for your reward is great in heaven." This too is a holy possession whereby the Holy Spirit not only sanctifies his people but also blesses them.

On the Councils and Church, 1539. LW 41:164; WA 50:641

I pray, O Lord, for all those throughout the world who are persecuted for righteousness' sake and for confessing your name. Amen.

The Unity of the Spirit through the Lord's Supper

The cup of blessing that we bless, is it not a sharing in the blood of Christ?
The bread that we break, is it not a sharing in the body of Christ?
(1 Corinthians 10:16)

Wherever you see this sacrament properly administered, there you may be assured of the presence of God's people. For, as I have said, wherever God's Word is, there the church must be. Likewise, wherever baptism and the sacrament are, God's people must be, and vice versa. For no one possesses or uses or observes these sacred things but the people of God, even though some false and unbelieving Christians are secretly among them. They, however, do not profane the people of God because they are not known.

See that you exercise and confirm your faith, so that when you are troubled or when sin is besetting you, you go to the sacrament and heartily desire it, and what it signifies, and do not doubt that it will be done to you as the sacrament declares, that Christ and all his saints will draw near to you with all their virtues, sufferings, and graces, to live, work, rest, suffer, and die with you, and be so fully yours that they have all things common with you. If you are willing to practice this belief and confirm it, you will experience what a rich and joyful marriage feast your God has prepared for you on the altar.

On the Councils and Church, 1539.   LW 41:152; 50:631

In your service, Lord, defend us; in our hearts keep watch and ward;
in the world to which you send us let your kingdom come, O Lord. Amen.
(Louis F. Benson, 1855–1930)

Teaching and Understanding

1 Corinthians 1:4-9

If Christ has not been raised, your faith is futile
and you are still in your sins.
(1 Corinthians 15:17)

When you want to preach the gospel, you must treat only the resurrection of Christ. Anyone who does not preach this is no apostle. For this is the chief article of our faith. And those books that teach and stress this most are indeed the noblest books. Thus the epistle of James is no truly apostolic epistle, for it does not contain a single word about these things. The greatest power of faith is bound up in this article. For if there were no resurrection, we would have no consolation or hope, and everything else Christ did and suffered would be futile.

Therefore one must teach as follows: "See, Christ died for you! He took sin, death, and hell upon himself and submitted himself. But nothing could subdue him, for he was too strong. He rose from the dead, was completely victorious, and subjected everything to himself. He did all this in order that you might be free from it and lord over it. We are not able to do all this with our own power. Consequently, Christ had to do it. Otherwise there would have been no need for him to come down from heaven." When we preach about our works, it is impossible for this message to be accepted and understood. Oh, how well we Christians should be aware of this! How clear this should be to us!

Sermons on 1 Peter, 1523.   LW 30:12; WA 12:268f.

Whether I live or whether I die, I am yours, O Lord.
Let me live in the hope of resurrection. Amen.

We Bear Witness through Our Infirmity

God chose what is foolish in the world to shame the wise.
(1 Corinthians 1:27)

Unless we are weak, Christ cannot exercise his strength on us. If we were to withstand our adversaries with our own power and strength, the glory would be ours and not Christ's. But our experience teaches that we are not our own saviors, but that God must help us. Thus God is honored in our weakness. Therefore when our enemies swagger and boast, and we are very weak by comparison, then God comes to our aid and proves his strength in our weakness.

Thus the Lord Christ also consoles us. He will have us know that our experience will be like his. At times we will be weak, while our enemies and adversaries will appear as strong and boasting blusterers. But Christ will still see us through.

Thus God deals with us when we ourselves and all that we stand for are yielding and going to pieces before the world, when we are outwardly weak in the eyes of the world, or when each single Christian is hard pressed, so that we are not afraid or dispirited. Here we learn that our Lord God does not jest when he feigns to be weak but is in earnest, for he will cast down the mighty through the weak and will exalt the weak. But we must not look upon these things with the eyes of worldly reason, as is generally done, or we shall be lost. We must know that it is God's will to overcome the mighty through the weak. We must believe this and then shut our eyes.

Sermons on John 6–8.   LW 23:215–16; WA 33:339ff.

In my weakness, in my finitude, O God,
let your presence give me strength and hope. Amen.

The Word Shows Whether the Church Is Present

They were yours, and you gave them to me, and they have kept your word.
(John 17:6)

There is no argument about whether there is on earth a church that we should obey. The battle begins when we must decide which is the true church. As long as we judge according to human words and understanding, we cannot settle this quarrel, nor can we find the true church, but we can reach certainty in the matter if we hear how Christ our Lord himself describes and portrays the church. Here he christens and depicts her as the little company that loves Christ and keeps his Word (for in this way is such love known and felt). "My Word," he says, "must remain and be kept, or there can be no church." The Word of Christ is here the rule and test whereby one can find and know the true church, and by which she must set her course, for there must be a rule and order according to which the church shall preach and act. It is not right that any one of us speak and act as we like and claim that the church has spoken and acted by the Holy Spirit.

That is why Christ binds his church to his Word and gives it to her as a sign whereby we may inquire and test whether she possesses the Word and teaches and preaches in accordance with it and does everything for the love of Christ.

Sermon on Pentecost, 1544.   WA 21:461

Lord, keep us steadfast in your Word. Defend your holy church that we may sing your praise eternally. Amen. (Martin Luther, 1483–1546)

The Preacher Shall Be God's Mouthpiece

Whoever listens to you listens to me.
(Luke 10:16)

God speaks through the holy prophets and other persons of God, as St. Peter says in his epistle, "Men moved by the Holy Spirit spoke from God" (2 Peter 1:21 RSV). God and humans must not be separated and severed from each other according to the understanding and judgment of human reason. Instead we must immediately say, "Whatever this man or woman, prophet, apostle, or sound preacher and teacher says and does by the command and Word of God, God himself says and does, for he or she is God's mouthpiece and instrument." Those who hear him or her should say with conviction, "At this instant I am not listening to Paul, Peter, or any human being, but I am listening to God himself speaking, baptizing, pronouncing absolution, punishing, excommunicating, or administering the sacrament."

Oh, my Lord God, what a great comfort a poor, contrite, and broken conscience may receive from such a preacher, when it believes that such words and comfort really are God's Word and comfort, and that God means it so. Therefore we most certainly believe that God works through his Word, which is like an instrument through which the heart may truly learn to know him.

Table Talk.   WA Tischreden 3:673f.

How beautiful upon the mountains are the feet of the messenger who announces peace, who brings good news, who announces salvation, who says to Zion, "Your God reigns." (Isaiah 52:7)

Try the Spirits

Beloved, do not believe every spirit, but test the spirits to see whether they are from God; for many false prophets have gone out into the world.
(1 John 4:1)

He is called the Spirit of truth because he is opposed to all lies and false spirits, for the world is full of spirits. As the proverb says, "Where God builds a church, the devil builds a chapel beside it." That is, where the pure Word of God is preached, the devil introduces sects and mobs and many false spirits that take to themselves the glory and the name of Christ and his church. But at bottom it is all false and there is no truth nor certainty in it. "But I will give you the Spirit," says Christ, "who will make you sure and certain of the truth, so that you will no longer doubt any article concerning your eternal blessedness but will be sure of the matter and will be able to be judges and judge all other teaching." Thus he will not only make you soldiers and victors but will give you a scarlet robe and make you doctors and masters who can discern with certainty which teaching is true and which false in the church. The devil will not be sufficiently clever and no traitor sufficiently nimble to make your teaching false or lead you astray.

Thus the Christian church has held her own from the beginning until now among innumerable false spirits that have been from the beginning and may still come. Yet she goes on standing firmly by her baptism, the Lord's Supper, the gospel, Christ, the Ten Commandments, and true and pure prayer, and thus she judges and separates from herself all false teaching that is opposed to her—yes, even though the devil should become an angel of light and as a beautiful and radiant figure should present himself as God.

Sermons on John 14–15.   LW 24:292; WA 45:727ff.

Lead me to a mature faith, O God, and let me avoid the lures of the preachers of false hope. Amen.

Let Us Hold Fast to the Confession of Our Faith

Let us hold fast to the confession of our hope without wavering;
for he who has promised is faithful.
(Hebrews 10:23)

Therefore, take care. Let nothing on earth, even if it were an angel from heaven, be so great as to drive you against your conscience and away from the teaching you recognize and regard as God's. St. Paul says in Galatians 1:8, "Even if we or an angel from heaven should proclaim to you a gospel contrary to what we proclaimed to you, let that one be accursed!" You are not the first, you are not even the only one, nor will you be the last to be persecuted for the sake of the Word of God. Christ says, "Blessed are those who are persecuted for righteousness' sake" (Matthew 5:10). Again, "You will be hated by all nations because of my name" (Matthew 24:9). Again, "An hour is coming when those who kill you will think that by doing so they are offering worship to God" (John 16:2). We have to take a firm hold of such texts and strengthen ourselves by them. In fact, we ought to praise and thank God for persecution, and pray to prove worthy of suffering for the sake of his Word. Remember, it is foretold that in the day of the Antichrist no one will be permitted to preach, and that all who speak and listen to God's Word shall be regarded as outcasts. That is what is happening now, and it has been going on for more than a hundred years.

Instruction to Penitents, 1521.LW 44:227; WA 7:295f.

In our time of competing voices, O God,
let your Word lead me on the right path. Amen.

In the Power of Christ

*Very truly, I tell you, the one who believes in me will also do the works
that I do and, in fact, will do greater works than these,
because I am going to the Father.
(John 14:12)*

Because we have such a treasure, we have everything and are lords over
all lords. On earth we are beggars, as Christ himself was; but before God
we are bountifully blessed with all good things. In comparison, the world
is poor and destitute, nor can it retain its goods without us. Now why
will the Christians do works just like, and greater than, those of Christ
himself? He says that there is no other reason than this: "Because I go to
the Father."

By "going to the Father" Christ means that he is to be made Lord
and placed on the royal chair at the right hand of the Father, that all
power and might in heaven and on earth are given to him. "You will
get the power to perform such works because you are my members and
believe in me; because you will be in me, and I will be in you. The power
that I shall have at the right hand of the Father—being of the same
divine majesty and openly transfigured and shown forth as very God and
Lord over all creatures—I shall work in you who believe in me and who,
having received my Word, baptism, and sacrament, steadfastly abide in
them. Just as I am Lord over sin, death, hell, the devil, the world, and
everything, so you shall also be lords over these and be able to glory in
the same power. This is yours, not by reason of your own worthiness or
strength, but solely because I am going to the Father. Through the Word
and through prayer, my Word will work mightily in you.

Sermons on John 14–15.   LW 24:85; WA 45:537ff.

*Lord of light, your name outshining all the stars and suns of space,
use my talents in your kingdom as the servants of your grace. Amen.
(Howell E. Lewis, 1860–1953)*

The Sanctifying Power of the Church

Ephesians 4:22-32

*We are putting no obstacle in anyone's way,
so that no fault may be found with our ministry.
(2 Corinthians 6:3)*

A Christian should be careful to give no offense to anyone so that the name of God shall not be blasphemed. It is a great thing to be a Christian—that is, a new person created after God, and a true image of God in whom God himself is clearly seen. Therefore, whatever a Christian does, be it good or evil (under the name of Christian), will be counted to the honor or dishonor of the name of God. Therefore, if you follow your lusts and obey the old person within you, you do nothing but give occasion to the blasphemer and cause the name of God to be blasphemed because of you.

In this respect Christians should take the greatest care, even if they care for nothing else, to protect and honor the name of their dear God and Savior, Jesus Christ.

Sermon on the Nineteenth Sunday after Trinity, 1544. WA 22:321.

Let me, O Lord, reflect your grace and mercy in all my dealings. Amen.

Stewards of the Mysteries of God

*Think of us in this way, as servants of Christ
and stewards of God's mysteries.
(1 Corinthians 4:1)*

St. Paul might well have said here, "We are stewards of the wisdom of God, or the righteousness of God," or the like. But that would be speaking in fragments. Therefore, to comprise everything that is offered in Christ, he uses the word "mysteries." It is as if he wished to say, "We are spiritual stewards and we distribute the grace of God, the truth of God, and who could count all his innumerable virtues? I call them mysteries and hidden things because they can be obtained by faith alone."

The mysteries of God are those hidden things that God gives and that dwell in God. The devil also has his mysteries, but there is nothing in them but death and hell for all who believe in them. But the mysteries of God contain life and blessedness.

Thus we learn from these words that the apostle regards the servants of Christ as stewards of the mysteries of God. That is, they should regard themselves and be regarded by others as persons who preach and give to the people of God nothing but Christ and what belongs to Christ. They shall preach the pure gospel and the pure faith, that Christ alone is our life, way, wisdom, power, prize, and blessedness, and that without him we have nothing but death, error, folly, helplessness, shame, and damnation. Whoever preaches anything else shall not be deemed a servant of Christ or a steward of the mysteries of God.

Sermon on the Third Sunday in Advent, 1522.   WA 10/1(ii):128f.

*Life itself is a great mystery, O God. Let my life be anchored
in the greater mystery of your steadfast love. Amen.*

Christians Save the World

*. . . as poor, yet making many rich; as having nothing,
and yet possessing everything.
(2 Corinthians 6:10)*

Every individual Christian is a human being such as the Lord Christ himself was on earth. He accomplishes great things and is able to govern the whole world in divine matters. He can help and benefit everybody, doing the greatest works on earth. For his sake God gives the world all that it has, and preserves it. If there were no Christians on earth, no city or country would enjoy peace; everything on earth would perish in a single day. That grain still grows in the field; that people recover from an illness; that they have their sustenance, peace, and protection—all this they owe to the Christians.

Indeed, we are poor beggars, yet we make many rich; although we have nothing, yet we possess everything. What kings, princes, lords, ordinary citizens, and peasants have is not theirs by reason of their golden hair but because of Christ and his Christians.

Christians have the gospel, baptism, and the sacrament, by means of which they convert people, snatch souls from the clutches of the devil, wrest them from hell and death, and bring them to heaven. With these they also comfort, strengthen, and preserve poor consciences that are saddened and troubled by the devil and others. They are able to teach and instruct people in all walks of life and to help them live in a Christian and blessed way.

All these are works that all kings and emperors in the world, all the mighty and the rich, all scholars and sages, are unable to do and could not purchase with all their wealth. For none of them can console and gladden a single conscience that is oppressed and aggrieved by sin.

Sermons on John 14–15.   LW 24:79; WA 45:532

*Give me strength, Lord God, to do the work you would have me do
in my time and place. Amen.*

The True Fellowship

Let all that you do be done with love.
(1 Corinthians 16:14)

True fellowship is divine and heavenly; it is the noblest, surpassing all the others as gold surpasses copper or lead; it is the communion of saints, in which we all are brothers and sisters, so near to one another that greater nearness could never be conceived. For there is *one* baptism, *one* Christ, *one* sacrament, *one* meal, *one* gospel, *one* faith, *one* Spirit, *one* spiritual body, and each one is a member of the other; no other brotherhood is so deep and close.

But if you say, "Unless I get something through the fellowship, of what use is it?" The answer is, "You serve the community and other peoples as love does, and you will have your reward without any seeking or desiring it." Love serves freely, which is why God in return also gives to it every blessing, freely and without charge. Because all things must be done in love if they are to be well pleasing to God, the community must also be in love. Yet what is done in love can by its nature not seek its own; instead it seeks the benefit of others, and especially the congregation.

As you find your trust in Christ and his dear saints growing in strength, your certainty grows of their love toward you, and how they will stand by you in all the troubles of life and death. Therefore your love goes out to each one and you desire to help everyone, hate no one, suffer with all, and pray for all. Again, if you take to heart the shortcomings and lapses of all Christians and of the whole church, or the fall of any one, and your love is given to them all, so that you would readily help anyone, hate none, sympathize with all, and pray for them, then all is well.

The Sacrament of the Body of Christ, 1519. LW 35:70, 72; WA 2:756f.

O God of mercy, God of light, in love and mercy infinite,
teach us as ever in your sight to live our lives in you. Amen.
(Godfrey Thring, 1823–1903)

The Unity of the Spirit in the Sacrament

For we being many are one bread, and one body;
for we are all partakers of that one bread.
(1 Corinthians 10:17)

To receive this sacrament in bread and wine is to receive a certain sign of fellowship and incorporation with Christ and all the saints.

Just as the bread is made out of many grains ground and mixed together, and out of the bodies of many grains there comes the body of one bread, in which each grain loses its form and body and takes upon itself the common body of the bread, and just as the drops of wine, in losing their own form, become the body of one common wine and drink—so it is and should be with us, if we use this sacrament properly. Christ with all saints, by his love, takes upon himself our form, fights with us against sin, death, and all evil. This kindles in us such love that we take on his form, rely upon his righteousness, life, and blessedness. Through the interchange of his blessings and our misfortunes, we become one loaf, one bread, one body, one drink, and have all things in common. This is indeed a great sacrament, says St. Paul, that Christ and the church are one flesh and bone. Again through this same love, we are to be changed and to make the infirmities of all other Christians our own; we are to take upon ourselves their form and their necessity, and all the good that is within our power we are to make theirs, that they may profit from it. That is real fellowship, and that is the true significance of this sacrament.

The Sacrament of the Body of Christ, 1519.   LW 35:58; WA 2:743

As we break bread together, O Lord, we rejoice in our fellowship
with one another and with you. Amen.

In Christ We Are Sure of the Teaching

So we have the prophetic message more fully confirmed.
You will do well to be attentive to this.
(2 Peter 1:19)

We have the comforting promise in defiance of all opposition that what we (as Christians) speak, and do, and suffer is true and comes from the Spirit of truth; and again, whatever is done, said, preached, and undertaken against it must be false and full of lies before God, however right it may appear, and whatever claim may be made by it as pure truth, highest holiness, and spirituality—yes, even when the world fights for it with all its might, to maintain it, and most cruelly slanders us and storms against us. For our gospel and deeds are not founded on us, neither are they for our sakes, but everything is for the sake of this Lord Christ, from whom we have all things and for whose sake we preach and live and suffer. Since, then, all things are for his sake, we leave the caring to him who says he will bring all these things to fulfillment and give us the spirit and the courage we need; and what he does through his Christians is pure and certain truth.

Sermons on John 14–15.   LW 24:120; WA 45:569f.

Lord, to whom can we go? You have the words of eternal life. Amen.
(John 6:68)

Before God We Are All Equal

God shows no partiality.
(Romans 2:11)

Thus all is made even and no one has more than another by which to glory before God, who will suffer no person to be despised, censured, or cast out. It is said, "Preach this gospel to all creatures." In this respect the greatest, wisest, holiest, noblest human being is no better than the meanest, simplest, and most despised one on earth. They are all lumped together, and no one is singled out or separated, for sorrow, or for love, or for praise and privilege. It is written plainly and without exception that those who believe, whoever they are, and no matter to what people, nation, or class they belong, and however unequal they may be in the eyes of the world, are in the same situation. But in the life of the world there must be inequality and variety, as there is among the creatures, where each is of its own kind and differs from the others.

Yet although all this works in perfect order, no one can say that whoever does this or that will be saved. Therefore in this kingdom of Christ all is heaped together and comprised in one word in one sentence: not this person or that person doing this or that, but "The one who believes . . . will be saved" (Mark 16:16). There you have it all in one, whether you be Jew or Gentile, master or servant, virgin or husband. "If you believe," says Christ, "you are in my kingdom, saved and redeemed from sin and death."

Sermon on the Ascension of Christ, 1544.   WA 21:393f.

Save me, O God, from seeking undue human praise and distinction,
for I know that we are all equal in your sight. Turn my thoughts outward,
toward those around me. Amen.

The Church's Worship

Ephesians 5:15-21

*. . . that together you may with one voice glorify
the God and Father of our Lord Jesus Christ.
(Romans 15:6)*

All that we can give to God is praise and thanksgiving. This is the only true service, as God himself says.

But how could we give God praise and adoration, the only true service, if we did not love God and accept his gifts? But how can we love God unless we know him and his gifts? But how can we know God and his gifts if no one preaches about them, and the gospel is left lying under the bushel? For where there is no gospel God cannot be known; hence there can be no praise or love of God. Thus there can be no worship.

St. Paul admonishes us that we should with *one* voice glorify God. That happens when we are of *one* mind and know that we are all equal, having received the same gifts in Christ, so that no one exalts himself or herself above another, and no one claims any special gift.

Sermon on the Second Sunday in Advent, 1522.   WA 10/1(ii):80f.

*O God, I know how easily pettiness and self-seeking can create divisions
among the believers. Help me to be a peacemaker. Amen.*

The Service

. . . how I went with the throng . . . to the house of God, with glad shouts and songs of thanksgiving, a multitude keeping festival.
(Psalm 42:4)

This multitude needs a certain place and certain days and hours suitable for listening to the Word of God; and therefore God has ordained and instituted the holy sacraments to be administered to the congregation at a place where all gather together for prayer and thanksgiving.

The advantage of this is that when Christians gather together, prayer is more powerful than at other times. We can and should most certainly pray at all places and hours, but prayer is nowhere so strong and powerful as when, in unity of Spirit, the whole congregation is gathered together to pray.

This is said that we Christians might know in what way, to what end, and to what degree we should use it, which means that we should gather at a certain place and time to study and hear the Word of God and to bring before God our own and other general and particular needs, and thus send up to heaven a strong and powerful prayer, as well as to join in praising and glorifying God for all his benefits. And this we know is the true service, which is well pleasing to God and which he honors with his presence.

Whatever is done at such a gathering of the congregation or church is pure and holy and divine—a holy Sabbath whereby God is worshiped in holiness and humans are strengthened.

Sermons from the year 1544.   LW 51:337, 339; WA 49:593f.

I was glad when they said to me, "Let us go to the house of the LORD!"
(Psalm 122:1)

The Church in Intercession

First of all, then, I urge that supplications, prayers, intercessions,
and thanksgivings be made for everyone.
(1 Timothy 2:1)

Common prayer is a precious and most powerful thing. That is why we gather together to pray. The church is called a house of prayer where we may gather together in unity of spirit and consider the needs and sorrows of all persons and carry them up in prayer before the throne of God and invoke his grace. This must be done earnestly and with genuine affection, because we feel the need of all individuals and therefore pray to God with real sympathy for them, in sure trust and confidence.

Would to God that some multitude might so pray that one common and genuine cry of the heart of the whole people should soar up to God! What immeasurable help and virtue would follow such a prayer! What greater calamity could befall all evil spirits? What greater thing could be wrought on earth, whereby so many sinners would be won, so many saints upheld?

Indeed, it is not that places and buildings are lacking where we can gather together—lofty, great, and glorious churches, spires or bells, but only this unconquerable prayer, that we should unite and offer it to God.

Sermon on Good Works, 1520.   WA 9:263f.

O Lord, let me join my voice with the faithful of all places that you would hear the cries of the suffering and all those who are bereft of hope. Amen.

The Catechism

Until I arrive, give attention to the public reading of scripture,
to exhorting, to teaching.
(1 Timothy 4:13)

My advice is that people should not dispute about secret and hidden things, but that they should stay simply by the Word of God and especially the catechism, for there is a good and true summary of the whole Christian religion and the most important articles put together in brief. For God himself gave the Ten Commandments, Christ composed and taught the Lord's Prayer, and the Holy Spirit set down the articles of the Creed in the shortest and most appropriate words. But it is despised as a bad, unworthy thing, because the children have to say it by heart every day.

The catechism is the true bible of laypersons; it contains the whole Christian teaching as all Christians must know it for their eternal blessedness.

The catechism contains the best and most perfect Christian teaching. Therefore it should be preached again and again without ceasing, and all the common preaching should be founded on it and related to it. I wish it would be preached every day and that preachers would simply read it from the book.

Table Talk.   WA Tischreden 2:523

Help me, Lord God, to follow your commandments, to pray as our Lord
taught us, and to trust the teachings of our creed. Amen.

Come, for Everything Is Ready Now

At the time for the dinner he sent his slave to those who had been invited,
"Come; for everything is ready now."
(Luke 14:17)

Friend, if you had no occasion or need to go to the sacrament, would it not be a serious and wicked thing to feel cold and disinclined toward it? What else could that mean than that you were disinclined to believe, to thank and to remember your dear Savior and all the goodness he has shown you through his bitter suffering, endured that he might redeem you from sin, death, and the devil, and justify you, give you life, and save you? But how shall you guard yourself against such coldness and disinclination? How shall you awaken your faith? How shall you stir yourself to give thanks? Will you wait until prayer breaks in upon you or till the devil makes a place for it? That will never happen. You must stir yourself by this sacrament and hold fast to it. Here is the fire that can kindle the heart. You must remember your need and thirst, and hear and believe the good that your Savior accomplished for you, and your heart will be renewed and your thoughts be changed.

The Sacrament of the Body and Blood of Our Lord, 1530.   EA 23:196

I need you every hour, O Lord. I thank you
for the blessings of the holy sacrament. Amen.

Preaching and Suffering

The sacrifice acceptable to God is a broken spirit.
(Psalm 51:17)

It is a very precious promise—if only we could believe it—that our afflictions are to God the most pleasing sacrifices. The Lord God delights in our preaching, suffering, and sadness; they are the highest sacrifice. But this psalm is not speaking of the sacrifice of praise and thanksgiving; it teaches that sorrow and contrition are the greatest sacrifices, for they temper our old selves. If I preach, I do it in praise of our Lord God, so that I offer the morning and the evening sacrifice, for God is well pleased when his Word is preached, and preaching is the loftiest sacrifice a person can give. All those who preach in the right manner give praise to our Lord God. If they are thrown into prison for it, they willingly offer the further sacrifice; and such affliction and suffering are well pleasing to God and are to him like a thousand sacrifices. The broken and contrite heart is to God a greater sacrifice than the whole Levitical sacrifice. Would that we could believe it!

Short Writings on the Psalms, 1530–1532.   WA 31/1:542

Be with me, Lord God, in the sufferings of this life;
let these experiences deepen my trust in your steadfast love. Amen.

The Sacrifices of the Community

Contribute to the needs of the saints.
(Romans 12:13)

How strange! Every day we ask and desire the saints to care for our needs, and St. Paul teaches us to distribute to theirs.

St. Paul mentions the needs of the saints in order to stimulate and inflame us all the more to do good to Christians. He points out to us the true saints, namely, those who are in dire need. That is, they don't look like saints at all; instead they look like poor, forlorn, hungry, naked, imprisoned people who are in need of everybody's help and cannot help themselves. The world regards them as wretched evildoers who deserve to suffer all kinds of misery. Christ will bring forward such saints on the day of judgment, saying, "Just as you did it to one of the least of these who are members of my family, you did it to me" (Matthew 25:40). Then the great saint-worshipers will stand in shame and fear before these saints, whom they would not look at on earth because of their disgrace.

"Extend hospitality to strangers"! Here Paul begins to enumerate some of the needs of the saints and to teach how we should care for them, namely, that this cannot be done by words alone but by deeds, such as to give them hospitality when they need it. It also includes all other bodily needs, such as feeding the hungry, giving drink to the thirsty, and clothing the naked.

Sermon on the Second Sunday after Epiphany, 1525.   WA 17/2:49f.

I thank you, Lord, for all those who work in our churches
for the relief of the homeless and the hungry. Amen.

The Church Militant

Ephesians 6:10-17

Finally, be strong in the Lord and in the strength of his power.
(Ephesians 6:10)

The writer acts like a proper God-fearing general who preaches a sermon to his troops drawn up in battle array, admonishing them to stand firm and fight boldly and confidently. This writing therefore might well be called a battle-sermon for Christians. For he shows here that those who are baptized into Christ and would hold fast to him must be warriors, always equipped with their armor and weapons, and that the lot of a Christian is no leisurely existence, nor one of peace and security; instead the Christian is always on campaign, attacking and defending.

Therefore the writer here warns and musters the soldiers, saying, "You are in my army and under my flag; see to it that you are on the lookout for the enemy, ready to defend yourselves against his angels, for he is never far away from you." As long as you do that, you need have no fear. For we belong to a Lord who has angels himself and power enough, and is called the Lord of hosts and the true victor over the dragon. He stands by us and fights for us. For the Word of the Lord abides forever. It may suffer temptation, and the church may have no peace from the enemy, and some who let the Word be taken out of their heart may fall, but the Word must abide forever.

Sermons from the year 1544.   WA 49:583f.

Lord, keep us steadfast in your word; curb those who by deceit
or sword would wrest the kingdom from your Son and bring
to naught all he has done. Amen. (Martin Luther, 1483–1546)

St. Michael's Great Fight

And war broke out in heaven; Michael and his angels fought against the dragon. The dragon and his angels fought back. (Revelation 12:7)

What is said about the fight in heaven must also come to pass here on earth within the visible churches, and the fight must not be understood in reference to the spirits in heaven but to all Christians who belong through faith to the kingdom of Christ.

They fight against the devil, who leads the world astray, and there is here on earth no other war than the fight against this seduction. That is why this war is not waged with armor, sword, pike, or musket, or with bodily or human power, but with the Word alone, as it is written, "They have conquered him by . . . the word of their testimony" (Revelation 12:11). With this testimony, the preaching of the Word and witnessing to it, they drive the devil out of heaven when he tries to go in and out among them to rob them of their salvation, which will be seen in the next life and now is believed.

Sermons from the year 1544.   WA 49:575f.

Deliver us, good Lord, from the cosmic powers of this present darkness, the spiritual forces of evil in the heavenly places. Amen.

Defending the Honor of God

The Jews answered him, "Are we not right in saying that you are a
Samaritan and have a demon?" Jesus answered, "I do not have a demon;
but I honor my Father, and you dishonor me."
(John 8:48-49)

What does Christ do here? He allows his life to be covered with shame,
and he endures it in silence. But he defends the teaching, for the teaching
is not ours but God's, and God must not suffer. There patience ceases and
I must venture for it all that I have and suffer all that they inflict upon
me, in order that the honor of God and God's Word shall not suffer. It
matters little if I perish, but if I let God's Word perish and remain silent,
I do harm to God and all the world.

Therefore, when they threaten our life, we must bear it and give love
for hate and good for evil. But when they attack the gospel, they attack
God's honor. Then love and patience must end, and we must not remain
silent but speak out and say, "I honor my Father; therefore you dishonor
me, but I do not seek my own honor. But be sure that there is one who
seeks my honor, and he will pronounce judgment; that is the Father
himself, and he will demand it of you and judge you." It is a comfort
to us that we can be cheerful if all the world heaps on us shame and
disgrace, for we know that God will demand our honor, and for the sake
of it he will execute judgment, punishment, and vengeance. Would that
we should believe it and wait for it, for he shall surely come!

Sermons from the year 1525.   WA 17/2:233

We praise you, O God; we acknowledge you to be the Lord.
All the earth does worship you, the Father everlasting. Amen.

The Importance of Truth and Unity

For we cannot do anything against the truth, but only for the truth.
(2 Corinthians 13:8)

This is so great a good that no human heart can grasp it (therefore it necessitates such a great and hard fight). It must not be treated lightly, as the world maintains and many people who do not understand, saying we should not fight so hard about an article and thus trample on Christian love. They say that although we err on one small point, if we agree on everything else, we should give in and overlook the difference in order to preserve Christian unity and fellowship.

No, my good person, do not recommend to me peace and unity when God's Word is lost thereby, for then eternal life and everything else would be lost. In this matter there can be no yielding nor giving way, no, not for love of you or any other person, but everything must yield to the Word, whether it be friend or foe. The Word was given to us for eternal life and not to further outward peace and unity. The Word and doctrine will create Christian unity or fellowship. Where they reign, all else will follow. Where they are not, no concord will ever abide. Therefore do not talk to me about love and friendship, if that means breaking with the Word, or the faith, for the gospel does not say that love brings eternal life, God's grace, and all heavenly treasures, but that these come from the Word.

Sermons from the year 1531.   WA 34/2:387

God's Word is our great heritage and shall be ours forever.
To spread its light from age to age shall be our chief endeavor.
(Martin Luther, 1483–1546)

The Weapons of Faith

Take . . . the sword of the Spirit, which is the word of God.
(Ephesians 6:17)

Christendom must also have people who can beat down their adversaries and opponents and tear off the devil's equipment and armor, that he may be brought into disgrace. But for this work powerful warriors are needed, who are thoroughly familiar with the Scriptures and can contradict all false interpretations and take the sword from false teachers—that is, those very verses that the false teachers use—and turn them back on them so that they fall defeated. But because not all Christians can be so capable in defending the Word and articles of their creed, they must have teachers and preachers who study the Scripture and have daily fellowship with it so that they can fight for all the others. Yet all Christians should be so armed that they themselves are sure of their belief and of the doctrine and are so equipped with sayings from the Word of God that they can stand up against the devil and defend themselves when others seek to lead them astray and so can help to fight the battle for the maintaining of true doctrine.

Sermons from the year 1531.   WA 34/2:378f.

In this confusing world, O God, let your Word be a lamp to my feet and a light to my path. Amen.

The Suffering Church

Resist [the devil], steadfast in your faith, for you know that your brothers and sisters in all the world are undergoing the same kinds of suffering. (1 Peter 5:9)

In such temptations St. Peter comforts the suffering Christians by telling them that they are not the only nor the first souls to be so tempted, as though they had to bear a peculiar, rare, and unheard-of cross and suffering and should think and feel that they alone had to bear it. Instead they should know that all their brothers and sisters in Christ scattered everywhere have at all times had to suffer thus from the devil and his onslaughts because they were in the world. For it is an immense help and comfort when the sufferer knows that he or she is not alone but is suffering with a great multitude.

Therefore none of us should regard our own anguish and distress as so horrible as if it were new and had never happened to anyone before. It may well be new to you and you may not have experienced it before. But look around at all the Christians in our beloved church from the beginning to this hour, planted in the world to run the devil's gauntlet and unceasingly winnowed and fanned like wheat.

For where God through his Word and faith has gathered together a church, the devil cannot be at peace. And where he cannot achieve its destruction through sectarianism, he strikes at it with persecution and violence so that we must risk our body and life in the fight, and all that we have.

Sermon on the Third Sunday after Trinity, 1544.   *WA 22:47f.*

Defend your church, Lord God, in the places where the faithful are persecuted and exiled. Give them strength and hope. Amen.

Christians, Arm Yourselves

Take the shield of faith. . . . Take the helmet of salvation,
and the sword of the Spirit. . . .
(Ephesians 6:16-17)

We must prepare for battle, and what we need most is a good, strong shield. Faith is such a shield, as the apostle indicates, as he takes it and clings to the Word of Christ, and answers the devil, "Though I am a sinner, though I have not lived as I ought and have done too little, yet there is the man, holy and pure, who gave himself for me and died for me and was given to me by the Father to be mine, with his holiness and righteousness. You must leave me unaccused and in peace. I hold fast to him. My life and deeds must remain as best they can."

"And the sword of the Spirit, which is the word of God." This is the last, but it is the strongest and the right weapon for smiting the devil and overcoming him. For it is not enough to have defended ourselves against the enemy and to be able to stand against him when he attacks us so that we are not defeated; that is called defense. We must also be able to take the offensive—that is, to pursue the enemy and put him to flight. Similarly, here it is not enough to ward off the devil with faith and hope as our shield and helmet, but we must draw the sword, hit back at him, hunt him down, and make him flee, thus gaining the victory ourselves. And that sword, he says, is the Word of God. For a sword of steel and iron would avail us nothing against the devil. It must be the sword of the Spirit.

Sermons from the year 1531.   WA 34/2:402ff.

God is our refuge and strength,
*   a very present help in trouble.*
Therefore we will not fear, though the earth should change,
*   though the mountains shake in the heart of the sea.*
(Psalm 46:1-2)

The Perfecting of the Church

Philippians 1:3-11

I am confident of this, that the one who began a good work
among you will bring it to completion by the day of Jesus Christ.
(Philippians 1:6)

Such is a Christian heart and such is its appearance and form, as St. Paul says in these words, namely, that from the bottom of his heart he is thrilled and delighted and gives thanks to God that others are coming into the fellowship of the gospel. He is full of confidence toward those who have begun to believe; he takes their salvation to heart and rejoices in it as much as in his own salvation and does not know how to thank God enough for it. He asks God unceasingly that he may live to see many come with him into that fellowship, and to be kept in it until the day of the Lord Jesus Christ, who will perfect all things and make whole what is deficient here. He prays that they will remain unobjectionable in such faith and hope until they reach that same joyful day.

Thus speaks the holy apostle as he pours out the bottom of his heart, filled with the rich and wondrous fruit of his spirit and faith, which is all on fire with joy and happiness when he sees that the gospel is understood, accepted, and honored. He is so filled with love for the church that he knows of nothing higher to wish it and to ask of God than that it may increase and abide in the gospel. He regards it as a great and precious treasure when people can hear the Word of God and keep it.

Sermon on the Third Sunday after Trinity, 1544.   WA 22:35f.

I love your kingdom, Lord, the place of your abode; the church our blest
Redeemer saved with his own precious blood. Amen.
(Timothy Dwight, 1752–1817, alt.)

The Blessings of Faith in Christ

I rejoice to see your morale and the firmness of your faith in Christ.
(Colossians 2:5)

Bodily blessings are common to all. But a Christian has other and far better blessings within, namely, faith in Christ. To have faith is to have the Word and truth of God, and to have the Word of God is to have God himself, the maker of all. If all these blessings in their fullness were revealed to the soul, it would in a moment break free from the body because of its exceeding abundance of sweet pleasure. Therefore all the other blessings of which we can speak are but monitors of the blessings that we have within us and that God would commend to us by them. Since this life of ours cannot bear to have them revealed, God mercifully keeps them hidden until they have reached their full measure. It is like loving parents who at times give their children foolish little toys with which they would lead their hearts to hope for better things.

At times, nevertheless, these inner blessings show themselves and break out, as when we with a happy conscience rejoice in our trust in God, speak openly about him, hear his Word with eagerness, and are ready and quick to serve him and do good works, to suffer evil, and so forth. These are all signs of the infinite and incomparable blessings hidden within, which, like a small spring, send forth little drops and tiny rills.

Fourteen Consolations.   LW 42:147

Oh, for a thousand tongues to sing my dear Redeemer's praise, the glories of my God and King, the wonders of his grace! (Charles Wesley, 1738)

TUESDAY

The Glory of the Church Is Still Hidden

Truly, you are a God who hides himself,
O God of Israel, the Savior.
(Isaiah 45:15)

The prophet Isaiah speaks the truth about God, for God hides his omnipotence, wisdom, power, and strength and makes it appear as though he could do nothing, know nothing, understand nothing, or does not wish to. Now God lets our enemies do as they like with his Word, sacraments, and the Christians. God lets us call and cry, and keeps silence, as though he were writing a poem, or were occupied with something else, or were out in the fields, or were asleep and could not hear us. But that day will come when God will manifest his greatness and power and omnipotence.

Meanwhile, Christians who are baptized in his name must keep still and endure being trampled on. They must be patient. For in the life of believing, it is God's will to appear small; but in the life of seeing, God will not be small but very great. Then he will show that he saw the suffering of his people and heard their cries and that his will was inclined toward them to help them, and that he had the power to help them. Now God hides his good will, his power and strength; but when he appears he will reveal his will and power and strength. God could help and save now. He has the power to do so, nor does he lack the will, but all this is concealed in the Word so that we cannot see it but must take hold of it by faith. But on the day of his advent he will take away the veil and he will appear as a great God and will do justice to his name, so that people will say, "See, God is the Lord and Savior."

Sermons from the year 1531.   WA 34/2:128

Along with the faithful of all ages, I wait with eager longing,
Lord God, for the day of earth's redemption. Amen.

In the Sign of Victory

The LORD says to my lord,
"Sit at my right hand
until I make your enemies your footstool."
(Psalm 110:1)

The prophet here depicts the kingdom of Christ as an eternal kingdom that is always engaged in battle. For it is written, "until I make your enemies your footstool." But that does not seem right to us. Such a king ought not to have many enemies, and he should drive them out swiftly with one stroke of his sword. Yes, and he will do so when the time comes, but while we are here on earth the warfare goes on. Schismatics, human wit and reason, our own flesh, conscience, death, and the devil press in on us to produce anxiety and fear. Therefore whoever wants to be a Christian should consider this and learn to know the nature of the kingdom.

There will be discord; it cannot be otherwise. Therefore when people rage and rave, I say, "It must be so. Don't you know who Christ is—a man whom the world, the devil, sin, and death and everything resist?" For he must have enemies, and here on earth his kingdom knows no settled peace. In the hereafter, in the life to come, there will be peace, but the kingdom on this earth shall not know peace.

Sermons from the year 1531.   WA 34/2:68f.

In this world of strife and contention, Lord God, give me strength
for each day and hope for the days to come. Amen.

THURSDAY

Wonderful Is Christ

He is named Wonderful Counselor. . . .
(Isaiah 9:6)

Christ is called "Wonderful" because it is wonderful and strange that he withholds from our eyes, reason, and senses all that he does for his Christian churches, and hides it away in his Word. Justification, holiness, wisdom, strength, life, salvation, and everything the church has in Christ is incomprehensible to reason and hidden from the world. If you judge the church according to reason and outward appearance, you are wrong, for you see persons who are sinful, weak, afraid, sad, wretched, persecuted, and hunted out of house and home. But when you see that they are baptized, believe in Christ, give evidence of their faith by bearing good fruits, and take up their cross with patience and hope, you have seen the truth. That is the true color by which we may know the Christian church.

The Christian church is holy and righteous, yet it does not appear holy and righteous. Human beings see nothing but sin and death and hear nothing but the slandering of the devil and the world. That is because Christian righteousness has its basis outside of us and is found in Christ and through faith in him. Therefore the whole Christian church and each single Christian confesses, "I know that I am sinful and impure, lying in prison, danger, death, shame, and disgrace, and I feel in myself nothing but sin. Yet I am just and holy, not of myself, but through Jesus Christ, whom God has made my wisdom, justification, sanctification, and salvation."

Sermon on the Festival of the Beheading of John the Baptist.   EA 6:281ff.

Just as I am you will receive, will welcome, pardon, cleanse, relieve;
because your promise I believe, O Lamb of God, I come. Amen.
(Charlotte Elliott, 1836, alt.)

Endure to the End and Win the Victory

The LORD is the stronghold of my life;
of whom shall I be afraid?
(Psalm 27:1)

Yes, God gives peace even in the midst of temptation, yet he does it in such a way that all the time you are going uphill and downhill and uphill again. One moment it is night, the next day, and then it is soon night again. It is not always night and not always day; it changes from one to the other so that at one time it is night, at another day, and soon it is night again. That is how God rules his Christian church, as we can see from all the stories of the Old and the New Testaments.

This is called the power of the Lord, that he is not a counselor and comforter who, when he has given us his Word, turns away from us and does nothing more for us, but God helps in order to bring our sufferings to an end. If we are led into temptation, he gives us his faithful counsel and fortifies us with his Word, so that we do not sink to the ground from weakness but are able to remain on our feet. But when the hour comes and we have suffered enough, he comes with power and we succeed and gain the victory. We need both counsel, to comfort and uphold us in our sufferings, and power to win through to the end. All the psalms give Christians strength in suffering; that is, they comfort us in our afflictions so that our backs do not break but we continue in hope and patience. Thus he leads all Christians. That is God's way. Anyone who does not know that does not know what sort of a king Christ is.

Sermon on St. Peter and St. Paul's Day. EA 6:294f.

In times of trial and testing, Lord God,
be the stronghold of my life. Amen.

Redemption from Strife and Suffering

He sent redemption to his people.
(Psalm 111:9)

"Those who have believed in me, suffered for my sake, and died in faith in me need have no fear. Those who have not believed may be afraid, but you need not fear, for it must come to pass so. If the world is to crash in ruins, there must first be some cracking and bursting; otherwise such a great structure cannot collapse. Everything must shake and sway, like a sick man, who when death strikes him, twists and writhes and rolls his eyes and twists his mouth. His face turns pale and his appearance changes. So it will be with the world.

"Therefore I tell you, don't fear, but lift up your heads, like people who rejoice to see it, for, see, your redemption is near."

So the Lord speaks to his saints, for they too will be afraid when the sun and moon so affect their eyes and the sky is filled with fire. For the saints are not so strong; even St. Peter and St. Paul would be afraid, if they were alive. But our Lord says, "Be of good cheer; it will indeed be a terrible sight, but it is not against you but against the devil and unbelievers. To you salvation is come and the joy of redemption, for which you have so long been sighing and praying, that my kingdom might come to you, cleansing you from all your sins and redeeming you from all evil. What you have so long been praying for with all your heart shall then be given to you."

Sermon on the Second Sunday in Advent, 1544.   WA 52:19

Lord God, with all the saints we wait with eager longing for the fullness of redemption and the time when your will is done in all creation. Amen.

Our Citizenship Is in Heaven

Philippians 3:17-21

Our citizenship is in heaven, and it is from there that we are expecting a Savior, the Lord Jesus Christ.
(Philippians 3:20)

We who are baptized into Christ and believe in him, he says, have not based our existence and our comfort on the righteousness of this temporal and worldly life on earth. We have a righteousness that clings in faith to Christ in heaven and stands and remains in him alone, for otherwise it would be nothing before God. This righteousness only aims to be eternally in Christ, that he through his coming may make an end of this earthly life and of this earthly body and give us another life, one that will be new, pure, and holy, and like the life and body of Christ.

Therefore we are no longer called citizens on earth, but whoever is a baptized Christian is, through baptism, a proper citizen of heaven. Therefore we should walk and bear ourselves as those who belong there and have their home there, and we should comfort ourselves in the knowledge that God has accepted us and will bring us to heaven. In the meantime we wait for the Savior who will bring down to us from heaven eternal righteousness, life, honor, and glory.

Sermon on the Twenty-third Sunday after Trinity, 1544.   WA 22:371

As a pilgrim looking for a heavenly home, O Lord,
help me use my time on earth wisely. Amen.

Behold, I Make All Things New

If anyone is in Christ, there is a new creation.
(2 Corinthians 5:17)

A Christian is a new creature, or newly created work of God who speaks, thinks, and judges all things in a different way from the world's speaking and judging. Being a new person, all things do become new, here in this life through faith, and afterward in the life to come, through openly revealing their nature. Now the world cannot do anything else but think of death according to its ancient custom and nature—that it is the most abominable and horrible thing on earth, the end of life and all joy.

But Christians, on the other hand, as new persons, are equipped with very different and even contrary thoughts, so that they can be courageous and happy, even when passing through hard times. In their hearts they remember that they possess a great treasure even though they might be poor. They are powerful princes and lords even when they are in prison, and surpassingly strong when they are weak and ill, and in highest honor when they are disdained and reviled. Similarly, they will be roused into newness of life if they now must die. In short, they win new hearts and courage through which they make all things new here on earth. They therefore have a foretaste here of the future life, where everything will become new before their eyes and in the full light of day made new, as they now think and picture it through faith, according to their new nature.

Sermon at the Funeral of Elector John, 1532.   *LW 51:244; WA 36:255*

Let my life, Lord God, reflect the newness that you have given me. Amen.

We Wait with Patience

If we hope for what we do not see, we wait for it with patience.
(Romans 8:25)

This advice is rightly taught but not soon learned; rightly preached but not soon believed; it is well advised but not easily followed; well said but hard to do. For there are very few people on earth waiting for the blessed hope and the coming eternal kingdom and inheritance, and waiting with such conviction as they should, being only lightly attached to this present life. There are few who look at this temporal life through a colored glass, as it were, blindly, but look at that eternal life with clear and open eyes. Unfortunately, the blessed hope and the heavenly inheritance are all too often forgotten, but the temporal life and the transitory life we have unceasingly before our eyes. We think about it and care for it and are happy in it, but we turn our back on the everlasting life. Day and night we pursue this earthly life, but the eternal life we throw to the winds.

But this should certainly not be so with Christians; the opposite should be the case. A Christian should look at this temporal life with closed or blinking eyes, but he should look at the future eternal life with eyes wide open and in clear bright light. We should have only our left hand in this life here on earth, but with our right hand, with our soul, and with our whole heart we should be in the other life, in heaven, and should wait for it always with certain hope and a joyful mind.

Sermons from the year 1531.   WA 34/2:110f.

Let me hope for the life to come, O Lord, but let me not become so otherworldly that I am no earthly good. Amen.

Strangers and Foreigners on Earth

They confessed that they were strangers and foreigners on the earth.
(Hebrews 11:13)

The apostle here wants to show that we should look on this life as a stranger and foreigner looks on a land in which he is a stranger or a guest. Strangers cannot say, "Here is our homeland," for they are not at home there. Pilgrims do not think of remaining in the land to which they make their pilgrimage, or in the inn where they stay the night, but their hearts and thoughts are directed elsewhere. They take their meals in the inn and rest, and then they continue their journey to the place where their home is.

Therefore conduct yourselves as guests and strangers in this strange land and strange inn, and take nothing from it but food and drink, clothing and shoes, and what you need for your night's rest, and keep your thoughts on your fatherland where you are citizens.

We must note this carefully. We must not seek to build for ourselves eternal life here in this world and pursue it and cling to it as if it were our greatest treasure and heavenly kingdom, and as if we wished to exploit the Lord Christ and the gospel and achieve wealth and power through him. No, but because we have to live on earth, and so long as it is God's will, we should eat, drink, marry, plant, build, and have house and home and what God grants, and use them as guests and strangers in a strange land. We know that we must leave all such things behind and take our staff out of this strange land and evil, unsafe inn, homeward bound for our true fatherland where there is nothing but security, peace, rest, and joy forevermore.

Sermons from the year 1531. WA 34/2:113f.

Guide me ever, great Redeemer, pilgrim through this barren land. I am weak, but you are mighty; hold me with your powerful hand. Amen.
(William Williams, 1717–1791)

God Makes Us Weary of Life

The hope of the righteous ends in gladness.
(Proverbs 10:28)

The world may inflict us with all kinds of plagues and sorrows, and pain our hearts and give us a bitter, sour drink—to say nothing of other daily troubles, such as accidents, illness, disease, hard times, and war, which hurt the body or our outward selves. But we must endure these misfortunes as though we were biting a sour apple and tasting a bitter draught, that the sweetness that follows may taste the better, and we be driven by this experience to yearn for that day with greater longing. Otherwise, we should continue our way so cold and numb that in the end we should no longer feel our misery, like the confident and unrepentant world, until at last we should no longer take notice of the Word of God and should perish with the godless. But now God in his grace makes us weary and tired of this life and gives us the comfort of a better life—that is, that he will soon appear in the clouds with great power and glory, and lift us up out of all misery to everlasting joy, so that as far as we are concerned nothing better or more to be desired could happen to us. But for the godless there will then be no such joyful sight.

Sermons from the year 1531. WA 34/2:472f.

Take my hand, precious Lord, lead me on, let me stand; I am tired, I am weak, I am worn. Through the storm, through the night, lead me on to the light. Take my hand, precious Lord, lead me home. Amen.
(Thomas A. Dorsey, 1899–1993)

Daily Mortification

I die every day!
(1 Corinthians 15:31)

How strange this saying sounds, "I die every day"! The world would say, "We don't see that you were ever buried. No, we see you walking and standing, eating and drinking, moving about and preaching and pursuing your occupation. Is that what you call dying or being dead?" Well, the apostle affirms this with an oath because he wants this regarded as certain. But not everybody knows or understands what Paul means with this, what this dying signifies, and how this takes place, that he constantly has death hovering over him and is perpetually harassed, feeling more of death than of life. And yet Paul says that he has a boast along with this, namely, a boast of life, although he feels this life but feebly and often not at all. Thus death and life, sin and piety, good and bad conscience, happiness and sadness, hope and fright, belief and unbelief—in short, God and devil, hell and heaven, engage in constant combat and contend with each other. It is of such a battle that Paul speaks here, which he alone understood, for he was a great apostle who constantly was involved in this warfare. Therefore it is necessary for him to affirm this with an oath that people believe he is telling the truth, even though others do not feel this so or understand it.

Commentary on 1 Corinthians 15.   LW 28:156; WA 36:610f.

*Straighten my priorities, O God. Remind me of what is ephemeral
and what is truly important. Amen.*

SATURDAY

They Will Never See Death

Very truly, I tell you, whoever keeps my word will never see death.
(John 8:51)

Here Christ makes a distinction between death, on the one hand, and seeing or tasting death, on the other. We must all die. But Christians do not taste or see death; that is, they do not feel it or fear it, but pass quietly and gently into death, as though they were falling asleep and not dying. But a godless person feels it and dreads it. Therefore to taste death may well refer to the power and might or bitterness of death.

It is the Word that makes this difference. Christians have the Word and hold firmly on to it in death. Therefore they do not see death but in the Word see life. Therefore they do not feel death. But the godless do not have the Word; therefore they see no life but only death, and therefore they feel it, for it is a bitter and eternal death.

Christ promises that whoever clings to his Word shall not see or feel death, not even in the hour of death. Here we see what a great thing it means to a Christian, that we are already eternally redeemed from death and can never die. For though the death and dying of a Christian appears outwardly like the dying of a godless person, they differ inwardly as much as heaven differs from earth. For Christians fall asleep as they die, and they pass through death into life.

Sermons from the year 1525.   WA 17/2:234f.

Even though I walk through the darkest valley, I fear no evil,
for you are with me. (Psalm 23:4)

The Inheritance of the Saints

Colossians 1:9-14

He has given us a new birth . . . into an inheritance that is imperishable, undefiled, and unfading, kept in heaven for you.
(1 Peter 1:3-4)

Our hope is not set on possessions or an inheritance here on earth but on an inheritance that is incorruptible, undefiled, and does not fade away. We possess this good eternally, only we cannot see it yet. These are mighty and precious words, and I contend that whoever can grasp their meaning will not be very concerned about temporal goods and pleasures. How can we still cling to temporal goods and pleasures if we really believe this? For earthly things last but a short time and then perish. But these things remain forever and do not perish. Moreover, earthly things are all impure and contaminate us, for no one is so pure and holy that earthly things do not defile us, but this inheritance is altogether pure and the one who possesses it is eternally undefiled. It will not rot or fade or wither. All things that are on earth, even though they be as hard as iron and stone, are perishable and cannot last. Human beings as they grow old lose their beauty, but the eternal good does not change; it remains fresh and green forever. On earth there is no pleasure so great that it does not fade in time. People grow tired of everything, but this good is different. This is all ours through the mercy of God in Christ, if we believe it, and it is given to us freely.

Sermons on the First Epistle of St. Peter, 1523.   LW 30:13; WA 12:269

Swift to its close ebbs out life's little day; earth's joys grow dim, its glories pass away. Change and decay all around I see; O thou who changest not, abide with me. Amen. (Henry F. Lyte, 1847)

Joy in Various Trials

*In this you rejoice, even if now for a little while
you have had to suffer various trials.*
(1 Peter 1:6)

Here the apostle indicates how Christians fare in the world. Before God they are dearly beloved children, certain of their heavenly inheritance and of blessedness, but here on earth they are not only sad and sorrowful and forsaken, but they must suffer also many temptations from the devil and the wicked world. What is their offense? Their greatest "sin" is that they believe in Christ and praise and glorify the unspeakable grace that God has shown in him to all the world, namely, that he alone can redeem us from sin and death and make us just and blessed. It is also that they believe that human reason cannot of its own free will, its own might and good works, prepare itself to receive the grace of God, much less merit eternal life, but with all its thoughts and deeds, however glorious and beautiful, it cannot reconcile God. Then the fire is kindled, for the world will not and cannot allow that its good opinion and piety, its saintliness and all its admirable works shall be punished and condemned as of no worth before God. So they strike and persecute and slay those who preach the Word and testify to it, and think they are rendering God a service. Therefore faith is not a dreamy thought in the heart, but all who have faith confess it and speak of what is in their heart, and for that reason troubles beset them. That is why St. Peter says, "even if now for a little while you have had to suffer various trials," thus uniting faith, hope, and the holy cross, for the one follows from the other.

Exposition of 1 Peter.   EA 52:21f.

When the trials of life overtake me, Lord, stand by me. Amen.

We Look for the Blessed Hope

*We wait for the blessed hope and the manifestation of the glory
of our great God and Savior, Jesus Christ.*
(Titus 2:13)

Let us meditate on these words. He calls it a "blessed hope" and sets it over against this wretched and unhappy life where there is nothing but misfortune, danger, and sin, which hunt and torture us so that everything that belongs to this life should become tiresome to us and should strengthen such hope in us. This happens with those who honestly try to live a sober, righteous, and godly life. Tribulation we esteem a precious thing, and we glory in it, for we know that sorrow helps to teach us patience, and patience brings us experience, and experience teaches us to hope, and hope does not put us to shame (see Romans 5:3-4).

Thus our eyes are kept shut toward earthly and visible things, and we hope instead for the things eternal and invisible. All this is accomplished by grace through the cross. This establishes the divine life in us, which is intolerable to the world.

Sermon for Christmas Eve, 1522.   WA 10/1(i):43

*Why are you cast down, O my soul, and why are you disquieted within
me? Hope in God; for I shall again praise him, my help and my God.*
(Psalm 42:5)

The Glory of the New Creation

I consider that the sufferings of this present time are not worth comparing with the glory about to be revealed to us.
(Romans 8:18)

The sun is now such a clear bright light that no one, however bright and keen the eyes, can steadily gaze into its brightness. But what will happen hereafter when the radiance of the sun will be seven times as bright as now? What bright clear eyes will be needed to bear such a sun! If Adam had retained the innocence in which he was created, he would have had clear bright eyes and would have been able to gaze into the sun like an eagle. But through sin and the fall we humans have become so weakened, poisoned, and corrupted in body, soul, eyes, ears, and everywhere, that our eyes are not the hundredth part as sharp as Adam's were before the fall. Our bodies are unclean, and all creatures have become subject to futility (Romans 8:20). The sun, moon, stars, clouds, air, earth, and water are no longer so pure and beautiful and lovely as they were. But on that day all things will be made new and will once more be beautiful, as St. Paul says, "The creation itself will be set free from its bondage to decay and will obtain the freedom of the glory of the children of God" (Romans 8:21).

Sermons from the year 1537. LW 12:119; WA 45:231f.

O Lord, I look forward to the day when sorrow and mourning will be no more, and all things are made new. Amen.

In Death, There Is No Other Way but Christ

I am the way, and the truth, and the life.
No one comes to the Father except through me.
(John 14:6)

When the hour comes when our life and work must cease, when we can no longer stay here, and the question arises, "Where can I find a plank or bridge by which I can pass with certainty to the other life"—when you reach that point, I say, do not look around for any human way, such as your own good and holy life or works. No, bury all this with the Lord's Prayer and say of these things, "Forgive us our sins," and so on, and hold fast to him who says, "I am the way." See that in that hour you have this word firmly and deeply engraved in your heart, as though you heard Christ really present and saying to you, "Why should you seek another way? Keep your eyes fixed on me, and do not trouble with other thoughts about how you may get to heaven. Thrust all such thoughts entirely away from your heart and only think of what I say, 'I am the way.' Only see that you come to me; that is, hold on to me with firm faith and the complete confidence of your heart. I will be the bridge and carry you across, so that in a moment you will pass out of death and the fear of hell into everlasting life. For I am the one who myself built the way or path, and I myself have trodden it and passed across, so that I might bring you and all who cling to me across. But you must put your trust in me, nothing doubting, must venture all on me, and with a joyous heart go and die confidently in my name."

Sermons on John 14–15.   LW 24:41; WA 45:498f.

Then let our songs abound, and every tear be dry; we're marching through Immanuel's ground to fairer worlds on high. (Isaac Watts, 1674–1748)

Death Is a Means of Grace

The righteous have hope in their death.
(Proverbs 14:32, a literal translation of the Hebrew)

If there were no death, sin would never die. Through death alone is sin restrained, and there is no other way of getting rid of it. Such gracious and wholesome punishment God gives to us that sin is slain through death. Therefore we should receive death with joyful hearts and bear it as coming from a gracious Father, as the faithful do. For our Father's goodness is so great that even death must serve to slay and to uproot all misfortune.

Therefore death is nothing but sheer grace, yes, even the beginning of life. For since it ministers to the restoration of the soul, our bodily system and all that is associated with it, such as illness, danger, pain, and labor, must also serve for our good, so that we could desire nothing better.

For Adam must die and decay before Christ can completely rise, and that begins with the life of repentance, and is perfected through death. Therefore death is a wholesome thing to all who believe in Christ, for all that is born of Adam death brings to decay and dust, that Christ alone may abide in us.

The Seven Penitential Psalms, 1517. WA 1:188

There no clouds of darkness gather, neither sorrow, tears, nor woe,
nothing harmful e'er shall enter, sin and pain we will not know.
(Joel Bloomqvist, 1840–1930)

Patience and Longsuffering

Grow in the knowledge of God. May you be made strong with all the strength that comes from his glorious power, with all patience and longsuffering with joyfulness. . . .
(Colossians 1:10-11, Luther's reading)

With such might and glorious power we too must be strengthened in faith, must strive for it and cling to it through the Word of God and pray that we may not only make a beginning but press on and persevere and so grow stronger and stronger in the power of the Lord.

But to be so strengthened and to overcome cannot be done without much patience—and not only patience but longsuffering too, which he distinguishes from patience as something greater and stronger. For it is the way of the devil, where he cannot overcome a heart with suffering and sorrow to beset it continuously, and so that it is too much and too long for the patience and it appears as though it would never end, so that at last it makes us weak and weary and robs us of courage and the hope of overcoming the enemy.

Against this not only is patience needed but longsuffering too, which holds on firmly and steadfastly and perseveres in suffering, and says, "You cannot trouble me too much or too long, even if it should last until the end of the world." This is the true Christian strength that can endure a long period of battle and suffering. But for that we most of all need the power and the might of God through prayer, so that we are not overcome in such hard fighting but reach the end. Such patience and longsuffering you should have and practice joyfully.

Sermon on the Twenty-fourth Sunday after Trinity, 1544. WA 22:386f.

Give me patience, O God, in the struggles and disappointments of life; let me not grow weary in well-doing, but let me persevere in faith. Amen.

The Resurrection of the Dead

1 Thessalonians 4:3-18

*For since we believe that Jesus died and rose again, even so, through Jesus,
God will bring with him those who have died.
(1 Thessalonians 4:14)*

He leads us out of death and the grave of sin to resurrection and life,
both of the spirit and of the body. But if we die, both spiritually to our
sin and bodily to the world and to ourselves, what are we profited? Do
Christians not fare otherwise than that they die and are buried? Certainly,
for we know through faith that we shall also live, as Christ rose from
death and the grave and lives, for we have died with him and with him
are planted in his death. For through his death he destroyed our sin and
death, and therefore we shall be partakers of his resurrection and his life,
so that there will be neither sin nor death in our soul and body as there is
no death in him.

This is our comfort against the weakness of the poor and wretched
flesh that is horrified at the thought of death. For if you are a Christian,
you know that your Lord Christ has risen from the dead and cannot die
again and death has no power over him, and that is why it has no power
over you.

Sermon on the Sixth Sunday after Trinity, 1544.   WA 22:103f.

*Have mercy on those to whom death draws near, O Lord,
and give them the certain hope of resurrection. Amen.*

The New Body

It is sown a physical body, it is raised a spiritual body.
If there is a physical body, there is also a spiritual body.
(1 Corinthians 15:44)

I live in hope that we shall also die in such a manner and pass as wretched sinners into heaven, if we can only keep this ornament and wrap ourselves in the death of the Son of God, and cloak and cover ourselves with his resurrection. If we stand firmly in him and do not waver, our righteousness is so great that all our sins, whatever their name and nature may be, are like a little spark, and our righteousness is like an ocean and our death is much less than a sleep and a dream. Moreover, our shame, which we shall bury so ingloriously, is covered with a glory that is called "the resurrection of Jesus Christ," and with this it is so beautifully adorned that even the sun will blush when it sees it and the dear angels will never be able to turn their eyes away from it. With such great beauty are we arrayed and adorned that all other filthiness of our poor bodies, like death and other things, does not count at all in comparison.

Therefore we must look upon the death of a Christian differently and we must not count Christians who have died as dead and buried. To our five senses it does appear so, and as far as they lead us it does hurt. Therefore we must listen diligently to what St. Paul says, namely, that they sleep in Christ and that God will bring them with Christ. Learn to comfort yourselves with such words. God cannot lie. Think only of this, for whoever lacks this comfort finds no other comfort and no joy.

Sermon at the Funeral of Elector John, 1532.   LW 51:239; WA 36:249f.

Asleep in Jesus, blessed sleep from which none ever wakes to weep;
a calm and undisturbed repose, unbroken by the last of foes.
(Margaret Mackay, 1832)

Resurrection Derived from the Creation

And as for what you sow, you do not sow the body that is to be,
but a bare seed, perhaps of wheat or of some other grain. But God gives it
a body as he has chosen, and to each kind of seed its own body.
(1 Corinthians 15:37-38)

Thus the apostle relates this article about the resurrection to the article about the creation, and he proves the one by the other. It is as if he would say: Whoever has God's word that there is a resurrection of the dead, and who believes and confesses that God who has spoken such a word is the Father almighty, the maker of heaven and earth, as the children say in the Creed, and of which the grain in the fields and all creatures are a convincing proof and example, he also believes and confesses that there is a resurrection of the dead. Whoever denies that there is a resurrection of the dead also denies that God is the almighty maker of heaven and earth and that he spoke this word about the resurrection of the dead. But whoever confesses this article that God is almighty does not dispute in subtle fashion whether it is possible that the dead shall rise, for there stands the word of God, which says that it shall be so.

God who says so is the almighty God, maker of heaven and earth and of all creatures; therefore the resurrection must come to pass and it cannot be otherwise, because God has said so. Otherwise he would not be an almighty God and creator.

Sermons from the year 1544.   WA 49:399f.

For the word of the LORD is upright, and all his work
is done in faithfulness. (Psalm 33:4)

We Follow Christ into the Resurrection

*. . . raised us up with him and seated us with him
in the heavenly places in Christ Jesus.
(Ephesians 2:6)*

If we had such faith, we should live well and die well, for it should teach us that he did not rise for himself only. We should cling together, knowing that this is also for us and that we too are contained in that resurrection. Because of it, or by means of it, we too shall rise and live with him eternally, which means that our resurrection and life in Christ have already begun and are as certain as if they were already perfected. But they are still hidden and not yet made manifest. From now on, we should fix our eyes steadily on this article, with which nothing else can compare—as though you could see nothing else in the whole heaven and earth. So if you see a Christian die and be buried, and before both your eyes and ears there is nothing but death, you will discern by faith in and beneath it all another picture instead of that picture of death. It will be as if you did not see a grave but unmixed life in a lovely summer garden or a green meadow in which there is nothing but new, lively, happy people.

For if it is true that Christ is risen from the dead, we already have the best and noblest part of our resurrection, so that the bodily rising of the flesh out of the grave (which is still in the future) must be counted insignificant in comparison.

Sermons from the year 1533. WA 37:68

*He has done all this in order that I may belong to him,
live under him in his kingdom, and serve him in eternal righteousness
and blessedness, just as he is risen from the dead and lives and
rules eternally. (Martin Luther, Small Catechism)*

Life Everlasting

For we know that if the earthly tent we live in is destroyed, we have a building from God, a house not made with hands, eternal in the heavens. (2 Corinthians 5:1)

This body is, as St. Paul says, only a tent of the soul, made of earth or clay, and like an old garment. But because the soul is already in a new, eternal, and heavenly life through faith, and can neither die nor be buried, we have nothing more to wait for than that this poor tabernacle may likewise be made new and incorruptible, for our better part is above and cannot leave our flesh behind. As he who is called *Resurrexit* ("he is risen") is risen from death and grave, so he who says "I believe" (*credo*) and clings to him must also follow. For he has gone before us that we should follow, and he has begun the work in us, that through his Word and baptism we may be daily raised in him.

If you receive the Word in faith, you are given other eyes that can see through death to the resurrection and apprehend the pure thoughts and image of life. If I would judge according to my reason that I can see and understand, I should be lost. But I possess an understanding loftier than what the eyes can see and the senses feel, which faith has taught me. For there stands the text that says *Resurrexit*, "He is risen," not for himself but for our sake, that his resurrection may be made ours, that we may also rise in him, and not remain in death and the grave, but with him may celebrate in the body an everlasting Easter.

Sermons from the year 1533.   WA 37:69f.

E'en death's cold wave I will not flee, since God through Jordan leadeth me. (Joseph H. Gilmore, 1861)

The Seed Is the Symbol of Resurrection

So it is with the resurrection of the dead. What is sown is perishable;
what is raised is imperishable.
(1 Corinthians 15:42)

Consider the farmer who sows seed in the field: he throws the grain on the ground, and it looks as if it were completely lost. Yet he is not troubled about whether it is in vain. He even forgets it entirely. He does not ask how it is getting on, whether the worms are eating it or it is lost for some other reason. On the contrary, he knows that toward Easter or Pentecost beautiful stalks will appear that will bear much more grain than he sowed. If you were to ask him about it, he would answer, "My friend, I knew that I should not throw the seed away, but I don't do it that the grain may perish in the ground, but rather that through decaying in the ground it may attain another form and bear abundant fruit." That is how anyone thinks who does the same thing or sees it done.

Christ rose from the dead. If we could see it before our eyes, we should not need faith, and God would have no means whereby to prove that his wisdom and power are greater than our wisdom and understanding. Therefore, in the midst of wailing and lamentation, the Christian can take comfort in knowing that God allows us to be buried in the earth and to decay in the winter so that we may shoot forth in the summer brighter than the sun, as though the grave were not a grave but a lovely garden in which roses are planted that are green and full of blossoms.

Sermons from the year 1533. WA 37:70

Despair not, O heart, in your sorrow, but hope from God's
promises borrow. (Prudentius, c. 413; Peder Hegelund, 1586)

This Song We Sing in Christ

*Death has been swallowed up in victory. Where, O death,
is your victory? Where, O death, is your sting?
(1 Corinthians 15:54-55)*

This song we sing now in reference to the person of Christ and of those who are risen with Christ from the dead, for they have passed through and have won the victory over death. But when we too rise we shall sing the song in reference to ourselves. Then we too shall laugh at death, and mock him and say, "Death, where are you now? Here is nothing but life, and I am lord and master over you. Previously you have devoured me and have lorded it over me; but now you leave me undevoured and I am lord over you. Previously I was in fear of you, but now you can no longer harm me. Previously you put me into the grave among the worms and you made my appearance horrible to behold; now I am risen from the dead and I shine brighter than the sun. How do you like me now? Before, you made me afraid; now I dare you to touch a hair of my head."

Sermons from the year 1545. WA 49:769f.

*O Lord God, you have been with me through life; sustain me also
in the hope of eternal life with you. Amen.*

The End of Time

2 Thessalonians 1:3-10

*Therefore we ourselves boast of you among the churches of God
for your steadfastness and faith during all your persecutions
and the afflictions that you are enduring.*
(2 Thessalonians 1:4-5)

St. Paul here praises his church in Thessalonica. Then he provokes them to further growth that he may present to others an example of the fruits that the gospel should yield. He shows what the building and increase of the true church of Christ consist of. He then comforts them concerning their sufferings and patience with the glorious advent of the Lord Christ for their redemption and the end of their sorrows with rest and joy, and eternal vengeance on those who persecuted them.

But it cannot be the will of God that the Christians should so suffer eternally and without ceasing and then die. For he testifies by his Word that he will be the God of the saints who fear and trust him, to whom he has given such great promises. Therefore his purpose must be to give a different gift, and this is one of the main reasons why he permits Christians to suffer on earth, namely, that his will to give to both their due reward may be revealed. Therefore both the Christians' sufferings and the world's wretchedness, tyranny, wrath, and persecution of the saints must become a clear testimony of another life to come and of the last judgment of God, through which all persons, good and evil, shall receive their due reward eternally and without ceasing.

Sermon on the Twenty-sixth Sunday after Trinity, 1544.   WA 22:407f.

*O Lord, let your Word guide me in this life and give me hope
for the life to come. Amen.*

The Inheritance of the Saints

If [we are] children, then heirs, heirs of God and joint heirs
with Christ—if, in fact, we suffer with him so that
we may also be glorified with him.
(Romans 8:17)

Because of such suffering with him, St. Paul here says that we are brothers and joint heirs with Christ. And now he begins to comfort Christians in such sufferings, and he speaks as one who has been tried and has become quite certain. He speaks as though he can see this life only dimly, or as through colored glass, while he sees the other life with clear eyes.

Notice how he turns his back to the world and his eyes toward the revelation that is to come, as though he could perceive no sorrow or affliction anywhere on earth, but only joy. Indeed, he says, when we do have to suffer evil, what is our suffering in comparison with the unspeakable joy and glory that shall be made real in us? It is not worth comparing with such joy nor even to be called suffering. The only difficulty is that we cannot see with our eyes and touch with our hands that great and exquisite glory for which we must wait, namely, that we shall not die anymore, neither shall we hunger nor thirst. Moreover, we shall be given a body that cannot ever suffer or sicken. Whoever could grasp the meaning of this in the heart would be compelled to say, "Even if I should be burned or drowned ten times (if that were possible), that would be nothing in comparison with the glory of the life hereafter." For what is this temporal life, however long it may last, in comparison with the life eternal? It is not worthy to be called suffering or thought of as a merit.

Sermons from the year 1535.   WA 41:302f.

Heaven's morning breaks, and earth's vain shadows flee; in life, in death,
O Lord, abide with me. (Henry F. Lyte, 1847)

We Wait for Our Redemption

We wait for . . . the redemption of our bodies.
(Romans 8:23)

Our Lord's Prayer teaches us that with joy we should long for that day and should cry to God, that at length he should avenge his name, goodness, and blood on the despairing, ungodly world, and that no Christian can or should pray otherwise. Who else should pray thus but Christians, who are thus tormented and afflicted because of their baptism and the gospel, or God's name and kingdom, that they have no other help or comfort on earth? Whoever has not yet learned by experience to long for that day has not yet a true understanding of the Lord's Prayer, much less can pray it from the heart. I myself used to feel that I was so hostile to the Lord's Prayer that I would much rather have said another prayer. But if you are in great tribulation, the Lord's Prayer will be sweet to you and you will gladly pray it from the bottom of your heart. For who would not wish and pray with the whole heart, "Deliver us from evil," that there may be at last an end to our grief and sorrow in this world? For we see that the world wills to stay as it is and will not cast off its old skin, and neither will nor can become better, but rather gets worse every day. Therefore there is no better thing than to flee away from it, and the sooner the better.

Sermons from the year 1531. WA 34/2:474f.

We pray, O Lord, for redemption and the end of all the forces of evil.
Amen.

As a Thief in the Night

For you yourselves know very well that the day of the Lord
will come like a thief in the night.
(1 Thessalonians 5:2)

The last day will come to all true and faithful Christians as a day of joy and glory. But it will be a day of dire distress for all unbelievers, godless persons and coveters, usurers, and false Christians. For it will happen this way: we shall not all receive the sacrament in our bed nor be laid in a coffin and carried to the grave. For Paul uses the term "fallen asleep" of one who gives up the spirit while lying in bed and afterward is carried out and buried in the earth. There will be no need of that (he says) on the last day. For then the word will not be, "Come, hear this one's confession, absolve him from his sins, administer to him the sacrament, bury him," and so forth. But as you sit at the table at mealtime or stand before the cash box counting your coins or lie in bed asleep or sit in the tavern drinking or are at a dance, suddenly in the twinkling of an eye you will be changed; that is, you will be dead and alive.

Whoever will receive advice should repent and become a better person. For the last day will come upon us and God's trumpet will sound before we expect.

Sermons from the year 1545.   WA 49:732ff.

Jerusalem, my happy home, when shall I come to thee?
When shall my sorrows have an end? Thy joys, when shall I see?
(F.B.P., sixteenth century)

Be Ready

Keep awake therefore, for you do not know on what day
your Lord is coming.
(Matthew 24:42)

No one is rightly prepared for the last day except the one who desires to be free from sin. If that is your desire, why are you afraid? For on this account you are in agreement with it. It comes in order to set free from their sins all who desire it, and you too long to be thus free. Give thanks to God and continue in that opinion. Christ says that his coming is your redemption.

But take care that you do not deceive yourself when you say that you would be free from sin, and do not fear that day. Perhaps your heart is false and you do fear it. Perhaps you do not truly desire to be free from sin. Perhaps you are deterred from sinning freely and confidently because of that day. Take heed that the light that is in you be not darkness. For a heart that truly desires to be free from sin rejoices in the expectation of the day when this desire will be fulfilled. If it does not rejoice in it, then is there no true longing to be set free from sin.

Therefore we must, above all, lay aside hatred and fear of this coming, and be diligent and earnest in our desire to be free from sin. If we do that, we may not only await that day with confidence but pray for it with great joy and with ardent hope.

Sermon on the Second Sunday in Advent, 1522.   WA 10/1(ii):111

In hope, in faith, and in love, O Lord, let me endure to the end. Amen.

Christ's Victory

Thanks be to God, who gives us the victory through our Lord Jesus Christ.
(1 Corinthians 15:57)

St. Paul speaks of two kinds of victory. The first is that of death, which overcomes and lords it over all humankind from the first man Adam until the end of the world. Of that victory he speaks in Romans 5:12: "Sin came into the world through one man, and death came through sin, and so death spread to all because all have sinned." That is death's victory and triumph, that death rules through sin and has power and authority over everyone, so that there is no one, neither emperor, king, prince, nor lord, nor however rich, strong, and great they may be, who must not admit that death will lord it over them.

The other victory is that of life, which rules in and through Christ, and is victorious over death. Of that victory, too, he speaks, in Romans 5:17: "If, because of the one man's trespass, death exercised dominion through that one, much more surely will those who receive the abundance of grace and the free gift of righteousness exercise dominion in life through the one man, Jesus Christ." That is life's victory and triumph, that in Christ life reigns and triumphs in opposition to death, and that death has no power to hold not only Christ but also those who are baptized in Christ and believe in him.

St. Paul means to say that death lies utterly defeated. It has lost its kingdom, might, and victory, for over against the kingdom and victory of death, our Lord God, the Lord of hosts, has brought about another victory, which is the resurrection of the dead in Christ. Here is pure life and no death. Death is conquered in Christ and is dead itself. Life has won the victory and retains it.

Sermons from the year 1545.   WA 49:767f.

Thine is the glory, risen, conquering Son. Endless is the victory
thou o'er death hast won! (Edmond Budry, 1854–1932)

Forever with the Lord

We will be with the Lord forever.
(1 Thessalonians 4:17)

There is for Christians no more precious thought than that they live in God while they do their work here on earth. But when the Great Day comes—and it does not matter when, because he is my Lord—then I shall be redeemed. Yet this comfort belongs to none but Christians.

This judge, who will come with such great power that he will awaken even the devil and all the dead, will be a brother and father and patron of Christians. Oh! the unspeakable joy when he will call us his friends and see in us his gift and the Holy Spirit. It will be a joyous thing to the dead. Though nature must be terrified by such divine majesty, yet the spirit will behold that majesty with joy. But whoever lacks this comfort will be tormented by the devil. May all bear this in mind and act accordingly. No one will find a hiding place. All will have to come forth, even though they lie a thousand fathoms down in the sea or under the earth or in the abyss of hell. When Christ is judge, all things must come forth into the light.

Sermons from the year 1525.   WA 17/1:221

Christ is risen! Henceforth never death or hell shall us enthrall.
Be we Christ's, in him forever we have triumphed over all.
All the doubting and dejection of our trembling hearts have ceased.
(John S. B. Monell, 1811–1875)

Christ the King
Matthew 15:1-13

Then they will see "the Son of Man coming in a cloud"
with power and great glory.
(Luke 21:27)

Here you might interpret "power" with reference to the host of angels, saints, and all the creatures that will come with Christ to the judgment. Or it might indicate that the second coming of Christ will be as impressive in its power as his first coming was insignificant in its weakness and poverty. Further, he not only says, "He will come," but "they will see" him come. For in his physical birth, he also came, yet none perceived him. He still comes every day in a spiritual way, in his gospel, into the hearts of those who believe, yet no one perceives him. But this coming will occur openly, so that no one can help seeing it, as it is said, "Every eye will see him" (Revelation 1:7), and they will perceive that he is none other than the man Christ Jesus in the flesh as he was born of Mary and walked on this earth.

Otherwise he might well have said, "They will see me," which need not have expressly referred to the physical form. But since he says, "They will see the Son of Man," it is clearly expressed that he means a physical advent, and a physical seeing of a physical form, yet in great power, with the multitudes of angels and all the heavenly glory, and he will be seated on a shining cloud and all his saints will be with him. Holy Scripture says much about that day, and all things are directed toward it.

Sermons from the year 1522.   WA 10/1(i):109

From the terror of judgment set me free, Lord God,
and let my hope rest on your steadfast love. Amen.

Blessings Even in Death

The sting of death is sin, and the power of sin is the law. But thanks be to
God, who gives us the victory through our Lord Jesus Christ.
(1 Corinthians 15:56-57)

Christians certainly have the greatest blessings of all awaiting them in the future. However, these are attained only through sufferings and death. They surely also rejoice in that common and uncertain hope that the evil of the present will come to an end and that its opposite, the blessing, will increase, but this is not their chief concern. Their chief concern is that their own particular blessing might increase, namely, the truth that is in Christ, for which they live and hope. But besides this blessing they have the two greatest blessings in their death. The first is that through death the whole tragedy of this world's ills is ended. For the believer death is thus already dead, and behind its cloak and mask it holds no terrors. Like a slain serpent, death still has its former terrifying appearance, but now this is only a mask, for it is now a dead and harmless evil.

The other blessing of death is that death not only puts an end to the evils of this life's punishments, but that death also—which is even more excellent—puts an end to all sins and vices.

Therefore, if we meditate on these joys of the power of Christ and on the gifts of his grace, how can any small evil distress us when in the great evil that is to come we see such a great blessing?

Fourteen Consolations.   LW 31:148, 150

Heavenly Father, have mercy on those to whom death draws near;
give me wisdom to bring comfort to those who face the end. Amen.

The New Glory

Then I saw a new heaven and a new earth.
(Revelation 21:1)

It is the brightness and glory of our Lord Jesus Christ here on earth that he is despised and rejected, but he will come again and will appear in glory. He will bring a brightness so wonderful that all creatures will be made more beautiful than they are now. The light of the sun will be seven times brighter than it is now; the light of the moon will be like the present light of the sun. Trees, leaves, grass, fruit, and all things will be seven times as lovely as they are now.

The Christians will then come forth from their graves shining like the loveliest and most radiant stars. A holy martyr who now for the sake of Christ and his gospel is persecuted and burned to ashes like a black dull star will then hover in the air and be drawn through the clouds toward the Lord and will go to heaven like a bright, shining, glorious star. In short, all the elect of God will be assembled in great and wonderful glory. And he himself, the Lord Jesus, will be seated in the clouds "on the throne of his glory [and] all the nations will be gathered before him" (Matthew 25:31-32). The whole world will be transfigured and will be a thousand times more glorious than it is now.

Sermons from the year 1531. WA 34/2:126

O Lord, I pray for the day when sorrow and sadness will forever vanish,
and your will shall be done throughout the cosmos. Amen.

The Resurrection of the Saints

*The Lord himself, with a cry of command, with the archangel's call
and with the sound of God's trumpet, will descend from heaven,
and the dead in Christ will rise first.*
(1 Thessalonians 4:16)

What will happen when the voice of the archangel and the sound of the trumpet are heard and Christ comes? In a flash the dead will rise in Christ, and we who are alive at that time shall be changed in the same instant and together with them be drawn on the clouds to meet the Lord in heaven, where we shall live with him forever. My words are brief and poor, but who can declare the meaning concealed within these words? Let each person meditate on them diligently and find in them comfort in all afflictions and especially in the pain of death.

From that day we shall no more be tempted but shall be delivered from all evil. There will be no more death, neither sorrow nor crying, neither shall there be any more pain, nor shall sin dwell in our flesh. It will be pure and unstained from all that is corrupt, from all evil desire and lust.

Christ is the judge over the living and the dead, whether they are good or evil, just or godless. But only to the faithful, that is, those who have fallen asleep in Christ, will be given the unspeakable grace and glory that they with Christ their bridegroom will be led into the new and eternal Jerusalem arrayed in a far more wonderful glory than all the world possesses.

Sermons from the year 1525. WA 17/1:225

*And, Lord, haste the day when our faith shall be sight, the clouds
be rolled back as a scroll; the trumpet shall sound and the Lord
shall descend; even so it is well with my soul. Amen.*
(Horatio G. Spafford, 1828–1888)

The Two Kingdoms

Then comes the end, when he hands over the kingdom to God the Father,
after he has destroyed every ruler and every authority and power.
(1 Corinthians 15:24)

The term "the kingdom of heaven" (as Christ himself uses it) applies not only to the realm of the blessed spirits and angels who have neither flesh nor blood, and to which we also eventually shall attain and be united with them in everlasting joy, but also to this life and among human beings. For a distinction is made between the two kingdoms, that of the Father and that of the Son. St. Paul says that Christ, God's Son, "must reign until he has put all his enemies under his feet" (1 Corinthians 15:25). "Then comes the end, when he hands over the kingdom to God the Father" (verse 24). Through one kingdom he reigns in this life, drawing a veil over our eyes so that we cannot see him but must believe. In the other kingdom faith is no longer needed but we shall see him before our eyes. In every other respect it is the *same* thing: what we now preach and believe we shall then look upon.

The preaching and believing must cease, and the veil must be taken away so that we shall then live with the dear angels eternally blessed with the beatific vision, which vision we have here on earth only in hearing and believing. Therefore this kingdom, which is of the Word and of faith, will be changed into a different kingdom where we shall no longer believe but shall see before our eyes God the Father and Christ the Lord. But now we must be content to be led by faith and the Word alone. Yet all who are baptized and believe that the Son of God is made man and in human likeness are already in the kingdom of heaven.

Sermons from the year 1544.   WA 49:573

Lord, as faith is the conviction of things not seen, I live each day
with the hope of the world to come. Amen.

The Kingdom of the Lord Christ Is Come

War broke out in heaven; Michael and his angels fought
against the dragon. The dragon and his angels fought back.
(Revelation 12:7)

See what we should learn here and what grounds we have for comfort, namely, the knowledge that we who have been baptized are truly blessed, and are seated in the kingdom of heaven where the Son of God himself reigns. Here, however, because we live by faith and not by sight, the battle is still going on and the devil is among the children of God—as he was also in Paradise in the beginning—and makes war against the Word, the sacrament, baptism, and all that belongs to Christ. For he seeks at all times to take possession of the kingdom of God and to become lord of Christendom. He wills to be seated and to rule in the pure and holy temple of God.

Therefore we, and especially those who preach the Word of God, should joyfully consider that we must hope for no peace here but should recollect that we are Christ's warriors in the field, always equipped and ready, for when one war ends another immediately begins.

We are called by Christ and already enrolled (in baptism) in the army that shall fight under Christ against the devil. For God leads his regiment in battle, not in heaven above among the holy spirits where there is no need of battle, but here on earth in his church. Yes, even though he is seated at the right hand of the Father, he is himself with his warriors leading them against the enemy, whom no human power and weapons can withstand, resisting and restraining him with his Word, which he has given to his people.

Sermons from the year 1544.   WA 49:579

Like a mighty army moves the church of God; let us boldly follow where
the saints have trod. (Sabine Baring-Gould, 1834–1924)

The Great Doxology

*Now the salvation and the power and the kingdom of our God
and the authority of his Christ have come.
(Revelation 12:10 RSV)*

When Satan is conquered through the struggle of the Christians and he is cast out of the heavenly kingdom of Christ, so great will be the joy that all the creatures will give thanks to God and sing, "Now the salvation and the power and the kingdom of our God and the authority of his Christ have come." There God himself sets both together so that the kingdom, the power, and the might of God belong also to his Christ; that is, there is one kingdom, power, and might of the Father and of Christ the Son.

This praise will certainly burst forth when the strife and struggle are ended, when Christendom is cleansed and purified and the lies of the devil have been put to shame. But this praise and thanksgiving will come from those who overcome by the blood of the Lamb and who for his sake do not love their own lives.

Yet it remains true that for this victory the Christians must venture their lives, as he says, "They did not cling to life even in the face of death" (Revelation 12:11). Therefore we must firmly and steadfastly continue in the faith and testimony through life and death until the devil is completely cast out through the strength and the victory of this Savior, Christ. To this end all the Scriptures point, and everything has to do with this Son of God, who for us was made man and shed his blood, and through his joyful coming should bring us out of this war of faith into eternal safety and to the glory of the blessed vision. Amen.

Sermons from the year 1544.   WA 49:588

*Lord, by the stripes that wounded you, from death's sting free your
servants too, that we may live and sing to you: Alleluia!
(Symphonia Sirenum, Cologne, 1695)*

Special Occasions

Psalm 145:15-21

The eyes of all look to you,
and you give them their food in due season.
(Psalm 145:15)

God makes the wheat grow, and we should praise him and thank him for that. It is not of our working but of his giving and blessing that wheat, grapes, and all kinds of fruit grow, which we all need for food and drink. The Lord's Prayer indicates this when we pray, "Give us today our daily bread." In the word "give" we confess that it is the gift of God and not our creation, and if he did not give, not a grain would grow and our tilling would be in vain. How soon might all the grain in the soil go bad or be frozen or rot or be eaten by worms or drowned by floods! Or if it is growing well, how soon might it be destroyed by heat or hail or cold or be eaten by beetles! How many perils the wheat must pass through before it is reaped! Even then it may be carried away or devoured by worms.

Therefore, when we look at a field of wheat, we should think not only of God's goodness but also of his power. We should think, "Oh, you dear grain, how God, out of his rich and gentle goodness, gives you to us so plentifully, and also with what power he protects you, from the hour when you are sown to the time when you come to our table!"

A believing heart well perceives how our plowing and sowing would be lost unless God's goodness were here at work. Even though we must do our work diligently and seek our food from the soil, we must in no way trust in our work as though our hands made the harvest. More is needed than our human hands. God's blessing and his mighty keeping are essential to growth.

Exposition of Psalm 147.   LW 14:122; WA 31/1:443

I thank you, Lord God, for the fruitfulness and abundance of our land and the marvelous blessings of my life. May I use these gifts wisely, with care for the natural world and for the benefit of others. Amen.

1 Corinthians 3:11-23

He answered, "It is written, 'One does not live by bread alone,
but by every word that comes from the mouth of God.'"
(Matthew 4:4)

The soul can live without all things except the Word of God; without the Word of God nothing can help us. But when we have the Word we need nothing else, for in the Word we have enough food, joy, peace, light, art, justice, truth, wisdom, and all good things in abundance.

What, then, is this Word that bestows such high grace, and how shall I use it? It is nothing other than the actual preaching of Christ as it is contained in the gospel. The purpose of the preaching is that you should hear your God speaking to you, telling how all your life and works are nothing before God and how you and all that is in you would perish eternally. If you truly believe how sinful you are, you will despair of yourself entirely. But in order that you may be saved from yourself and out of yourself—that is, out of ruin—God presents to you his dearly beloved Son, Jesus Christ, and bids you, through his living and comforting Word, to yield yourself to him with a cheerful heart. For the sake of such faith all your sins will be forgiven, your ruin overcome, and you will be just and true, content and devout, fulfilling all his commandments, and set free from all things.

On the Freedom of a Christian, 1520.   LW 31:345; WA 7:22f.

God's Word is our great heritage, and shall be ours forever. Through life it
guides our way, in death it is our stay. Lord, grant while worlds endure,
we keep its teachings pure throughout all generations. Amen.
(Nicolai F. S. Grundtvig, 1817)

Repent.

Matthew 3:2

There can be no repentance when I want to pay and atone for sin by my own deeds, for since I am by nature a sinner and a child of wrath, as the Scripture says, I cannot blot out sin with sin. I can only increase it.

Repentance means that I believe the Word of God, which accuses me and tells me that I am a sinner before God and am condemned, that I am afraid, that I have always been disobedient to my God, that I have never truly regarded his commandments, and never meditated on them, much less obeyed the greatest or the smallest. Yet I must not despair but turn to Christ, seek grace and help from him, and firmly believe that I shall receive it. For he is the Lamb of God chosen from eternity to bear the sin of all the world and to atone for it by his death.

But if you wish to maintain that you are right, turn to other things. Turn to worldly rule, where you may well be right in opposition to your enemy who has wronged you and taken what belongs to you. There you may appeal to your rights, seek for them and demand them. But if you are dealing with God and have to stand before his judgment, do not think of your rights at all. If you would find grace, acknowledge that you are wrong and that he is right. This you do if you say with all the saints, "O Lord God, I confess, feel, and believe that I am a condemned sinner; therefore, I pray, absolve me and wash me clean and baptize me for the sake of Christ. Then I shall know that you are gracious to me, that I have been forgiven, and that I am pure and as white as snow."

Sermon preached on the Thursday after Easter, 1540.   WA 49:119f.

Search me, O God, and know my heart;
*   test me and know my thoughts.*
See if there is any wicked way in me,
*   and lead me in the way everlasting. Amen.*
(Psalm 139:23-24)

SCRIPTURE INDEX

Biblical references for weekly readings (listed on the pages for Sundays) and those for responses at the bottom of the pages are not included here.

INDEX OF MOTIFS